The Corporation
A Theological Inquiry

Edited by Michael Novak and John W. Cooper

American Enterprise Institute for Public Policy Research
Washington and London

Cover illustration by Karen Laub-Novak.

Library of Congress Cataloging in Publication Data

Main entry under title:

The Corporation.
  (AEI Symposia ; 81C)
  Proceedings of the third annual seminar sponsored by the American
Enterprise Institute and the Syracuse University Department of Religion;
held July 6–12, 1980 at Airlie House, Va.
  Bibliography: p.
  Contents: The development of the corporation / Oscar Handlin—
The taxonomy of the corporation / Oscar Handlin—The corporation
and the liberal order / Paul W. McCracken—[etc.]
  1. Corporations—Congresses. 2. Industry—Social aspects—Congresses.
3. Church and economics—Congresses. I. Novak, Michael. II. Cooper,
John W. (John Wesley), 1953–   III. American Enterprise Institute
for Public Policy Research. IV. Syracuse University. Dept. of Religion.
V. Series.
HD2711.C73   338.7′4   81-2802
ISBN 0-8447-2203-0   AACR2
ISBN 0-8447-2204-9 (pbk.)

AEI Symposia 81C

Contents

Foreword

The private corporation is an institution unique to modern history, and one that plays a special role in democratic societies. Whether the corporation is organized for reasons of business and profit, or for other purposes (such as those of labor unions, universities, and civic organizations), it is a type of vital mediating structure, a part of the system of social and political checks and balances that stand between the individual and state. The private corporation is, in fact, a historically crucial component in the development of democracy; economic freedom and political freedom go hand in hand. Much has appeared in the literature of economics about the structure and functions of the corporation, but very little has been said about the broader historical, sociological, and theological aspects of the corporation—and most of what has been said has been one-sided and critical. Until recently, that criticism has largely gone unanswered, because friends of the corporation have considered history, sociology, and theology to be rather exotic and forbidding realms. That state of affairs is gradually changing, and a more balanced view of the corporation is emerging, as this volume should make clear.

With the publication of *The Corporation: A Theological Inquiry*, the American Enterprise Institute seeks to help fill the need for a deeper, theoretical, and balanced understanding of the significance of corporations in a free society. This edited text of the 1980 Summer Institute on theology and economics forms the third in a series of conferences cosponsored by AEI and the Department of Religion at Syracuse University. The conference was held at Airlie House in Warrenton, Virginia, from July 7 to 11, 1980. The conferences held the previous two summers resulted in the publication of *Capitalism and Socialism: A Theological Inquiry* and *Democracy and Mediating Structures: A Theological Inquiry*.

Special thanks are due to Dr. Ronald Cavanagh, associate dean of the College of Arts and Sciences, and Dr. James B. Wiggins, chairman of the Department of Religion, both at Syracuse University, and to Michael Novak, resident scholar at AEI, for their work in organizing, shaping, and directing the conferences.

The private corporation is one social structure among others which serves a legitimate function and helps to preserve the checks and balances in a pluralistic system. We need a theory—indeed, some would say, a theology—of the corporation if we hope to maintain the differentiation of powers which preserves us from tyranny.

WILLIAM J. BAROODY, JR.
President
American Enterprise Institute

Preface

This volume constitutes the third in a series of proceedings of Summer Institutes on theology and economics which have been jointly sponsored by the Department of Religion at Syracuse University and the American Enterprise Institute. The first volume, *Capitalism and Socialism: A Theological Inquiry*, tested the validity of commonly accepted theories about the ethos, practices, and institutions of competing social systems. In the second volume, *Democracy and Mediating Structures: A Theological Inquiry*, the exploration focused upon the social institutions—family, church, voluntary association, labor union, business corporation—that mediate between the individual in his private life and the megastructures of government. The present volume provides a more specific analysis of the mediating function of the corporation and its unique role in a free society.

The sponsors of the 1980 Summer Institute were confirmed in their expectation that the corporation would prove to be a lively subject for reflection and debate. Many serendipitous insights were generated in the formal and informal discussions through an intensive week at the Airlie House conference center in rural Virginia. The participants included theologians, economists, historians, philosophers, business executives and consultants, officers of foundations and church agencies, and graduate students in various disciplines. The group comprised both practitioners and theorists, all eager to explore the origins, nature, and function of corporations in relation to cultural and religious values. The texts of the proceedings presented here retain much of the effect and immediacy of their original oral delivery.

We begin this study with the recognition that corporations, especially large or transnational business corporations, are frequently targets of attack by social critics and religious ethicists. We are particularly interested, therefore, in achieving a dispassionate understanding of the facts about corporations. What constitutes a "large" corporation? How significant is the effect of large corporations on the American economy and the world economy? Do corporations foster or impede balanced economic development? Secondly, we wish to explore the overall meaning of the corporation as a unique institution in modern Western society. Is the corporation a beneficial or nefarious social structure? Can corporate executives be brought to a fuller ethical awareness and can corporations be made to render greater service to the common good? What distinguishes the business corporation from the nonprofit corporation, and what do they have in common? Finally, what can be said about the future of corporations in the United States and abroad?

We hope this volume will raise the level of discussion about the corporation above the simplistic paeans and jeremiads frequently encountered in the current literature. Perhaps these proceedings will in some way help to make our understanding of the corporation more concrete, more balanced, and more attuned to historical contingencies. They may also help to point the way toward new horizons in the broader study of mediating institutions and social processes.

Many participants of the three annual Summer Institutes to date have made favorable evaluations of this project and have encouraged us to continue this line of investigation. Consequently, the 1981 Summer Institute will examine official church documents addressed to questions of economics and economic justice, with special emphasis on the relevant documents of the Roman Catholic Church, the World Council of Churches, and the National Council of Churches (U.S.A.).

Gratitude is owed to all who contributed to the success of the Summer Institute of 1980, and especially to the key organizer of the conference, our moderator, Dr. Ronald Cavanagh, associate dean of the College of Arts and Sciences at Syracuse University, and to Dr. James B. Wiggins, chairman of the Department of Religion at Syracuse University.

Michael Novak
John W. Cooper

The Development of the Corporation

Oscar Handlin

As a historian, I do not presume to make a theological inquiry into the corporation; I intend to speak about the past of the corporation, about how it got to be the way it is now. A lawyer or an economist might have been chosen to open this discussion; these are the scholars who usually deal with the corporation. But my approach will be radically different from those that either the lawyer or the economist would take.

Lawyers who deal with the corporation seek uniformities and consistencies. They look at the statutes, at the decisions of judges, and try to find a regularity that makes the corporation comprehensible from their point of view and permits them to proceed on into the future with a secure knowledge of what the essence of that institution is. In doing so, of course, they tend to overlook the inconsistent, contingent elements in the way this institution actually came to be what it is.

The economists tend to look at the corporation functionally, that is, in terms of what that kind of body does within the system of production, and to make the rather gross assumption that it came to do what it does because people intended it to be the kind of institution that it became. Such an assumption is not justified by the actualities of the way in which the institution developed.

The corporation, as we know it—and we know it from every aspect of our lives—was invented; it did not come to be of itself. It was not invented to serve present needs or to fit into present concepts of justice, although the way in which it was invented did affect its capacity to meet present needs and does affect how we think of its position in relationship to government and the various kinds of power in our society.

So I will not apologize for casting back into history; I think we need this exposure to the past in order to be able better to understand what the present offers us and what the future may offer.

I like to use, as the point of departure in discussing the corporation, a fairly recent year—say, 1800, a quarter of a century after the foundation of the republic—and recall what the corporation was at that point.

1

The Corporation in 1800

In 1800 the United States was only beginning its history as an independent nation. It was an underdeveloped country, primarily agricultural, with a population of perhaps 4 or 5 million along the Atlantic coast. Already, however, the United States had more corporations, and more explicitly business corporations, than all of Europe put together; this is an astounding circumstance if you look at it from the point of view of the economist.

The economist thinks of the corporation as a way of amassing capital and applying it to the needs of modern productive systems. Certainly, in 1800, countries like Britain and France, even Germany, were far ahead of the United States in manufacturing, commerce, and banking—all the areas in which the corporation has traditionally appeared. They remained far ahead of the United States, through, say, the first half of the nineteenth century. And yet, during that period, American corporations proliferated, whereas the corporation in Europe remained a very rare and specialized form of enterprise, almost until the end of the nineteenth century.

This presents us a puzzle; how did this body, this way of organizing and carrying forward an enterprise, take its form so early, so quickly at the very beginning of the republic when economic circumstances hardly justified it?

The concept of the corporation, of course, is much older. It is medieval and even Roman in its origins. We know that charters in the twelfth and thirteenth centuries had already created what was called a body politic and corporate, essentially a corporation. The kind of body was not a business institution, as we know it; it was more likely to be, for instance, a borough or a municipality. One still speaks of the corporation of the City of London or the corporation of any other large borough in England. It has a mayor, who with the aldermen forms the corporation.

That idea remained prevalent in European political thinking, down until modern times. Basically, it assumed that the chartering authority—usually the king—could delegate to some subsidiary body some of the power to govern and could create a body politic, that is, a body that was competent to use political power for ends that were specified in the instrument that created it, the charter.

Other very rare kinds of corporations were formed in the premodern period, generally associated with the monopoly or a privilege or a grant of some sort. And that, indeed, was how the first corporations came to the New World.

The Years prior to 1800

In the early seventeenth century, Virginia, Massachusetts, and some of the other colonies were settled by chartered companies, by bodies politic and corporate, in exactly the same legal terms, although with different functions. These companies consisted of investors who put up capital; they had boards of directors called by various names; they were run by a governor; and they operated in terms very similar to those of traditional medieval chartered companies.

These chartered corporations did not last long. The Virginia Company lasted from about 1607 to 1625, and the Massachusetts Bay Company fell apart within a decade. Somehow, it was not possible to transfer that kind of institution to the remote areas of settlement in North America, although in another part of the world the East India Company retained control over British India down until the nineteenth century. The British Muscovy Company traded with Russia and the Turkey Company, with Turkey. Those enterprises continued within accepted forms. Those forms did not work in North America, where large bodies of settlers began to insist on making decisions that could not be controlled from London. Because of the remoteness and underdeveloped nature of the area the population acquired many powers that corporations traditionally had exercised from a central directory.

Thus arose an underlying sense of local hostility to the corporation, which persisted down through the seventeenth and eighteenth centuries, a general and not always well-articulated feeling that this was an alien institution operating from London or somewhere else overseas— the Dutch West India Company tried to run New Netherlands in the same way—and that the local powers were susceptible of mobilizing themselves sufficiently to become ungovernable when the decisions were made from those remote sources of authority.

On the other hand, there were points at which the colonists themselves wanted to use the corporation form. For instance, in 1636 when Massachusetts people decided to establish a university in Cambridge, the local assembly issued a charter of incorporation to set up the body that became known as the President and Fellows of Harvard College; that corporation still exists. This action evoked hostility from the mother country, because the grant of a charter of incorporation was a privilege that the king and Parliament wanted to hold in their own hands. And it was one of the reasons why the Massachusetts Charter was itself revoked, and thereafter no colony was able to establish a corporation through its own governing body.

As a result, for 150 years there existed a situation in which the kinds of corporations that could be chartered by the royal authority were resisted and rejected in the colonies, whereas the colonies themselves were not allowed to form corporations of their own.

Now, throughout that whole one hundred fifty years of development, the colonists had unfulfilled needs which they believed only a corporation could supply and which could not be met because neither the local authorities nor the royal government could create corporations. For instance, conceive what it would be like, in an economy that was thriving, growing, engaging in a great deal of trade, to have no banks and no money, no coins, no paper, no facilities for credit. Over and over again, plans were made in different colonies to establish a bank, but none of these plans could be satisfactorily completed because the royal government would incorporate no such entity; and people could then conceive of no way to establish a bank, other than through a chartered body.

Alternatives to Incorporation

Instead, there was a series of spontaneous cooperative devices which did, in an informal way, the kinds of things a chartered corporation would do, in a formal way, in the Old World. Of course, in any settlement close to the frontiers, habits of cooperation were necessary; no individual could live alone, and on numerous occasions in life neighbors, villagers, and townspeople had to help. But the various kinds of cooperative actions had to be structured in ways that people worked out for themselves, because they had no legal forms that they could use.

For instance, all issues involving property rights required some kind of legal decision. Take, for instance, a parish. In the Old World, the position of a parish that owned a building, other church property, and a graveyard was regularized by the government and by law. The church and the state were united in ways that established the parish as well as the whole set of other ecclesiastical institutions that rose above it to the apex at the episcopal or royal level. But in America, it became difficult to deal with parish problems in that fashion, partly because establishment in the colonies in which it existed was contingent and qualified, partly because in other colonies, like Rhode Island, churches were not established at all, and partly because there appeared a great number of dissenting churches that could not be established and yet were property holders. In Philadelphia, the wealthiest churches belonged to the Friends. Who held the property on behalf of the Society of Friends? No individual could claim to be the owner; the meeting had no legal status. In towns like Newport and New York, Jews owned the structures in which their own religious functions were carried forward, not only as individuals but also as communities. In Maryland and

Pennsylvania, the Jesuits, until they went underground for reasons connected with events in Europe, were property owners, and yet there was no episcopal authority in whose name the property could be held. Instead, a series of devices developed that focused on trustees, who held property not as their own but on behalf of the commonality for which they dealt.

Another kind of problem arose in places like the New England towns that were originally political and also economic entities. They were political entities because they made rules and exercised the powers of local government; but they also owned the common fields and many of the undivided lands that remained available along the frontier and even in some of the eastern towns.

When new people came in, the old inhabitants were sometimes willing to accept them as townspeople, but the question arose, did these newcomers have a right to the common fields? Did they have a right to the undivided lands? To be overly generous was, in a sense, to deprive the next generation of its heritage.

Hence there appeared a body called the proprietors of the common fields. Its members were sometimes the same people who met in the town meeting and who governed the town. But in their alternative capacity they formed an abstract body that had property rights in that area. In time, not all members of the town meeting were also proprietors.

So too, a distinction was made between the parish and the church that became increasingly anomalous. In the Puritan colonies, the parish included all the people who lived in its area. They were all supposed to come to meeting on Sunday. They did not all worship together, because only the church members took communion. The church members were a smaller, narrower group of the population, set apart by the special act of conversion that Puritans recognize as separating the saints from the sinners. Here was another kind of grouping distinction between church and parish.

People often went off by themselves and formed bodies politic without waiting to receive a charter because they knew they would not get a charter—the earliest example is the people who came on the *Mayflower* and who settled in a part of the New World where they knew they had no right to be. They aimed for Virginia, but their navigation was off and they ended up in New England. Before they settled, they executed a covenant. They mutually agreed among themselves that they would be a body politic and corporate and would act in ways that were spelled out in what amounted to a constitution or bylaws.

By the middle of the eighteenth century, people had spontaneously created numerous small bodies of this sort. England, the home country—civilized, stable, with a long history—had two universities. By the time of the revolution, the colonies had six. They had no abundance of learned men or anxious scholars, and none of the colleges had valid charters. They were self-constituted bodies in Rhode Island and New Jersey and New York, which set about the business of doing whatever it was without the formal power that gave them the right to do what they were doing.

There were a whole clutch of cooperative associations. People wanted to build wharves. They got together and formed the proprietors of Long Wharf or of Broad Street Wharf. These were not partnerships; they were not individual enterprises; they were kinds of cooperative arrangements that were related to trusteeships or the kinds of management that the other institutions developed. Self-devised, rudimentary, illegal in strict terms, they kept sprouting up and filling the needs of the actual population at that time.

Corporations after the American Revolution

Then came the revolution. It broke out in 1774, and went on till 1783, but it was really settled in the first two years. The immediate impact of the revolution was to persuade significant numbers of people, who were close to the levers of power in the new government, that they ought to do what Britain had prevented them from doing for a century and a half, namely, form legal chartered bodies politic and corporate. They looked for guidance to what they knew about precedents for this in England and on the continent. The body politic and corporate was an agency that the government formed by issuing a charter for a stated purpose and connecting to it various valuable privileges, monopolies, and other perquisites.

Consider a bank. Everybody knew that the Bank of England was an important institution in Britain. It seemed plausible to charter a Bank of North America, as was indeed done, in a very early measure, in 1781. So, too, other charters emerged from the Continental Congress and later from the Federal Congress and the various state legislatures. The trouble was that, although it was possible for the new government to issue these documents, somehow they did not work the way they had in Britain, and certain very simple conditions in the character of American life were responsible for this discrepancy between actuality and intention.

First, and perhaps most important, was ignorance. The people who secured the charter to set up the Bank of North America in Philadelphia realized when they had this piece of paper that they had no idea how to run a bank, no more than any merchant would know about how a banking institution runs. They had to improvise, and the process of improvisation continued for almost half a century, until a banker appeared who knew what a bank was supposed to be like.

Ignorance also extended to the law, because most American lawyers were self-trained. They read a few books like Blackstone and Coke on Littleton, all of which dealt with the past. They had had no experience with how to draw up charters, with what went on within the corporation, or with how to resolve the various problems relating to the contact of the corporation with the state. The result was much looseness of terminology concerning how powers were disposed, and much carelessness that later provided generations of lawyers ample opportunity to exercise their ingenuity.

Secondly, there was the federalism in American government. This meant that it was unclear who had the right in the new United States to issue these charters. In England, there was no question: it was the king in Parliament. But in the United States, there were fourteen sovereign entities, and the number increased every time a new state came in. Within a year of the chartering of the Bank of North America, Massachusetts had chartered the Bank of Massachusetts and New York soon chartered the Bank of New York—both of which are still going. Pennsylvania chartered a bank of its own. Soon there were a multiplicity of banks, each in a separate state.

This federalism grew out of the original ambiguity about sovereignty in the United States. People spoke about the United States as a sovereign power but they also spoke about the sovereign states, and that ambiguity meant that the power to create corporate bodies could never be centralized, systematically controlled, or regulated.

Finally, there was a very general popular attitude, which was logically inconsistent, perhaps, but which was nevertheless powerful and very important during the century that followed. It was not that people were ever against corporations, because corporations were chartered to do worthwhile things; but they were against confining corporate authority to a few individuals. They were not against privilege, but everybody had to have a right to have privilege.

In other words, when the Bank of Massachusetts was chartered in Boston, the people in Salem came round and said, "Why shouldn't we have a bank?" And before they were in business, the people in Newburyport and, within ten years, a rival group in Boston, had said, "Well, those chaps have their banks, but we ought to have one also." There was no political capacity for control effective enough to contain the desire for a share of the power to act as a corporation.

As a result, by 1800 there were many more corporations in the United States than in all of Europe, and year after year, the number increased in every area in which people felt that a cooperative task remained to be performed. Churches were incorporated, as were educational and eleemosynary institutions, manufactures, canals, and later railroads and turnpikes. Any enterprise that someone thought worthwhile had access to this form of organization.

Incorporation as a Right

This diffusion of the capacity to incorporate led to startling, but hardly noticed, changes. In Europe, and at the beginning in the United States, each charter of incorporation was the subject of special legislation. An act of Parliament, of the Congress, or of a state legislature was necessary to create a corporation. But as time went on, incorporation in America ceased to be a privilege and became a right. Any qualified group of individuals, by some general set of standards, was entitled to be incorporated; because the press of legislation became heavy, the corporation was born not by a law but by a simple act of registry. The proper people came in, filled out certain pieces of paper, and that was it; they were a corporation.

This small change of detail affected the very substance of what was involved in incorporation. If that was all incorporating meant, what did it really mean? It was one thing to incorporate the Bank of England; a whole array of privileges went with that incorporation, and nobody else but the Bank of England could be the same kind of bank. It was another thing when any six individuals who claimed that they had the requisite capital could put their names down on a form and set up business as a bank. The same was true of universities and churches and charitable institutions. Incorporation did not signify a privilege, but the opposite of a privilege; it simply meant an opportunity. It meant an opportunity to assemble cooperatively, whatever the nature of that enterprise demanded.

Negative Aspects of Corporate Development in America

This change had both positive and negative effects. The negative effects are easier to perceive. It meant, for instance, that there was a good deal of wastefulness. If you set up, in a primitive economy, in nineteenth-century Ohio or Illinois, twenty or thirty different banks, half of them were bound to fail; in many cases more than half, and in some cases all, the banks in a state failed. Aside from there being no qualifications, the competitive nature of the situation led to the taking of untoward risks, and that was wasteful.

It meant that when the transportation network was laid out in the middle of the nineteenth century, there was no coherent set of routes. The railroads in France, by contrast, were laid out like the spokes of a wheel, radiating out from Paris. The whole system followed a national plan, coherently laid out and structured. Almost the same obtained in England. Nothing like that happened in the United States. Any set of local entrepreneurs could get together and create a railroad between any two towns. In the 1870s, there were six different railroad routes between New York and Boston, four of which were actually running at one time. (Three of the four, of course, went out of business before very long.)

The change also meant that no centralization was possible. The United States, at the end of the nineteenth century, experienced a tremendous wave of hostility toward trusts and the kinds of large enterprises that took similar forms. This phenomenon had no counterpart in Europe, either in Britain or Germany or France, where there were also big enterprises and where there were very powerful critics of industry, business, and banking. Hostility did not break out in Europe because the trusts there were institutionalized. They were encouraged by the government. The act of Parliament that created a corporation endowed it with the powers to act in ways that made cartels and similar arrangements possible. And no one could protest against the acts of the sovereign body.

In the United States, the trusts were not incorporated. The trusts appeared because corporations could not do in America what they could do in Europe. Since American corporations were all separate little entities, they had to be brought together either in trusts, strictly speaking, or through holding companies or other artificial devices, and then they became targets of popular attack. That is another wasteful feature of American corporate development.

Positive Aspects of Corporate Development in America

There are, however, certain positive sides to this development. For one thing, since the government had lost the power to incorporate, institutions that were not totally dependent on the government were set up, and these were not totally creatures of politics.

This appears most clearly in the areas of education and philanthropy. Toward the middle of the nineteenth century there was an important and stimulating move to create state universities of various sorts. Those universities did not preempt the field of education, because at the same time, and on an even larger scale, autonomous, independent educational institutions were being created; these were run by corporations that acquired charters in the same way that all other corporations did, namely, by registration. And the government did not have the capacity to favor some at the expense of others, to favor its own creatures at the expense of those that operated autonomously.

9

This was likewise true of a whole range of other corporations which might have fit under last years' rubric of mediating institutions—hospitals, philanthropic bodies of various sorts, religious bodies and bodies associated with religion. These institutions all used the same devices of incorporation, yet did so without becoming dependent on the state because the state had, in effect, lost the capacity to control them once the right to act as a corporation became a simple matter of registry.

The same freedom from state control operated in the economy. Offsetting the wasteful way in which the corporations competed with and fought against one another was the rapid exploitation of new opportunities that was made possible by the resources mobilized in the corporation.

The railroad was invented in England, and within ten years there were more miles of railroad in the United States than in all of Europe. They were not all going somewhere. But some of them were; and they permitted the penetration of areas even before the passengers and the freight that they would carry appeared. In the same way, a whole series of new economic opportunities were able to be exploited at the end of the century because the device of the corporation permitted the rapid mobilization of large amounts of capital, of managerial ability, and of the enterprise to bring these processes to a successful conclusion.

In sum, what happened in the long process of development was this: the corporation, which had been an instrument of privilege and a kind of exclusive body, tightly controlled by the state for reasons of its own, now became an instrument by which its members—and anyone could form a corporation—could serve whatever ends they wished. The corporation was therefore not in the position of depending upon its privileges in order to survive or thrive. It could survive or thrive only if it efficiently served the interests of its own members and those to whom it wished to render services. This meant that it had to be attuned to the marketplace, in which its clients or dependents or customers operated, and to its own members, who supplied it either with capital or funds or other resources; and while a large number of them failed, they failed not for want of privilege but for an inability to accommodate themselves to the dual demands of their clients or of their own members.

By the twentieth century, this course of development had brought into being a remarkably flexible instrument, which could serve, as it did in the nineteenth century, a multiplicity of functions and do so in a way that was attuned to the needs of the times and of the population with which it dealt.

Discussion

QUESTION: Did these charters define the responsibilities as well as the privileges of the corporation? How did these companies become business enterprises?

PROFESSOR HANDLIN: The charters were, in a sense, like miniconstitutions—this was in England, where they knew how to do it. They created a body politic and corporate. They stated what its purpose was. They stated how it was to be governed, how bylaws were to be made, what the rights of members in the corporation were, what the members owed the corporation, and what privileges the corporation had; so they anticipated, as it were, all the governmental questions that might arise in the operations of a corporation.

Some of these corporations had always been business enterprises. For instance, the Virginia Company was a joint stock company, which meant that in addition to running the government, individuals invested in it and expected—although they never got—a profit from their investments. The company was to own land and exploit it, and so on, so it was a kind of business enterprise.

There were other joint stock companies of that sort, like the East India Company. What is interesting is how Americans got into kinds of economic activities that did not involve privilege. Say, for example, that if a person were going to build a railroad or a canal or a turnpike, he had to have certain privileges—for instance, the right to acquire land by eminent domain. It was understandable that in such a situation a corporation would appear quite logically. But in manufacturing there was only an enterprise, and in Europe, manufacturing companies were not incorporated until the end of the nineteenth century. The corporation appeared in manufacturing in the United States for a different set of reasons, which had very little to do with privilege. The first large-scale American enterprises in manufacturing were in textiles. The textile mills were built by merchants. They did not want to run the mills themselves; they were in commercial business. What they wanted was a way in which to invest in the mills without actually being responsible for

11

running them, and the corporation provided that instrument. They could buy shares and let the corporation run the mills in a way that would enable them to profit from it, if there was profit, but not be directly involved. So, in what could then have been considered an underdeveloped economy, incorporating was a way of mobilizing capital and accumulating the resources permitted business enterprise to take form. Incorporation then became useful in other kinds of businesses, as well, because it permitted the use of capital in a pointed, specific way that did not get people involved directly but enabled them to act through cooperative intermediaries.

QUESTION: Is there a sense in which what was a unique and limited privilege in Europe became a democratized form in the United States by limiting personal liability?

PROFESSOR HANDLIN: I do not like *democratized* in that sense. It gives a misleading impression that the great masses could go out and form their own corporations. Actually, some of the masses did, but I would prefer to say that anybody who could afford to do so was able to incorporate without passing through a governmental filter that could favor some and discriminate against others.

QUESTION: Could a chartered company in England be charged with unfair practices?

PROFESSOR HANDLIN: The terms of the charter were generally sufficiently broad, so that the corporation was not liable to charges of monopoly, restraint of trade, or unfair pricing practices. Indeed those were among the privileges given to the corporation, and it could not be held accountable under the common law. The only cases that would come up would be against officials of a company who exceeded their powers; but the very act of creating the corporation created an agency of the government that was therefore free of the restraints nongovernmental agencies faced. It was not until late, toward the middle of the century, that any action was taken, and then the East India Company was dissolved and made a formal branch of the government. Some of the corporations, however, still exist.

QUESTION: How does this analysis fit the large, modern corporation and to what extent is that still a mediating institution?

PROFESSOR HANDLIN: The great corporations in terms of size, however we measure it—capital, sales, profits, number of employees, of 1930 are not the same as the ones that are at the top in 1980. How did that happen?

All the enterprises of the last ten years were incorporated, and yet incorporation did not provide a stone wall behind which any could simply entrench itself. Indeed, it sometimes exposes enterprise to a kind of vulnerability that an individual does not have. I would say that there is therefore a prima facie case against the argument that the large corporation has become so large that it is a different order of being from what it was twenty years ago, or since the war.

QUESTION: I have a kind of theological question, one for a historian, not a lawyer. In describing the corporation, you began by saying it was something that had been invented, but in the historical account, it just seems to have grown in actual strength. Leaving the legal protection aside, is it really strong?

PROFESSOR HANDLIN: Let me explain what I meant by saying that it had been invented. It was not an institution that existed of itself or was simply a product of a long line of development. One can point to dates at which certain changes came in response to the will and intention of individuals. In that sense, it was a kind of invention. On the other hand, it was not independent of the circumstances and surrounding conditions, any more than any other invention was. Every invention is conditioned by the time and the place and the stream of development in which it occurred.

QUESTION: Was there in this country a deliberate decision, at the founding, to cause the creation of corporations, as you described?

PROFESSOR HANDLIN: There was a deliberate decision not to prevent the proliferation of corporations.

QUESTION: What were the advantages of incorporation once incorporation was no longer a privilege of the government?

PROFESSOR HANDLIN: Incorporation became a very convenient way of acting. It was not the only way one could act; but it was effective. For instance, if twenty people invested in an enterprise, all twenty could be partners; but that was cumbersome, because if one partner died, then the whole partnership was in trouble. Alternatively, the twenty people could choose one to be a trustee, or choose two or three to be trustees, to act on behalf of the whole group. That was also cumbersome, although it could be done, and it was done. The advantages of incorpora-

13

tion, other than those connected with the government, included perpetuity, for instance, a corporation went on whatever happened to its stockholders. If it had twenty stockholders and they died, the corporation still went on and the stockholders' interests passed to their heirs.

The corporation also has limited liability. That means that if a corporation cannot pay its debts, the creditors cannot proceed against the individual investors. The individual investors will lose their investment, but they will usually not lose more. There are also advantages to having a corporate seal and a corporate identity. These are conveniences. They are not essential; incorporation is not the only way businesses can operate, but it is a convenient way, and it becomes more and more convenient as it develops.

QUESTION: It seems to me that what you are describing as an accident or a convenience might really be part of a rather deliberate, though not necessarily self-conscious, change in ideology. For example, corporations in England during the Middle Ages were chartered by the government, and they were in charge of the public interest. A corporation would be chartered to do something that would be useful for the public —take the East India Company, for example.

What you described as happening in the United States shifted the focus from the corporation as having a public usefulness to the corporation as being convenient for individuals. That was the new focus of the organizing principles, to limit the liability of individuals. Hasn't what happened to the Amercan corporation seemed entirely consistent with America's general liberal ideology?

PROFESSOR HANDLIN: I would agree with that, as long as we understand what we mean by public interest in its original sense. Among the chartered bodies in England were certain schools that were called public schools, like Eton, Rugby, Harrow, and so on. A description of their function usually appeared in their charters. But public in that sense did not mean open to everybody. It meant that these schools held a certain privileged position by virtue of their relationship to the authorities of the state.

Now, when one reaches a point at which anyone can get a charter, then nobody is in the public interest in the original sense. Later in the nineteenth century, however, people began to talk of the public interest in the United States and to some extent in Europe also, in a completely different sense, meaning the interest of a heterogeneous body of consumers against the corporation that served them. That old idea of the public interest had died away, and no one really thinks of the words in those terms, but a new idea has appeared, a really different concept.

QUESTION: May I offer an illustration? Doesn't the Hamilton Bank of the United States illustrate the old notion of incorporation, and doesn't what happened illustrate the new idea?

PROFESSOR HANDLIN: Right. Under Hamilton's plan, however, there should have been no other banks; there should have been just the Bank of the United States. But even when it was going in the 1820s, lots of other state and local banks competed with it.

QUESTION: In the early charters of the corporations, were there instances of theological language?

PROFESSOR HANDLIN: The English charters had a certain formulaic language. They would say, "James I, by the grace of God." The overseas ones often had clauses about converting the heathen. That is about the extent of the theological language I can find in those charters.

QUESTION: How would you characterize the events that defined the differences in corporate development? For example, have these events been in the area of ethics, or in what we now have as profit/nonprofit, or banks, or different kinds of corporations, or in the struggles between or among the different private corporations trying to get hold of public licensing authority to make sure they were licensed in a way that would give them the greatest flexibility? Was it any of those or was it just chaotic?

PROFESSOR HANDLIN: It was mostly chaotic. For instance, the big cases that settle the nature of the business corporation do not deal with business. The most important one was the Dartmouth College case, and everybody knew what was involved because high-powered lawyers, like Webster, were involved. The issue was whether the government had the right to alter the charter of the corporation after the charter had been granted. The decision held that a charter was a contract between the government and the incorporators and that a state could not alter the conditions of a contract once it had been granted. It applied in the first instance to a college. But it would apply to business corporations of all sorts as well. Another case, a few years earlier, dealt with property rights in a parish, but by extension also reached over into business corporations.

15

The concept of profit/nonprofit, which is a very ticklish concept anyway, did not arise until the twentieth century, and then it came in with legislation that was designed to give nonprofit corporations certain privileges that corporations defined as profitable did not have. It is not a distinction that had much meaning until the income tax amendment and the appearance of the Internal Revenue Service, which can rule on what is and what is not a profit-making enterprise.

QUESTION: Can one render a judgment about the efficacy of planned as against unplanned growth?

PROFESSOR HANDLIN: In the nineteenth century, planning would have been a straitjacket in the United States, because one would always have been planning for conditions that were out of date by the time the plan was implemented. Given the rapid growth and great expansion of this society, it is unlikely that a plan could have looked ahead a decade and guessed what would happen. Besides, the tools of analysis for devising a plan that would have been effective did not exist then.

Most of the plans for railroads, for instance, envisioned railroads that would run from east to west, and in time, that is how the transcontinentals were built. A lot of that was very romantic; it looked interesting on the map. Actually, the most profitable railroads in the nineteenth century ran north and south, but they did not show up in that interesting way on the map. The most profitable single railroad in the history of railroading was probably the Illinois Central, which ran north and south from Chicago. From a planner's point of view, it had to compete with the Mississippi River and all its tributaries, and it did not make sense; but it did make money.

The Taxonomy of the Corporation

Oscar Handlin

I want to say something about the taxonomy of corporations as they exist in our time and as they may affect our future. At the beginning of this century, the corporation, as a result of the kind of evolution it had undergone in the United States, stood in a contrapuntal relationship to government. It was separate and apart: sometimes it harmonized with what government wanted to do, sometimes it was in opposition; but it proceeded along an autonomous line of development.

Consider the way in which corporations came into being. They were no longer chartered by the government as agencies to perform a public service approved by the state; instead, they were registered. Anyone could register, and the government did not presume to pass judgment upon what was a valid object of action and what was not. In registering, however, a corporation accepted general rules, which applied to all other bodies of the same kind. These rules had to do with how the corporation was governed internally, regardless of whether it was a business corporation, a charitable or an educational corporation, or a foundation. There were members, who were defined by the initial act of incorporation, and these members chose directors by some process also spelled out in the initial act of incorporation. The directors chose an executive. Among these three categories of people the work of the corporation was to be done. It is such corporations that have descended to our times.

The Size of Corporations

The most important distinction among types of corporation, it seems to me, is that of size. There are large corporations and there are small ones, and they all operate according to the same rules derived from common historic antecedents. A corporation with fifty thousand or more members will elect its directors under one set of conditions, and the relationship of the directors to the management and of the management to the whole body of members will be affected thereby. There are also corporations whose membership may number forty or fifty, and no more, and that creates a totally different set of conditions for everyone.

17

The distinction between large and small obtains in all corporations. A small, closely held business corporation operates in much the same way as a small foundation does. Everybody who has a stake in it knows pretty much what is going on, is close to the decision-making process among the directors, and can maintain some level of contact with the management or the executive.

By contrast, in a very large corporation the membership fluctuates as people enter and leave, and the process of selecting the directors loses its meaning for the membership. The directors tend to become a body which co-opts itself and which annually presents a slate of new directors to the membership, for a *pro forma* election. Often the executive acquires a kind of independence of both the directors and the membership that enables it to continue in office as long as it maintains some minimal level of satisfaction in both.

Great size means impersonality and the dilution of contact among the members, directors, and management, whereas small size means that personal relationships which affect the way in which the corporation functions can be preserved. And size, as I said, imposes its imperative on every corporation, be it General Motors, the Metropolitan Museum of Art, or a great hospital, each of which functions in very much the same way.

Corporations: Public or Private?

The second important distinction to be made is between public and private corporations, with regard to both their ends and purposes and their ownership. In the early corporations, this was not a meaningful distinction, because all corporations had a public purpose, at least on the face of it; that was what justified the act of incorporation and the charter. Whether it was the establishment of a university or the creation of a bank, the preamble of the charter stipulated that this organization existed for the public good and the common welfare, and was therefore worthy of the special grant of privileges by the state.

As that link to the government dissolved, however, corporations tended to become private, that is, to become voluntary associations of their own members without a clear link to the state. Nevertheless, public corporations have appeared—and in increasing numbers—in the last half century. They are often no different in their purposes from the private corporations, but they are public in the sense that the government is actively involved in financing and controlling them.

The first large and important modern American public corporation was the Port of New York Authority. It came into being in response to a very special situation. The Port of New York existed in three different states, and it was impossible to charter a corporation in Connecticut or New York or New Jersey that would deal with the affairs of the entire port. It took a special set of treaties and enabling legislation to create this body, which was independent of any one of the states, had its own charter and its own *modus operandi*, and yet was a creature of the states in the sense that they created it. The directors, instead of being elected by the members, were nominated by the governors, and functioned in this curious middle ground between the governmental and the private sectors.

The constitution of this body freed it from direct intervention by the states. The governor of New York appointed some directors, but he could not interfere with decisions made by the Port Authority. It thus had a limited kind of authority, which stemmed from how it was financed. Such agencies were usually financed, not by the states directly, but by private money assembled through the issue of bonds, and, in order to maintain both the confidence of the bondholders and their own capacity to borrow, these agencies had to provide assurance that they would be free of political interference.

The number of such public corporations, which are public in the sense that I have just defined but which are autonomous, has increased steadily in the past decades. These corporations are responsible for the operation of many of the nation's toll roads, bridges, tunnels, and airports, and for Amtrak. A large variety of these agencies are playing an increasingly important part, in the sense that they can perform functions which investors and users do not trust to the government and which the government wishes to have performed more efficiently than it could itself, yet which it does not wish to relinquish to a purely private corporation.

By contrast, there are corporations that are private in the sense that they have bodies of members who elect their directors. It is often hard to distinguish between public and private on a superficial level. The person who pays a toll at a bridge has the same relationship to that authority as has the person who pays a fare on the subway to that authority, as has a person who buys a ticket on the Greyhound Lines to Greyhound, which is a private corporation. From the point of view of the consumer or the fare-payer, it is all the same. From the point of view of financing, it is also much the same; the private corporation and the public corporation both draw funds from capital markets that operate freely in the country.

One does it largely through bonds and the other through equity issues; one promises fixed and regular rates of interest, the other less regular and less fixed dividends; both sets of securities fluctuate in the market as people gain or lose confidence in their futures. The differences are of another sort, and are not even differences in management, because management in the large public corporation is usually a self-contained, self-perpetuating bureaucracy, just as it is in the large business corporation. The difference lies, rather, in the nature of the linkage to the state and to the political system. In the public corporation, there remains a set of connections through the capacity of the government to nominate directors and thus, in the long term, to influence the policy of the corporations. In the private sector, corporations operate with a greater degree of autonomy and without interference.

Corporations: Profit and Nonprofit

The third important distinction to make is between corporations that operate for profit and those that do not. This distinction can best be seen in the abstract. It is easy to conceive, say, of a hospital or a museum or a university operating not-for-profit, and it is easy to conceive of General Motors or Westinghouse operating for profit. On that rather abstract plane, the distinction is clear-cut.

When you approach it in practice, however, this distinction is not all that real, except in a few limited respects. The large, nonprofit organization often operates in much the same way as does the large, for-profit corporation. Each has to keep its members pleased, interested, and involved, the one through the hope of dividends, the other through the achievements or performance it can display to its members. There is even a great deal of similarity in the way in which these organizations function in terms of the relationship of the members to the directors and of the directors to the management.

Let us look first at the profit-making organizations—because nonprofit is the negative side of profit—to understand what the objective of the actual functioning corporation in this society is.

Profit is a simple concept in classical terms; it is earning more than one spends. In a large corporation, however, many more considerations are involved than that of simply showing a set of black figures on a balance sheet. When one thinks of how corporations operate and of the public accounting systems that are thrust on them, and to which they have to conform, the end result of a balance sheet often seems to depend as much on almost theological concepts like the rate of depreciation and the reserve set aside for various purposes, as it does on adding up gains and losses.

In any case, by the time the profit and loss statement is translated into dividend checks there is a remarkable distance between the bottom line of the statement and the return to stockholders. Dividends often have very little to do with annual profits and losses. Some corporations that continue to lose money nevertheless continue to pay dividends;

others make money and do not pay dividends. The rate of pay-out may not depend on the profitability of the corporation in any specific sense. The fact that Gulf Oil profits in 1979, as they were reported by the newspapers, doubled from the previous year really had no effect on the amount of the dividends that Gulf stockholders received. During the year in question, the dividends did not go up, but the value of the stock doubled, and that was far more important than the expectation of profit in the narrower sense.

The set of expectations that investors have about the future of an enterprise is what matters most, not the rewards that they hope immediately to receive from its operations. Management knows this very well. The burden on management, therefore, is not to pay out large amounts of profit at a given moment, but to sustain a quality of operations that will give investors confidence in the future of their securities over the longer term. In a nonprofit organization, of course, there are no dividends, no pay-outs to the members. On the other hand, the quality of expectations about the future of the organization is as important as it is in the profit-making corporation, because what sustains the interest and support of the members is a sense of the importance of the task that is being performed by the corporation and the likelihood of the corporation's future survival.

This applies at all levels and sometimes creates curious similarities between profit and nonprofit organizations. If the public relations department of a hospital or a museum, for instance, were compared with that of a business enterprise, the modes of operation would not appear strikingly different.

Large, Private, Profit-making Corporations

What we know in general, shorthand terms as the business corporation is usually a combination of three elements in that set of dichotomies I have presented; that is, it is large and involves massive amounts of capital, many stockholders, and impersonal bureaucratic management; it is private and set apart from the public sector rather clearly; and it operates for profit in the sense in which I have described it.

Now, largeness, privateness, and profitability are potential targets in our society, and the managers of all large, private, and profitable enterprises have to be conscious of their vulnerability, particularly to interference by the government. The relationship between these particular kinds of corporations and government is curious, because although they need one another, they are potentially hostile to one another in many ways.

A whole set of regulations has been designed to protect the mem-

21

bers—that is, the stockholders—of large corporations, beginning with security legislation in the 1930s and continuing into the present. This legislation is directed primarily at opening the internal accounting and procedural matters of the corporations to public inspection and has, in a sense, because it is so difficult for them to keep any secrets, created an unexpected confidence in what goes on inside these organizations. More is known about the internal affairs of the large corporate enterprises than is known about any other kind of large enterprise anywhere in the world, and it is rare indeed for investors to have second thoughts about the quality of information they receive about these corporations.

A good deal of governmental effort has also gone into protecting the consumers and establishing rules according to which these industrial giants are expected to deal with one another. Most important of all, perhaps, the system of taxation drastically affects the way these large enterprises function. The tax-gatherer helps determine how the corporations recruit their capital, manage their own funds, and devote themselves to their own purposes. It is in this last respect that corporations that can define themselves as not-for-profit organizations can acquire a great measure of freedom.

Thus far, I have been speaking primarily of corporations as they function within the United States and as they have grown up as creations of our society. But it is necessary to say something about what are commonly known as the multinational corporations, because these bodies are little understood, although a great deal of scholarly work has been devoted to describing their operation. (It is curious that the gulf between what scholars have discovered and what the public has learned is probably wider in this area than in any other aspect of the economic system of the United States.)

Multinational Corporations

Multinational corporations began to appear at the end of the nineteenth century, and they were distinctively American; that is, Americans were the first to create this kind of body. They appeared for reasons that were peculiar to this country also. In order to understand those reasons, we have to look first at what these corporations did and where they appeared.

The first American firm to have an overseas operation of any consequence was Tiffany and Company, the New York jeweler, which established a branch in Paris. That was significant, at least symbolically. Why should a company like Tiffany, jeweler, silversmith, and later glassmaker, set up an establishment in Paris? There were already many other jewelers in Paris. The American market was not overstocked, so that a surplus of jewelry had to go abroad. It made no sense in ordinary terms. In fact, competition among jewelers would be far more intense in Paris than in the United States.

The second large company to go overseas was Singer Sewing Machines, which was developed in the United States shortly after the middle of the nineteenth century; by 1900, there were Singer plants all over Europe and later all over the world. The third was International Harvester, which makes reapers and other agricultural machines. These were followed by companies like International Telephone and Telegraph and Standard Oil. By 1914, when war broke out in Europe, many of these companies professed to be international in their make-up and in their operating methods.

It is worth looking at what motivated these ventures, because many of the motivating factors still exist. But first let us consider some factors that were not involved.

The kind of classic motives that are usually ascribed to imperialists were not involved. American investors did not go to underdeveloped countries. The biggest areas of American investment were Western Europe, then Canada and Mexico, which were contiguous and closely related. There were practically no investments in Africa or Asia; the biggest flow of capital to these continents was for the support of missionaries and philanthropic institutions.

Nor were the first multinational corporations set up to extract natural resources from the countries in which they functioned. Even Standard Oil, when it went overseas, went to sell oil, not to import it, because in all the important areas of raw material production, the United States at the time was producing a superabundance, and when Standard Oil began to deal in China, it went to supply kerosene for Chinese lamps, not to import oil.

Why, then, did these corporations go overseas?

Motives for Overseas Expansion

Tiffany and Company opened its showroom in Paris *because* of the competition there. The people at Tiffany felt that they were the best jeweler in America, and they wanted to show that they could compete with the best in Europe. These people were not abstract calculating machines; they were human beings with human motives, among which was the desire to demonstrate, in a competitive way, their own excellence. One of the things that moved them, as citizens of a newly industrialized nation, was the desire to show that they could deal with, compete with, produce better and more cheaply than, their peers among the more advanced nations of Europe.

Some of these businessmen were eccentric romantics. William H. Harriman, for instance, wanted to build a transportation system that would circle the globe. He wanted to be able to get on a railroad in New York and go all the way around the world, through China, Russia, and Western Europe, crossing the water by steamship, and return to New York all on the same line. This idea made neither economic nor political sense, but Harriman spent years of his life and millions of dollars trying to realize it.

Multinational corporations were born, then, in an age of big entrepreneurs, and part of the quality of entrepreneurship was to demonstrate its capacity, having conquered the country, to conquer the world. It was as simple as that. And they began with the hard ones, not the easy ones.

A second element came into play owing to the nature of these enterprises, which required some degree of technical competence. Even a sewing machine has scores of little parts. In order to sell a sewing machine in Germany, a manufacturer must have people there who will know how to repair it and who will provide spare parts. The same for a reaper or a harvester or for telephones, elevators, and the like. The more American technology developed, the more it demanded that, along with the goods that were produced, there should also be exported the technical ability and capacity to service and, in time, produce the same products.

When Ford and General Motors went overseas after World War I, or when Union Carbide and IBM went after World War II, it was partly to expand operations but also partly to safeguard the quality of their product; one simply cannot send goods overseas and expect them to take care of themselves in the hands of buyers in a foreign land.

Overseas Expansion on a Wider Scale

As these companies began to operate overseas, of course, particularly in the areas they first penetrated—Europe and Canada—they had to deal with government in entirely new terms. The necessity of meeting governments accustomed to a different relationship with corporations presented a challenge to American businessmen overseas.

German and English corporations had a close, intimate relationship with the government, and American corporations did not, either with their own government or with the governments of the host countries in which they operated. This meant that, over and over again, American companies had to stress—and this is how the concept came into being—their multinational quality: they were autonomous entities, not arms of the American government in the sense that German or British corporations were; they were free-standing bodies which happened to have their headquarters in New York but which were multinational in their own operations.

After World War II, the operations of these companies expanded beyond Western Europe and the contiguous areas of the United States. They did so for a combination of very different reasons.

First, there was a crying demand for products. Markets that had long been supplied by Britain, Germany, and France now presented a vacuum because those countries had suffered during the war and were incapable of supplying even themselves. This was particularly true in Latin America, which had always been more closely related economically to Europe than to North America. To a lesser extent it was also true of Asia and Africa; as those parts of the world ceased to have colonial relationships with Europe, they began to offer tempting markets to the multinational corporations of the United States.

Second, particularly in the Near East and to some extent in Africa, there was a reversal of relationships, and American corporations began to look for extractive raw materials—oil, cobalt, and other products—to bring to the United States, instead of exporting these materials from the United States.

Third, American corporations were under heavy political pressure to move abroad, a pressure they did not always welcome but one that was real and genuine. After the war, a series of policies, beginning with President Truman's Point Four Program, accepted it as a duty of the United States to lead what were then called the underdeveloped countries toward a more developed position in the world, and, as part of that duty, the multinational corporations were to export their techniques and methods of production to these countries, even if there was no immediate profit—as there usually was not. Throughout the 1950s and 1960s politically motivated pressure in this direction continued.

Finally, there was a fourth, and in some ways overriding, element, which was expressed graphically at the end of World War II in a widely read little book by Wendell Willkie called *One World*. This concept posited the development of a global system that would, as the result of advances in transportation and communications, form a single global entity, within which multinational corporations would perform the work of the world, providing a unifying economic system that would spread the methods of American production, raise the standard of living everywhere, and ultimately level the importance of political differences among various parts of the world. The development of a common economic stake, the common sense of participating in a single productive system, would make all political differences shrink in importance. Commitment to this concept of one world was a further important animating element in the diffusion of multinational corporations overseas.

This is a very brief and sketchy conspectus of the various ways in which corporations still function in 1980. As in all the other institutions in a vital society, there are often residues, things which appeared for now-forgotten reasons many years ago but which still persist because they have an impetus and importance of their own. As we look at these institutions, it is important to try to understand how they came to be what they are, what functions they once served, and what they are still capable of serving.

Discussion

QUESTION: You have said that the distinctive American experience in the evolution of corporations was breaking away from state control or charter. In the twentieth century, did the American experience in turn affect the quality and nature of corporations in Europe and elsewhere? Do you see an influence in reverse?

PROFESSOR HANDLIN: Not really. European corporations are still closely linked to the government, and indeed, as a result of postwar developments, they are often more closely linked than they were earlier. Compare, for example, DuPont with ICI, the big chemical company in Britain, or I. G. Farben, in Germany. There they have a set of linkages between the government and the corporation which not only often makes the corporation an instrument of government policy but also gives them all sorts of privileges in dealing with the marketplace that DuPont or Union Carbide in this country would not have. The closest approximation here would be, say, the government bail-out of Chrysler. Such action would be normal practice in most European countries.

In addition, many European enterprises that we would regard as private are closer to public corporations like the Port of New York Authority than they are to our private corporations. In France, Renault is an automobile manufacturer, but it is really a public corporation, run by the state. The large commercial banks in France all have directors who are appointed by the state. The biggest Italian corporations also have state directors.

Ties to the state have been cemented and solidified in Europe, and the kind of practice we have has not really taken hold at all, except in a very few cases. Japan is different. Japan is more like the United States.

QUESTION: How do foundations fit into the picture?

PROFESSOR HANDLIN: The foundation is generally a corporation. Of course, there are big foundations and little foundations; there are literally thousands of foundations now in the United States, so the size varies.

27

A foundation usually has a board of trustees or directors which has intermittent importance. This means that they are very important on a few occasions—when there are big changes in management, for example. If there is to be a new director of the Ford Foundation, the board of directors plays a critical part in choosing him. In the normal operations of the foundation, however, the directors are not very important. This is a situation in which the management generally runs things and secures approval from the board of directors at quarterly or more regular meetings, and all the important decisions are made there.

A foundation is not public, although it serves a public end, in that the state has no role in managing or even doing very much to control how it functions. Occasionally, there may be investigations to verify that the foundation does what its charter says it will do. It is not profit-making, and that is primarily a matter between its management and the tax authorities, because its ability to escape taxes and to receive tax exempt gifts depends on its status with the Internal Revenue Service.

So the foundation is another type of corporation that has a character of its own, based on a combination of these different elements.

QUESTION: Would you compare American corporations with the Japanese?

PROFESSOR HANDLIN: Japanese corporations, partly because of the American occupation, are in many ways similar to ours. And not only the business corporation; Japan is the only country that has a university system comparable to our own with state universities and also literally hundreds of private colleges and universities, some run by religious bodies, some autonomous—the same kind of situation we have here in the United States.

The Japanese have foundations, and so on. But somehow they also have a greater rapprochement with government than we do. Not particular corporations—the government does not protect a particular automobile or steel company; but it sets up barriers to competition with outside steel and automobile companies. It allows big corporations to go bankrupt, as one of them did just recently. There is also a paternalism, which is a different set of relationships between management and labor; but I really do not know much beyond that, never having done much with Japanese corporations.

QUESTION: What was the situation in other parts of Asia?

PROFESSOR HANDLIN: The French had a colonial relationship in China. A section of Shanghai was owned by France, and in that French colony, as it were, French companies operated, until 1949, just as British companies operated in British colonies and the Dutch operated in Indonesia, and so on. That was a characteristic feature of the kind of colonial system of Europeans in that part of the world.

There were some early understandings, for instance, between the British and Dutch. The Royal Dutch–Shell combination appeared just before World War I, and it represented a working understanding between a British company, which is still independent, and a Dutch company, which is still independent, but having a common management and a cartel-like system.

There were efforts to develop other kinds of cartels of this sort throughout the interwar period. Lever Brothers was another Anglo-Dutch joint venture, based on colonial possessions. But these examples were not multinational, they were Anglo-Dutch, and there was no mistake about their national quality, even though the union was one of convenience.

After World War I, a number of genuine multinational enterprises arose in imitation of the American multinational corporation, mostly companies like Nestle of Switzerland. But even those were not multinational in the American sense; they were Swiss corporations operating in many parts of the world, generally run by Swiss and managed from Switzerland.

QUESTION: Do you interpret the Chrysler bail-out as a turning point in our conceptualization of the corporation?

PROFESSOR HANDLIN: This is not the first instance of a bail-out, and there are areas in which corporations and government have cooperated very closely in the past. A small, individual entrepreneur cannot set up autonomously to produce tanks and then take the tanks around to the Pentagon and offer to sell them. Chrysler is the biggest manufacturer of tanks in this country and works intimately with the Defense Department, so there is a set of relationships that goes back a long way.

The same thing happened some years ago with Lockheed Corporation, which makes aircraft and missiles. They had a serious financial problem and got a government guarantee and so on.

Whether two cases makes a precedent or not—all depends on the future. It could be a significant development, or it could just be a minor deviation.

QUESTION: With regard to the beer industry, six corporations now control 90 percent of the market, whereas twenty years ago, there were dozens of small companies. Do you see this historical trend, that is to say, the monopoly trend of American capitalism, as continuing on through the latter part of the twentieth century?

PROFESSOR HANDLIN: Monopoly is a much abused word. At one time it had a clear meaning, namely, that the government said to an individual or a group, "Only you can do this." That was a monopoly. Now, of course, that almost never happens. There are a limited number of firms, however, in many sectors, that satisfy a large part of the market.

In a strict sense, six companies do not form a monopoly. In the days when every town had its own beer company, every town might be said to have been the victim of a monopoly because there was only one company in that town.

There are limited cases—for instance, the American Telephone and Telegraph Company, which was as close to a monopoly as we had. It was never a total monopoly because there have always been private telephone companies in the United States, including some in big cities like Rochester, which has always had its own telephone system. Now, as the result of changes in telecommunications, the role of AT&T has been diminishing. It no longer serves all long-distance telephone communications, and an increasing number of private companies have begun to operate in that field. On the other hand, AT&T is now becoming involved in enterprises related to what it used to do but separate, like satellite communications. That will change its whole situation.

Exxon now has a subsidiary dealing with a device called Quip, which is a long-distance way of transmitting typewritten material. This means that the activities of Exxon have diminished the kind of monopoly that AT&T once had.

So we are dealing with a very fluid situation. In order to see it even more clearly, we have to understand that technology has changed in many ways, and those changes have affected the command of the marketplace.

For instance, we now have only three big air-frame manufacturers —Boeing, Lockheed, and Douglas. Among them, if we leave out the small, private plane manufacturers, they command the whole American market. But these companies no longer manufacture the whole airplane. They subcontract large parts of it. The motors come from one place, the navigation systems from another. At one point, Boeing had twelve thousand different subcontractors for various parts of its enterprise, because it was more economical for them to allow a lot of competition among subcontractors than to do the job themselves and be locked into their own way of doing things.

Looking at the position on the top, then, there are only three manu-facturers; but when it comes to the actual fabrication of the airplane, there are literally thousands of small companies at work. This is also true of automobiles. When Ford built the River Rouge Plant in Michigan, that was the last time that anybody thought of having a plant in which the whole automobile would be manufactured. Now, all the big automobile companies regard manufacturing as the way of planning, assembling, and coordinating the whole machine, but not necessarily as producing it all themselves.

We could go back to 1920, when there were fifty large automobile companies, and say that there are now only four. In terms of where the work is actually being done, however, there may be thousands of producers. The control rests in fewer hands—and that is important, too—but it is not a simple matter of monopoly.

QUESTION: What do you think of the tendency of corporations to form conglomerates and multinational enterprises?

PROFESSOR HANDLIN: Conglomerates are a very complicated subject. Partly as a result of tax policies, it has become difficult for successful corporations to do very much other than hand over a large part of the rewards of their success to the federal government. Therefore, they are constantly being tempted by opportunities to use excess funds in ways that may not be directly related to the enterprise.

Second, because of federal antitrust policy, it is extremely difficult for a company to expand laterally. Suppose, for example, that Mobil Oil were doing very well. It could not go ahead and merge with Exxon or Texaco or any other oil company, because that would expose it to an antitrust suit. Therefore, it would be tempted to diversify. If Mobil Oil were to buy Montgomery Ward, no one could accuse it of attempting to set up a monopoly in energy.

Third, most enterprises need competent management more than anything else, and often in a corporation a bureaucracy develops that is just hanging on and is not exploiting opportunities. A merger is often a way of shaking up that enterprise and making more of it than it was.

Fourth, there are opportunities to challenge a near monopoly. For instance, at one time there was only one national rental car system, Hertz, and it really had the whole country sewed up. It would have been very difficult for a small rent-a-car operation to challenge Hertz, but when ITT acquired Avis, it put a lot of muscle behind it, thus permitting it to present a serious challenge to Hertz. At that point Hertz sold out to RCA. So there was, for a while, a kind of competition financed by two conglomerates for interests of their own.

There are many factors contributing to the formation of these bodies. The only sensible way to think of them is to see them as means of disposing of capital resources and management skills across the lines of particular industries.

Multinationals, by their very nature, are not as susceptible to control by national governments as are nationalized enterprises. If we believe in a world that consists of sovereign and mutually exclusive states, which ought to control everything within their borders, then multinationals are a threat. It is interesting that people who think of the multinationals as a threat often also think of national governments as a threat. They cannot have it both ways.

Take multinational oil companies, for instance. It is perfectly true that people who manage Texaco, Mobil, Exxon, and Gulf can circumvent national regulations by moving their stocks around, by directing the flow of exploration capital, and so on. Generally, people who attack these multinationals do so on the assumption that the alternative would be to have them run from Washington in some enlightened fashion that would be more advantageous to the people of the United States.

It is questionable whether it would be a good idea to have them run from Washington. But that would not happen. What would happen is that they would be run from Riyadh, from Caracas, by all those national entities which would create their own apparatus and which might not have the interest of anybody's people, including the people of the United States, at heart at all.

If we conceive that there are areas of life that ought not to be totally subsumed under national authority, we must at least consider the possibility that economic enterprise, like education or religion or anything else, ought not to be so totally subsumed—which does not mean that economic enterprise ought to have no controls, any more than it means that education should have no controls.

QUESTION: You made reference to Chrysler and Lockheed, and the moves that have been made to prevent their total collapse. This is true not only of major corporations; we see evidence of that movement with regard to municipal corporations in the establishment of the municipal assistance corporation, which prevents a city like New York from going under. Isn't the distinction between public and private corporations and between European public corporations and American private corporations in the process of disappearing? Isn't the distinction today perhaps more apparent than real?

PROFESSOR HANDLIN: Not necessarily. You see, socializing risk can be a form of insurance. We all know that everyone runs the risk of being hit by an automobile or falling victim to a disastrous illness or dying young, and we are accustomed to thinking of insurance as a way of averaging out those risks, so that instead of running the whole risk, as an individual, we pay something each year to take the burden off disaster when it strikes.

A bail-out is something different, because it is, in effect, a kind of subsidy to compensate for past mistakes. Now, this poses big problems. If it happens a few times and is thought to have been worthwhile in those particular instances, then it is tolerable, and becomes a kind of exception to normality. Or we might say that the disaster that would result from a contrary policy would be so great that we do not want to consider the possibilities.

If bailing-out becomes a habit, however, instead of just a temporary pain-killer, then it creates great danger. A city like New York or Los Angeles is probably bound to go bankrupt, sooner or later, and what one does to stave off the day will not be very helpful unless, at the same time, one takes steps either to cushion or to avoid that bankruptcy. But if the help, at a particular moment, only deepens the dependence, it is certain to have negative long-term effects.

The Corporation and the Liberal Order

Paul W. McCracken

Colloquies between theologians and economists, one might reasonably infer from literature, would have a somewhat uneasy and rickety status. The Bible itself has some harsh words about mammon, and economists spend a good deal of their time and earn a substantial portion of their paychecks preoccupied with things that are presumably in the mammon department.

On the other hand, the frequent "lay" presumption that economics is concerned with such matters as how to sell vacuum cleaners or how to get rich in the stock market is far wide of the mark—quite evidently so, since the incidence of rich economists is not notably high, and corporations seldom look to an economics faculty when recruiting a marketing vice president. Economists, though they themselves study what might be called the material side of life, have never taken the position that only material things matter. In Adam Smith's *Inquiry into the Nature and Causes of the Wealth of Nations*, a book some of you might assume (quite mistakenly) to be a bald rationalization of greed, there are twenty-six pages devoted to the subject of religious instruction. Over a century later the great English economist, Alfred Marshall, observed in the preface to the first edition of *Principles of Economics* (a book that generations of students were to study), that "attempts have indeed been made to construct an abstract science with regard to the actions of an 'economic man,' who is under no ethical influences and who pursues pecuniary gains warily and energetically, but mechanically and selfishly. But they have not been successful. . . ."[1]

Even so, the "stuff" of economics has never elicited many glowing tributes from the poets. You will all remember Wordsworth's dictum:

> . . . high Heaven detests the lore
> Of nicely-calculated less or more.

Now that second line does seem to come close to capturing the essence of economics. The discipline is concerned with what constitutes rational

---

[1] Alfred Marshall, *Principles of Economics*, 8th ed. (New York: Macmillan, 1925), p. vi.

strategy in the face of scarcity. Would it be better for a family to cut back on vacation spending and paint the house? When the corporation would like to spend $200 million on new facilities but only $150 million of financing is available, how should it decide what to cut out? Would the church be better off to settle for a less expensive minister in order to fortify the music budget? Perhaps it would be better to squeeze the music budget, hoping to get better preaching. If you were to ask an economist what projects the corporation should cut out or which way the church should go on its budget, he would (or he should) respond that he does not know. What the discipline of economics is concerned about are the logic and the principles by which an optimal decision can be reached when everything that people would like to do cannot be done.

That means that the discipline is inherently concerned with "less or more." For that we practitioners of the profession have no apology. Scarcity is a fact of life. We occasionally hear some such words as that the problems of production are solved and the only remaining item on the agenda is distribution. That is, of course, nonsense. Material levels of living will be improved in the poor countries, and for the lower income groups both there and here, as economies become more productive.

People do not like to be reminded of this, which is probably why the poets are irked by the practitioners of my discipline. Thus Wordsworth's poetic exasperation, or Thomas Carlyle's allusion to those "Respectable Professors of that Dismal Science." Even though high Heaven may detest this lore, the fact remains that what people would like to do always extends beyond what they have to do it with. Questions about whether it would be wise to do less in one direction in order to do more in another must, therefore, be faced and answered. In that sense economics is not out to spoil the party but to minimize the danger of "it might have been."

Corporate Businesses and the National Income

In 1978, the last year for which some of these data in table 1 are available, national income in the United States is estimated to have been $1,724 billion, and in that year 61 percent of the national income originated in corporate businesses. This share has been rising slowly during the half century for which we have the data, having been only 53 percent in 1929. On the average the corporate share has increased roughly one and one-half percentage points per decade. (A significant part of the decline in the noncorporate share, of course, is accounted for by the diminishing share generated by farms—now roughly 2 percent.)

What are we to make of these organizations within which about

35

TABLE 1

U.S. NATIONAL INCOME, 1929–1978
(dollar amounts in billions)

| Year | National Income | From Corporate Businesses | | Price Index[a] |
		Amount	% of National Income	
1929	$ 84.8	$ 44.6	52.6	51.3
1940	79.7	42.2	52.9	42.0
1950	236.2	130.2	55.1	72.1
1960	412.0	233.6	56.7	88.7
1970	798.4	470.9	59.0	116.3
1978	1,724.3	1,051.3	61.0	195.4

[a] Consumer price index (1967 = 100).

SOURCE: U.S. Department of Commerce and U.S. Department of Labor. In 1978 national income was equal to 81 percent of the more familiar gross national product. The principal difference is that national income excludes depreciation and certain taxes.

three-fifths of our national income is now generated? Have they been enjoying some sort of unjustified status in our economy? Is a major restructuring of them or of the economy needed to have corporations serve the public interest? These are some of the questions that are being asked in the contemporary scene, and they are questions that many of you have undoubtedly thought about as you prepared for this conference. They are certainly live items on the agenda of national debates today.

Role of Government and Shareowners in the Modern Corporation

There is a considerable element of scholasticism in the current discussion, much of it stridently polemical in nature, about the basic rightness or legitimacy of the modern corporation. These matters have been thoroughly explored elsewhere, and only a brief review is pertinent here.[2] A foundation stone of the case for the view that corporations are somehow "getting away with something" is the assertion that corporations have been created, and accorded certain privileges, by the state. They have received some sort of "concession" from the state, and they should

---

[2] Cf. Robert Hessen, "Corporate Legitimacy and Social Responsibility," *Hastings Law Journal* 30 (May 1979): 1327–50.

therefore be operated for the public benefit, not "just for the benefit of the owners and managers," as it is often put.

Although this concept of the corporation was stated by the Supreme Court at the beginning of the century, it seems to reflect in part the ancient custom of the Crown's awarding to a consortium the right to exploit trade—in, for example, a given colonial area—in return for which the Crown itself would receive an appropriate recompense. The recipient organization would thus be operated importantly for "the public benefit," as it would then have been defined, as well as for the benefit of the group. Except for such "natural monopoly" situations as public utilities or the licensing of radio and television stations, where the state does award the recipient something of value—for example, an exclusive right to broadcast on a wave length or to market electric power in an area—the privileges of the modern corporation operating in competitive markets are more elusive. Two are, however, frequently mentioned. One is that the liabilities of the company do not reach through and become personal obligations of the owners. The other is that a corporation has an ongoing life in the sense that its charter for operation continues indefinitely (unlike a partnership, which terminates when a partner dies). The corporation, as it is sometimes said, has been accorded the status of an entity on its own.

If these are the bases for the assertion that somehow the corporation has some special obligation for eleemosynary activities, the case is weak and superficial. The state does not award eternal life to a corporation, and the roster of once-illustrious corporate names now on tombstones in the bankruptcy graveyard attests to the mortality of corporate life. The uncertain future of Chrysler, a once-great corporate name, is simply a contemporary reminder that a corporate charter does not assure perpetuity.

As for the limitation of liability, it is not clear whether this is more advantageous to the owners of the business or to the creditors or other claimants. An individual can readily and easily sue a corporation, and the long roster of cases confronting most corporate legal staffs suggests that in this litigious age there is little reluctance to do so; but having to sue each shareholder would be quite another matter. Indeed, if prospective creditors and plaintiffs could choose, when extending credit to a company or suing it, between holding the company liable or having to collect from the shareholders, there is little doubt about which would be their choice.

The fact is that the state, by issuing a corporate charter, is doing little more than recognizing a relationship among individuals that makes for a more effectively operating economy. This is really no more an award of privilege than is the issuance of a marriage license, which is also a formal recognition of a relationship between individuals that makes for a more effective society.[3] In any case, indefinite (though not necessarily eternal) life is also a possibility for other business organizations, for example, law firms or CPA partnerships.

The other fundamental criticism of the concept of the corporation is that it has metamorphosed into something that was never intended, in which managers have wrested control from owners. Adolph Berle and Gardiner Means in their book *The Modern Corporation and Private Property*, published almost fifty years ago, articulated this case and drew the conclusion that the corporation should serve all of society, not just owners or management. Irving Kristol has also explored this phenomenon of corporate metamorphosis, and he comes to a dour conclusion. "Every day, in every way," declares Professor Kristol, "the large corporations look more and more like a species of dinosaur on its lumbering way to extinction."[4]

Why?

There are two reasons. First, the modern corporation "doesn't understand that, whereas the American democratic environment used to perceive it as being a merely economic institution, it now sees it as being to an equal degree a sociological and political institution, and demands that it behave as such."[5] Moreover, every institution ultimately faces an environmental crisis. This makes too much out of contemporary development. On these bases most of our major institutions are apparently not long for this world since public confidence in them (including government and the church) has decreased dramatically. This decline in confidence does, however, also pertain to corporations. The days of the *American Magazine*, with its glowing biographies of corporate heroes, belong to a distinctly earlier stage in our history. (Just how much earlier is indicated by the number of you who probably do not even know that there was once a popular, widely circulated *American Magazine*.)

That the very concept of the corporation is being subjected to a more critical review is clear enough if one simply listens to the pertinent debates and hearings in Washington. As we probe this further, however, the substantive case "against the corporation" becomes less clear. If managers had wrested control from the owners, the owners themselves would be expected to be quite up-tight about it, demanding a return of their lost prerogatives. In fact, owners seem to be remarkably satisfied. In a study conducted by the Opinion Research Corporation of Princeton,

---

[3] Ibid., pp. 11–12.

[4] Irving Kristol, *Two Cheers for Capitalism* (New York: New American Library, 1979), p. 69.

[5] Ibid., p. 70.

TABLE 2

PRIMARY REASON INDICATED FOR BUYING STOCK

(percent)

Stockholder	Add to Income	Make Money Grow	Participate in Management Decisions	Other
Professional, proprietor, managerial	14	76	5	6
Sales, white collar	16	74	6	6
Blue collar	17	69	10	8
Housewives	19	72	8	4
Retired	34	60	6	4

SOURCE: "Shareowner Attitude Survey", mimeographed (Princeton, N.J.: Opinion Research Corporation, Study 63068, 1978). "Other" includes no opinion.

shareowners were asked to rank three objectives in buying stock—to add to current income, to make money grow, and to participate in management decisions (see table 2). It is clear from this survey that participating in management decisions was a decidedly weak, tertiary objective in the stock-purchasers' decisions. At 10 percent, the highest vote indicating an interest in managing was among blue-collar shareowners, but even in this group the other two investment objectives combined received an affirmative vote from 79 percent of the respondents. Evidently shareowners are themselves quite satisfied with the arrangement by which management manages "their" corporation and their investment.

Shareowners were also asked their views about the wisdom of the federal government's requiring that representatives of interest groups such as unions, consumer movements, environmentalists, and minorities be included on boards of directors. Interest in such a requirement is inversely correlated with education. Even among blue-collar shareowners, where there might presumably be substantial interest in union representation, sentiment about such a requirement was heavily negative.

Whatever the other implications of this mosaic of shareowner sentiment may be, there is clearly little evidence here of owners seething with resentment about some sort of usurpation of their ownership rights. Nor does there seem to be much inclination to believe that further government involvement in the procedures of corporate governance would improve matters. Moreover, all this cannot be dismissed as simply the narrow views of the elite rich or the well educated. Indeed, the "vote" among blue-collar shareowners or those with no more than a high school education was still overwhelmingly opposed to such government action and overwhelmingly uninterested in management participation. This is all the more significant since at one remove, as it were, shareownership is spread widely across the population through extensive ownership of common stocks by pension funds.

Corporations and the Public Interest

Does this all mean that what we might call "corporate America" has no interest in anything except money? I do not interpret the contemporary scene, including the results of shareowner surveys, in this way. What we are observing is that the concept of larger community interest evolves through time, and it also has far deeper implications than much of the contemporary discussion might seem to imply.

The notion of what constitutes a good corporate citizen of the community is clearly changing. Corporations today are, for example, aggressively recruiting women and members of minority groups for management positions and membership on boards. That this was not done in an earlier era reflects less the changes in the mores of corporations than in those of society itself. Indeed, blacks have long been making their way in competitive markets (for example, in professional sports), because where competition prevails there is pressure for performance to be the route to success. By contrast, it may even still be true that the most segregated hour of the week is 11:00 A.M. on Sunday. A predominantly black college, so an official there told me, became a member of the local chamber of commerce before the college chaplain became a member of the local ministerial association. In any case, corporate efforts here reflect less a reluctant and grudging acquiescence in what society all along has been demanding than responsiveness to changes in the perception of these matters within society itself.

Most corporations today have a contributions budget, many have a Board contributions committee, and corporate funds are flowing not only to community chests but also to art museums, colleges, hospitals, and other eleemosynary activities. Corporate managers are expected to give time and energy to civic projects. Their predecessors of a half-century ago would be bewildered indeed to see how their successors spend their time and how some company funds are expended. This is not to imply that the managers of yesteryear were particularly benighted sinners or that modern managers are children of light; what constitutes good corporate community citizenship today reflects today's view of things just as yesterday's corporate ideals reflected yesterday's views.

What, however, is the meaning of the statement that the corporation should serve the public interest? We can all think of good works whose substantially increased corporate support each of us would welcome. Beyond the list of things and amounts considered "by common consent" to be appropriate for corporate support, however, who should make the decisions? It is paradoxical that Berle and Means, having worried about the usurpation of shareowners' rights, seemed then to suggest the use of corporate resources in eleemosynary ways that would in fact usurp the very prerogatives of ownership about which they were originally so concerned. The problem is that, beyond a common-denominator list, shareowners naturally would not agree on what to support. You might want heavy support for your favorite divinity school while I would opt for, say, the American Enterprise Institute for Public Policy Research. The case is strong, therefore, for paying out the earnings (beyond what is required for growth of the company) to the owners, letting each make his own decision.

There is, however, a more fundamental point, yet one often missed in much of the discussion. In the most basic sense the corporation must serve "the public interest." Its most basic function is to use labor and other productive resources to produce and sell an array of products and services responsive to the preferences of customers freely expressed in open and competitive markets. If the corporation is not responsive to these expressions of what the public considers beneficial to them, it will not survive. Too often we—and particularly we in the intellectual arena —criticize corporations when the source of our vexation is the preferences being expressed by the public and to which businesses are responding. Those expressing these preferences can rightly retort that in a liberal society their preferred ways of spending their incomes have just as much inherent legitimacy as the preferences of those who have appointed themselves to be the intellectual and cultural elite. The company that in this most fundamental sense ignores the public interest will not and should not survive.

This is true because ours is still an economy disciplined by competition. In spite of superficial rhetoric to the contrary, this competitive discipline remains strong. Indeed, with the growing proportion of world output moving in international trade, these competitive disciplines have almost certainly intensified. Furthermore, there is no persuasive evidence that domestic markets in the United States are becoming more concentrated and monopolistic, except where government has intervened (for example, the Postal Service monopoly of first-class mail).[6]

---

[6] See Yale Brozen, "Are U.S. Manufacturing Markets Monopolized?" in *Is Government the Source of Monopoly* (San Francisco: Cato Institute, 1980).

The Corporation and Enlightened Self-Interest

As indicated at the outset, the corporation is the basic means by which we organize ourselves and assemble the productive resources to put on the market products and services that people want. It is the means by which an economic activity, with capital and labor requirements extending far beyond the cottage-industry dimensions of an earlier age, can be made viable. At the same time the corporation must exist in an environment or as part of a system so that its striving for profits, and its employees' striving for better and better incomes, can succeed only as the organization responds to the preferences of buyers in terms of the nature of the product or service and its price. It must be able to achieve success only through performance.

There is something that is probably troublesome to theologians. The corporation is a part of an economic system that proceeds on the assumption that people are going to have regard for their own self-interest. The system should be designed, therefore, so that these efforts can succeed only as they serve the general welfare as people themselves see it. A world in which it is assumed that we will all try selflessly to serve the wants of others might somehow be more attractive to contemplate (though it would pose some difficult logical problems), but things will work out better if we have a system that serves the general welfare even assuming that something less than such exalted altruism motivates people. This does not mean that economics advocates selfishness or materialism. It simply means that, taking man as he seems to be, this is the way to make it all work out.

D. H. Robertson, the wise and witty economist of Keynes's generation, commented on this in discussing some presuppositions of economics.

> One of these beliefs is concerned with human motive, and is crystallised in a sentence of Marshall, to which I often find myself recurring (the italics are mine): "Progress mainly depends on the extent to which the *strongest,* and not merely the *highest,* forces of human nature can be utilized for the increase of social good." If that seems cynical, it is surely cynicism of a very gentle and mellow kind, calculated to promote right judgment and to forestall disillusionment.[7]

The corporation, being the predominant organizational unit in our system, stands or falls with the track record of this liberal, market-

---

[7] D. H. Robertson, "The Economic Outlook" in *Utility and All That* (New York: Macmillan, 1952), p. 45. Presidential Address read to Section F, British Association, August 1947.

organized economy more generally. The reverse is probably also true. If the corporation has lost its legitimacy, as some have suggested, our liberal, market-organized economic system is probably also in its latter days.

Market- versus State-managed Economic Systems

The corporation, as we found at the outset, is the basic unit within which much of our economic activity takes place. The case for it, therefore, rests heavily on the track record of the liberal, market-organized economic system of which it is a basic unit. Suppose we stand back for a moment and look at the world economic scene. There are, broadly speaking, two alternative systems for organizing economic activity in the world today: the state-organized economic system and the liberal, or market-organized, economic system. Within each category there are, of course, wide variations, and each contains elements of the other. A substantial proportion of the U.S.S.R.'s food, for example, is grown on private plots and sold in free markets, but the U.S.S.R. would rightly claim that it is a state-managed economy. There are important and widely varying elements of government presence in the economies of Japan, France, and Canada, but these countries could reasonably claim to belong in the liberal, market-organized category.

Now if we mentally look around the world, we cannot fail to be struck by the extent to which the economic success stories are to be found in nations with liberal, market-organized economic systems. Indeed, the modern world provides a laboratory in which the important ethnic variable can be held constant. There are two Germanys, and clearly the Federal Republic of Germany (West Germany) provides the economic success story. There are two Koreas, and clearly South Korea's is the economic success story. There are Chinese economic success stories, but they are to be found in Taiwan, Singapore, and Hong Kong—not in the People's Republic of China.

There are two strong, logical reasons for expecting this result. The liberal, open economy has a clear strategic advantage in each case. First, the liberal economy can more effectively take advantage of the knowledge and creativity that does not exist in its totality at any one place. New ideas often emerge from unexpected sources. Who would have expected an erstwhile geophysical exploration company (Texas Instruments) to pioneer the integrated circuit—the foundation of the modern electronics industry. Was it logical that Henry Ford, with no background in the transportation industry of his day, would pioneer the automobile? The liberal economy in effect says to all: "Have at it; most new ideas are no good, but you will be well-rewarded if yours is one of the winners."

43

Second, the liberal economy has a way to diffuse or spread across the economy the new that is better. If the something new is offered in open and competitive markets and if consumers and customers prefer it, that new will prevail, because in open markets the status quo will lose out. The new of today will thereby become the standard of tomorrow, in spite of the usual (and often sincere) opposition by the status quo. This system has a logical, built-in process for continuing disestablishmentarianism.

On both counts the state-managed economic system has an inherent disadvantage. Incentives for coming forth with a new idea are weak, and the perils of thus assaulting the status quo are real. Indeed, it is the status quo that would have to give the permits to go ahead in any case. These economies, therefore, are perpetually playing catch-up ball when it comes to innovation and progress. Their problem is not that they are avant-garde, but that operationally they are so ultrareactionary.

There are other things to say about the liberal economy that may be relevant here. For one thing, by its inherent logic the liberal economy is forced into a particular solicitude for consumers generally rather than for the rich. Through the automobile the man on the street joined the carriage trade. Dupont put all women in the silk-stocking class. If Messrs. J. C. Penney or Sebastian S. Kresge had gone high-hat and aimed their merchandising efforts at the carriage trade, they would never have been known outside their hometowns. If two decades ago the Kresge Company had decided to become another Brooks Brothers, it would at best have had a few stores in a few cities. Instead, it opted to become K Mart, with a strategy of low-markup margins and large sales volume. It was thereby transformed from an undistinguished variety store company into the nation's second largest retailer, and in the process it kept the consumer price index from being yet a few points higher today. It is intelligent, not merely benevolent, to aim at the mass market, because, quite simply, that is where most of the national income is.

Moreover, the liberal, market-organized economies are better organized to tailor limited resources more effectively to the enormous diversity of people's wants and preferences. The top-down economy tends inherently toward the drab sameness of a limited range of products offered to consumers. By contrast, in the liberal economy the person who wants a hot rod and the person who wants a good suit can both be satisfied.

There are some noneconomic dimensions worth pointing out, too. The liberal economy has an essential morality in its basic insistence that performance be the route to success—not membership in The Party or having been born into the right family or the right race. Markets in the United States were generally color-blind before the churches were. (This all, of course, does not exclude sharing with those who cannot fully participate in the economic process.)

Moreover, government-managed economies tend to produce corrupt societies in the purely conventional sense. This is to be expected. In an economy of diktats, permits, licenses, and decrees the decision of some official or functionary has enormous value, and it should surprise no one that the price gets paid. Indeed, these economies could not function without their expediters and black markets. It is a fact worth pondering that most of the cases of questionable corporate payments that have come to light have involved a government or a government functionary as the recipient.

John H. Bryan, the able and sure-footed young chairman of Consolidated Foods Corporation, had some words in his commencement address at Millsaps College that are worth pondering here.

> The most important advice that I or anyone can give you is to cultivate in a very conscious way and abide by at all times a very high standard of values in everything that you do. . . . The business world, with all of its intricate dealings and relationships, has a fundamental dependence on integrity. . . . Clearly, it is the character possessed by a person that is the most distinguishing trait which makes for success.[8]

A country with a state-managed economy tends also in the direction of military power because a military program can more readily be managed from the top by government than can the civilian economy with its changing and complex patterns of consumer preferences. Production for a military program, in short, "fits" the system more comfortably. This we see if, once again, we simply look around. The major military disturbances taking place today are in parts of the world with state-managed or command economies.

Finally, a liberal, democratic political system apparently cannot exist with a state-managed, command economy. A liberal economic order does not, of course, assure a liberal political order—as we see in such countries as Taiwan or South Korea. Even in those countries, however, a wide measure of economic freedom exists—a broader choice of things to buy, of places to work, of businesses to go into. The aggregate of freedom, economic and political, which people in those countries have enjoyed is, therefore, far greater than in those countries with government-managed economies because in the latter there are neither economic nor political freedoms.

---

[8] John H. Bryan, "The World You Enter Today." Commencement address, Millsaps College, May 11, 1980.

The Future of U.S. Economic Management

These more general concluding comments may have seemed to be a diversion but they are relevant to our topic. Developments of the last decade have clearly moved the United States further in the direction of government management of the details of economic life. The number of people involved in such government regulation and management has been rising 20 percent per year, according to the journal *Regulation*, published by the American Enterprise Institute.[9] International experience clearly indicates that we should expect such an increase to produce an increasingly inflexible, unprogressive economic performance. This has indeed occurred. The American economy now has virtually no capability to deliver gains in real income, and its rate of gain in productivity has for years been the lowest of the major industrial nations in the Free World.

Unable to accept that their strategy for social and economic policy may be fundamentally wrong, influential interest groups have attempted to off-load responsibility onto "the corporation." Thus overregulation, which produces a deteriorating economic performance, has tended to beget yet more regulation.

The great danger is not yet that democracy in the formal sense will be jettisoned in some blinding flash. The danger is that citizens will begin to feel that the opportunity to choose at the voting booth between two people for a few jobs is of little significance when their lives are increasingly enmeshed in regulations by bureaucracies over which neither they nor the elected officials seem to have any control. Educational institutions are finding to their discomfiture that a government that tells its citizens what to eat or what to wear seems also to have no hesitation about telling educators how they are to educate.

If these trends are allowed to continue, is it far-fetched to wonder if the Central Authority might at some point add religion to the agenda? Would it not be desirable for people to be protected from poor-quality sermons, perhaps by an expanded Consumer Protection Agency, or protected from unsubstantiated claims in church literature, perhaps by a Federal Trade Commission ever anxious to expand its bureaucratic empire?

---

[9] *Regulation* (March/April 1980), p. 8.

Discussion

QUESTION: You mentioned some of the social responsibilities that corporations accept. Would you agree with Milton Friedman that the social responsibility of corporations is to earn as much profit as they can?

DR. McCRACKEN: I think if Milton Friedman were here he would want to add to that statement. I think he would say that the major social responsibility of corporations is to earn as much profit as possible within the context of the competitive economic system. That would not include, in other words, shooting the competitors and whatever else might be helpful to profits but would go against the general welfare.

At this point, I will not try to comment on where Milton and I might agree or disagree. I would agree that, clearly, the basic responsibility of the corporation is to operate for profit, but, once again, within the context of a competitive environment, because then the only route by which profits can be improved is either through reducing costs—in other words, becoming more productive—or becoming more innovative in terms of offering new and better products and services.

We see the other side of this coin when things are not working out very well, as they have not been in recent years. In the annual economic report of the Council of Economic Advisers, there is a table —the data are from the OECD in Paris—which shows that for the last five years and beyond, we have had virtually no gain in productivity— defined as output per worker. If you take the so-called Big 7—Canada, France, Germany, Italy, Japan, the United Kingdom, and the United States—our rate of gain in productivity for years has been the slowest, even below that of the U.K.

Now, the other side of the coin of sluggish gains in productivity is that the economy has lost its capacity to deliver gains in real income. That, I think, is the fundamental difference in the contemporary scene vis-à-vis economic performance. Historically, people have been able to feel that, even if they were not doing so well now, their real incomes would rise, on the average, 2½ percent per year. This has been the historical average—a gain of at least a third every decade. In addition, each individual would be rising along the life-cycle phase of his earnings.

Think of the vast difference it makes in people's planning and in their own economic problems when they cannot make any progress in terms of real income. I think this is one—but only one—element of the extraordinary and unpredicted increase in second and third income-earners in families; the normal process by which incomes would, in real terms, be enlarged no longer seems to work very well.

You can see why I make no apologies for saying that when it comes to a Hewlett-Packard or a K-Mart or whatever the company is, their basic contribution is to perform their job effectively. Let me say, by the way, in regard to K-Mart, that a case could probably be made that had that innovation in merchandising not come along, the Consumer Price Index, with incomes remaining where they now are, would be perhaps 2 to 4 percentage points higher than it now is. In other words, our levels of material living would be that much lower.

Having said that, I am myself impressed with the evolutionary nature of what corporations consider to be appropriate good works or public activities, in the more conventional sense. Twenty-five years ago, if a director had suggested that we ought to give X percent of our profits in contributions, he would probably have started a rash of stockholder suits. Beyond that, even had it been legal, it just was not done. Now it is.

I am a director of a few companies, and I detect no argument when it comes to our focusing on a contributions budget; that is the current environment. It will be different ten years from now; I do not know how, but the situation is never static.

QUESTION: Would you, as a corporate director, be inclined to enlarge that sphere then?

DR. McCRACKEN: In general, yes. By the way, this is a delicate matter; my base, after all, is a university professorship. But in general, my push has been in that direction. I do not think this is a parochial attitude; I think it is the trend of the times.

On the other hand, I think one does have to recognize that there is a point at which the question arises whether the common fund, as it were, ought to be allocated or whether the stockholders, or people themselves, should be relied upon to support those things.

There is a rapidly growing practice of corporations matching, up to a certain limit, the contributions that people make to educational institutions. Incidentally, that does have a certain practical advantage; it relieves the corporation from deciding that, for example, Harvard will get money but not Yale. To say that we don't make that choice, or that we will match whatever our people give, is not a bad way to do it. And people tend to give to the institutions that contributed to their education, which institutions, one hopes, are now contributing to the company.

QUESTION: You associated the decreasing productivity in a large number of industries with regulation and compared that with the situation in other Western industrial countries. Does that mean that you oppose regulation?

DR. MCCRACKEN: I did not mean to give the impression that that is all there is to it. I think the shift to a much greater, much more detailed management by government of the details of economic life is a factor here, and we have moved rapidly in that direction, whereas we do not find an analagous situation in other countries.

Not that regulation is absent. This is why I indicated earlier that one can go to France or Japan or any other country and find varying degrees of government presence, taking varying forms, although these countries still have fundamentally liberal economies.

I would stress, while we are on this subject, the key fact that the American economy has become a very low-investment economy. The pace of what economists call capital formation, the putting into place of new machinery and equipment and facilities, is low, relative to the size of the American economy, compared with the same type of activity, particularly with such high-growth economies as those in Japan, Germany, or for that matter, France and even Italy.

We tend to get mostly political news about Italy, and, of course, the Italians stagger from one political crisis to the other. But the Italian economy has not done too badly; there is a high rate of inflation, but they have adjusted well to that.

In Japan, the percentage of the total economic activity accounted for by adding to the stock of productive assets would be two or three times our own, which would be, say, 10 percent or so of our gross national product. It would be at least 25 percent in Japan and 15 to 18 percent in Germany.

This is evident at the grassroots level. If one is involved in a process in which every few years a farmer moves from a smaller tractor to a larger tractor, the number of acres he can get over in the course of a day will rise. If that process stops, there will be implications for agricultural productivity.

Even more important, however, a low-investment economy introduces new technology into its economy slowly, because it is often new

49

equipment that introduces the latest technology. There may be technology that is known, but that will not be introduced until the time comes to add equipment. So it is not only that our stock of capital is not rising fast enough; it is that the whole process does not enable us to have as much of our productive capability at the frontier of technology as some other countries do.

I predict that unless there is a major change, by 1990, Japan's per capita income will be higher than that in the United States, probably by a significant margin. And per capita income in the Pacific basin area generally, including not only Japan but also Singapore, Taiwan, South Korea, Malaysia, and so forth, will, by the year 2000, probably be equal to that in North America. It could be higher. So we are not talking about little deflections in trends. These are major differences.

QUESTION: It seems to me that the kind of theory from which you are working is predicated on two things that I'm not sure can be assumed. First, can we continue to talk about the world economic situation in terms of growth? Second, what happens to so-called externalities or environmental effects?

DR. MCCRACKEN: Let's take the specific matter of externalities first, and a classic illustration of how economics could have been put to work to achieve the same level of improvement in the environment, with much less in the way of resources committed. Or, to put it the other way around, with the amount of resources committed, we could have moved further in that direction.

When it comes to air quality, for example, the important thing is that we achieve an appropriate level, however we measure it. Now, resources are scarce. If we commit more resources to achieving our goal than are really needed, we have in effect taken resources from some place else, where they could have been used more productively.

How would government tend to approach air quality? It would go to all the companies in an area and require that they reduce their emissions by X percent—90 percent or 50 percent or whatever the regulation is. Now an economist will instinctively feel that this is a very crude way to go about it, that it is wasteful. Some of those factories will be able to reduce their emissions by 90 percent with very little additional expense, while other factories will pay dearly for every percentage point of reduction. Therefore—and this may offend some of you—why not sell the right to emit pollutants? To say that emissions must be cut by 50 percent is another way of saying that half of the emissions can remain. K-Mart, for example, could probably cut out what few particles it puts in the atmosphere with pennies, so it would not have to pay anything to reduce its pollution. But it might be better for some other operation, which would find it extremely costly, to buy that right and let other companies reduce their pollutants not to 50 percent but to 90 percent.

QUESTION: Wouldn't they then price themselves out of the market?

DR. McCRACKEN: Not if this was a general requirement. But it is a problem when a local community does this, because the costs for production may approach the point where it is not economic in a national market. Let me give you a specific illustration.

The problem of leaded gasoline came up when I was Chairman of the Council of Economic Advisers. There was a proposal to eliminate lead from gasoline, and another to apply a stiff tax to gasoline containing lead. The council recommended a different approach: not to impose a tax on gasoline that uses lead, but to impose a stiff tax on lead used in gasoline. Why? Because that would have created an incentive to cut back sharply on the amount of lead that was used in gasoline. Technical evidence at that time suggested that if 75 percent of the lead was cut out of gasoline, the remaining lead would still accomplish about 75 percent of what lead was put in gasoline to accomplish in the first place. We could make significant progress toward eliminating lead in the atmosphere, without imposing dislocations on the economy and the enormous costs of tooling up refineries, and so forth. Obviously, that proposal did not get very far, but it would have been a more effective way to achieve the same result.

So I do not see any particular problem with externalities; indeed, one can make a strong case that if those externality costs are not internalized, the result will also be a misallocation of resources; that if the production of widgets is creating severe pollution in the community, then the cost is borne, not by the factory, whose profits may be no more than average for industry, but by the residents of that community. They are subsidizing the people who use widgets, and that ought not to be. People who are going to use widgets ought to have to pay the full economic cost.

The economic literature on how to handle externalities is enormous, and one can really say that the failure to handle externalities is more nearly a failure to have this kind of system work properly.

QUESTION: What about the growth question?

DR. McCRACKEN: In a way, as an economist, I can stand to one side and say that it is fine to want an economy that is not producing further increases in per capita income; the basic logic of economics can be equally applicable. But I have not noticed that environmentalists have been able to persuade people that this is what they want.

QUESTION: I hope we do not feel that it is really what we want; it is a question of the limitation of resources.

DR. McCRACKEN: Resources have always been limited. In fact, at no point in American history were basic economic resources more limited than when the colonists first landed in America. We had uranium and all that sort of thing, but it had no significance for them. And in the early days, a high percentage of them died.

Resources have always been limited, and that is part of the pressure to try to improve technology in order to be able, in time, slowly to make progress toward enlarging the total capability to produce real income and real output.

I think it is very important to realize that if our economy begins to be unable to generate gains in real income, it will be very difficult to avoid having the major impact of that inability fall on the lower income groups.

If we travel, mentally, from here to Taiwan, and perhaps wind up in India, we will have gone from a fairly high-income country to a middle-income country to a low-income country. It is not an accident that we will observe a growing inequality in the distribution of income as we move to the poor country.

QUESTION: I understand from the nature of your argument that, basically, we in the West should be satisfied with as free a work room as possible; that is, at least as free a room as possible for different kinds of corporations to buy their wares and invest their efforts in competition.

For one or another reasons, a sufficient number of people are not convinced of this, and they continue to seek regulations through the government, which, from your point of view, only raises further problems.

You have asserted also that it is essential to have some basic kind of rules of the game. It seems to me that an increasing number of issues that confront all of us have to do with drawing up these rules rather than simply with an issue such as whether we should eliminate, let's say, the corporations. I question whether the way in which corporations have carried on their business generally has allowed us, as a society, to look very far down the road toward what is not only economically healthy but socially beneficial in the long run.

52

Let me give an example. You come from Iowa. I am conscious that in the Midwest, in places like Iowa, prime agricultural land is being eliminated, owing to the development of towns and cities, at an alarming rate. From an economic point of view, this can only mean higher and higher food costs in the long run.

I do not see any evidence that, say, utility companies or housing developers or other people who are interested in economic growth are doing anything in the public drawing of the rules of the game to help protect that agricultural land.

I can see, though, that it would be economically beneficial in the long run if we, as a society, could come to grips with this problem earlier rather than later. Perhaps we could redraw the rules of the game and say, all right, we need a market in agricultural land, but it should be for farmers only, not for land developers. We also need a market in developed land for houses, but then that would be for housing developers and not for farmers.

I do not see the push to go into other resources for that kind of advantage coming from the people who are now in the business and who play by the present rules of the game. Is it legitimate for many of us, even if we do not know how to get at public policy, to be concerned about regulating or somehow taking control of enterprises that seem not to look after the long-run good of all of us or the short-run good of the poor and others?

DR. McCRACKEN: You have raised a great many issues.

I do not yet see any evidence that this removal of agricultural land for urban purposes is confronting us with a kind of shortage that will constrain agricultural production or increase food prices relative to prices generally; it may happen. If one goes back a hundred years, the proportion of the area preempted by streets and roads and cities was lower than it is today, and of course, it is absolutely correct that if that kind of a trend were extended indefinitely, at some point there would be no land left for agriculture.

But most of us are not inclined to carry logic to quite that extent. It is striking that for as long as I have been an economist, there has been far more worrying about agricultural surpluses than about our inability to produce enough. Indeed, I think it was Ted Schultz at the University of Chicago who rather aphoristically said that all poor countries have a food problem and all rich countries have a farm problem.

Technology, in terms of better equipment, better seeds, better fertilizer—better land management generally—has enormously increased the output per acre. The time might come, of course, when that becomes a problem. There are, however, two other points to keep in mind. One is that the market mechanism is responding to this phenomenon that you are talking about.

When I went to Ann Arbor, it was not at all difficult to get a building lot, of a half to two-thirds of an acre, at a rather modest price. What is the typical land use for residential development today? Condominiums, townhouses, various ways whereby a given tract of land can accommodate a much denser population than anybody ever thought about when I paid just a few dollars for a lot that, if it were empty, would now sell for a price I do not even like to think about.

I am not so sure that I want corporations deciding what land use is going to be—that we will not allow developers to develop land because it might preempt it from some other, more important use. That is still a function for government, and I would be inclined to abide by the usual rules of zoning. But we must remember that the main reason land developers are building new residential units is that you and I decided to have enough children that the population is expanding. As these children get married, they have to live some place.

Some communities decide they are not going to grow any more, and you know what happens to residential values in a case like that. Inevitably, the price of residences rises sharply, simply in response to the fact that there will be no new supply. We do have to have land use planning. I do not think, however, that Detroit Edison or Commonwealth Edison should be making those decisions. The market itself—in addition to government—is responding powerfully to this.

QUESTION: You referred to a national opinion research poll about interested shareholders. I am sure the polls are dead right about individuals, but I wonder if there aren't some other trends we should look at, too; trends concerning institutional investors, be they foundations or universities or college teachers' pension funds (such as TIAA-CREF) or even state and municipal pension funds, who now, at least, are giving lip service, if not serious program attention, to the companies they invest in, and who look at some of the social obligations or social injuries these companies cause.

I am suggesting not that one trend overcomes the opinion polls research but simply that we must look at that trend and see that if, in the 1980s, there is a surge of interest among trade union pension plans, which I guess amount to hundreds of billions of dollars. We may really be talking about a different set of rules evolving from investors.

DR. MCCRACKEN: I think you are right that the prevailing procedure for pension funds and trust holdings and that sort of thing a decade or two ago generally was to take an almost completely passive view in the sense of simply signing the proxy card, or perhaps not even doing that, on the grounds that if an owner did not like the stock or what the company was doing, he would sell—which is, incidentally, a powerful discipline. If enough people do that, the price of the stock comes down.

But that has changed, and trust departments, pension funds, and so on, are much more active. For example, I suspect that these funds would vote pretty readily against management that advanced some kind of incentive compensation plan that seemed too rich. There are such cases, no question about it. As one moves more into what might be called the social area, it is less certain how far that will go, because the trustees of a pension fund are themselves a corporation, and if social awareness starts to move very far, they are going to find themselves with their "shareholders" much more conscious of what the pension fund is doing. And there will probably be less and less agreement as to what the pension fund, or whatever it is, ought to do.

There is no doubt that that trend has been rising. Once again, I am always skeptical of linear trends. If you project them and they are rising, they will ultimately reach the sky. I think what it really means is that by 1990 or 2000, there may well be some things in what I call the common denominator list that would not be there today. I see nothing strange about that. We have things on our list today that corporations do as a matter of course that would have been very controversial twenty-five, or even ten years ago. I suspect that metamorphosis will continue.

QUESTION: You stated that the only real monopolies in the corporate world occur when government intervenes, but it seems to me as if the opposite should be true; if anything, government should intervene to slow down the long-term trend.

DR. MCCRACKEN: The rate of increase in international trade has been about double the rate of increase in the output of the individual economies. I am sure the American automobile market is far less concentrated now than it was twenty years ago, when General Motors had half the market. Now when you shop for a car, all kinds of alternatives are available.

I did allude to government actions, which frequently do have the effect of exacerbating monopoly. I would not want that translated into: Anything that government does will make the economy more monopolistic. I do not mean that. I have said and written many times that we certainly need an antitrust program.

Incidentally, another thing we need is for somebody to review the record to try to evaluate what the results of antitrust activity have been. Surprisingly, that kind of an analysis has really not been done.

On the other hand, I think we do have to recognize that, to a far greater extent than we might realize, the actions of government are apt to create or enhance monopolistic situations. I alluded to the Postal Service monopoly of first class mail; that was just an example. What about marketing orders in agriculture? There is no question but that they make prices higher. When I was Chairman of the Council of Economic Advisers, the department we had to watch like a hawk was the Department of Agriculture; all kinds of devices were used to try to create a more monopolistic price situation.

I do not want to give the impression that I think the only good government is a dead government; that is certainly not true. And the concept of what constitutes the proper role of government is itself an evolving thing. Having said that, I do not think one needs to apologize for saying that the role of government can go too far, and then it starts to be counterproductive in the economic scene. I think there is accumulating evidence that that is the case.

QUESTION: You indicated that one of the roots of our problem is the inability to establish capital formation, which, in turn, leads to the problem of generating gains in real income. What do you think the root of that problem is; why the paralysis of capital formation? Is there some kind of psychological basis for it?

DR. McCRACKEN: Inadequate capital formation is producing a problem, and you are asking what caused the cause? I would hold the accounting profession more responsible here than anyone else, because of the convention in accounting of not properly accounting for depreciation charges as a current cost.

If a company invests a $1 million in a facility that is going to last ten years, there are various ways of depreciating. Let's just say that for the next ten years, $100,000 will be charged each year as a cost. Suppose that, by the seventh or eighth year, the value of the dollar has been reduced, through inflation, by 50 percent; in other words, the price level has doubled. That is about what the current rate of inflation would do. Any economist worth his salt would say that the current value of capital expiring in the current year is $200,000; that is the current value of the capital that is expiring, that is "used up" in production. Therefore, the cost of the product ought to be charged with $200,000 of cost, $200,000 worth of current resources at current prices that have had to be used up to produce this year's output.

But the accountants do not do that, and the result is that profits have been significantly overstated via our accounting conventions, and corporate profits, therefore, and taxes, as a percentage of true corporate profits, have been rising.

Interestingly, according to the president's economic report, last year the corporate profits tax was reduced 2 percentage points, but because of inflation, corporate profits taxes, as a percentage of true corporate profits, rose.

This is so generally accepted in the profession that in the national income accounts there is a regular estimate of what is called capital consumption adjustment, which is really that understatement of depreciation—and it is now running at around $15 billion to $20 billion per year.

QUESTION: To a layman like myself, that seems like an elementary problem, one that could easily be solved.

DR. McCRACKEN: Do not forget that the initial step in the solving of it is the Committee on Ways and Means. It would require legislation, and any kind of legislation like this takes a lot of time. But it is finally being perceived that this is a problem, and I predict that in the next session of the Congress some kind of action will be directed to this problem.

QUESTION: Several times now the low-investment economy has been identified as the last hurdle. Why do you think that is? Do you agree with that?

DR. McCRACKEN: Our comments here in regard to taxes are very important. I think you would find, if you were sitting on the board of a corporation that was planning its capital budget for the next year—that is, the amount it will spend on new facilities and new machinery—that a key item in that budget would be the company's so-called internally generated funds. These are the earnings retained after paying taxes and dividends and, of course, what becomes available through depreciation charges.

Now, this tax problem has substantially reduced retained earnings. Actually, retained earnings of corporations, in real terms, are well below what they were ten years ago, even though the national income, in real terms, is well above what it was ten years ago. So, that has been a factor. In various other ways, too, we have become a rather low-savings society.

The normal percentage of after-tax individual income saved, in the aggregate, is about 6 to 7 percent in the United States. It is about

15 percent in Germany, and 20 to 22 percent in Japan. And that flow of savings into the capital market constitutes the money that others can borrow for financing.

QUESTION: What makes people in this society save less? Why do managers in corporations decide to do something else with their retained earnings and not put it back into the physical plant, or whatever.

DR. MCCRACKEN: In some cases they might be better off to buy another corporation. One of the curious features of a stagnant economy is that once stock market values become sluggish, the cadaver value of a corporation can exceed its going-rate value. Many companies can be bought at costs well below their book values. Fortunately, that has not yet gone too far, but it could. When interest rates rose as high as they did in early 1980, it was much better to buy Treasury Bills; there was absolutely no credit risk.

Beyond that, there is some evidence that social security and other income maintenance programs will tend to reduce the inclination to save. Japan, for example, does not have anything like the highly developed income maintenance programs that we have, and that may help to explain why, throughout their lifetime, the typical Japanese family will save much more of their income than is true for an American.

The very low savings rate that we have seen in the last year—the figure got down to 3 percent—is, I think, largely a function of inflation; the surveys at the University of Michigan made it quite clear that people were saying, "Go ahead and spend, because the prices are just going to get higher yet." With the crunch this year, that anticipatory buying has almost disappeared.

QUESTION: This may be closer to theology, but I hate to lose the opportunity to address this point. When the values that people personally think are important in their lives change, dramatic economic effects follow. I believe this is one phase where the corporations have been remiss in understanding their own positions in the environment.

I once told Ray Kroc of McDonald's that I could not understand a good Czech immigrant like him telling Americans, "You deserve a break today." He surely did not want people to begin believing that, because if they did the system would be sunk. I think that corporations have played a nefarious role in teaching people to buy now and pay later, escape, enjoy, without recognizing the damage they were doing. It is a theological point, but in shifting people's psychology and value systems, they were undermining their own future.

DR. MCCRACKEN: You say that corporations are teaching people to buy now and pay later, buy this, buy that, or whatever. In fact, if you go through the advertising of any magazine or of any other sample, what do you find? An enormous welter of cross-currents. You do find an automobile dealer who says you can buy a new car for only $500 —in other words, finance the rest of it on credit; and right next to it is an advertisement of a savings and loan association urging you to save money.

In other words, I see all kinds of messages in advertising. Some point this way, some that way. Moreover, I do not have much confidence in the ability of good corporate managers, who are good at their jobs, to be sure what it is they should be encouraging in the arena to which you allude.

Let me be very blunt. Values are the theologian's job. If you do not like the messy value judgments that you see in society, I would hold the churches responsible more than any other institution.

I would even go further. I do not want the corporations arrogating to themselves the responsibility to decide what the proper values of society are. They participate in the decision, and I want them to be sensitive to what is going on in society. But beyond that point, I think the corporate executive is out of his proper role. In just the same way, I am not sure that I want either a university professor or a theologian to be running the corporation. In general, I do not think the corporation should have central responsibility for the value-shaping and creating processes in our society. It is not unrelated to them, but it is not their central function.

Churches and
Corporate Responsibility

Timothy Smith

It is my privilege to serve as the executive director of the Interfaith Center on Corporate Responsibility (ICCR), a fascinating coalition of 170 Roman Catholic orders and 17 Protestant denominations that put considerable time, effort, and energy into inquiring into the policies and practices of corporations. As churches motivated and informed by Roman Catholic or Protestant theology, ICCR's members spend much time reflecting theologically upon the actions of corporate America and working to change any policies and practices that cause social or individual injury. For ten years, this has been a growing priority for American religious institutions. I hope the thinking and experiences of this decade will be useful in these discussions.

I am fully aware that this audience includes theologians and economists much more schooled than I in analyzing corporations; nevertheless, I trust the thoughts of this "practitioner" will be useful grist for the discussion mill.

I have been asked to reflect upon the stance and attitude, the positions and actions, the analyses and statements, of the churches upon the affairs of the economic creature called the corporation.

In thinking about the most appropriate thoughts to highlight, I decided I would *not* provide a mere academic review of the statements issued by churches on economic and corporate responsibility questions during the last decades. While that exercise has its use, I felt it would be much more interesting, to describe some actions of the churches in the area of corporate responsibility, on the assumption that "by their fruits ye shall know them."

A church policy statement has some reality if it is translated into a meaningful program; otherwise, it runs the danger of being a mere "tinkling cymbal" or words "full of sound and fury, Signifying nothing." What have the Sisters of Mercy or the United Presbyterians, the Jesuits or the United Methodists, the Sisters of Charity or the United Church of Christ, done? Have they made a difference, have they alleviated suffering, have they been a prophetic voice in the board rooms of corporate America? Or does the church run the risk of being an ecclesiastical Don Quixote, tilting at corporate windmills, tolerated but not taken seriously?

Attitude of the Church toward
Issues of Corporate Responsibility

Let us look, first, at the premises that lead churches to be involved in issues of corporate responsibility in the first place. Shouldn't churches stick to religion and let corporations run their own affairs? What do nuns, priests, and the clergy know about the internal workings of America's giant corporations? Why is the church involved in board rooms and corporations at all? It is important to share some of the basic premises that explain why the churches feel mandated, and compelled, to concern themselves with corporate social responsibility.

For the Roman Catholic orders and Protestant denominations that form ICCR, there is a basic belief that to be relevant to people's needs, one must examine the systems and the organizations that affect people's lives. I am sure there is no disputing the assumption that U.S. corporations influence and affect our lives in several ways every day. We all know this. To ignore the power of U.S. corporations would be tantamount to becoming an ecclesiastical ostrich, our heads stuck in the sand, ignoring reality. Churches relate to companies and try to raise issues of social responsibility because corporations exist, they are powerful, and they affect our lives so profoundly.

As you all know, Pope John Paul II, during his recent trip to Brazil, called for land reform, including the right to own land for those who work the fields in order to feed themselves: "The right of property must, in the Christian vision of the world, serve social ends. The needs of the common good must prevail in the use of private property over the comforts and advantages and sometimes even the necessities of those who own it." He supported the right to unionize and argued that "a society that is not socially just and does not intend to be, puts its own future in danger." He urged the Catholic Church to "serve the cause of justice" by using its voice to "summon consciences, guard people and their liberty, and demand the *necessary remedies.*"[1] This is clearly a mandate to act for social justice and implicitly a call to look at any companies that impede these principles.

This is a glimpse at some of the theological thinking that propels churches into the arena of corporate responsibility.

---

[1] Warren Hoge, "Pope, in Brazil, Hints the Poor Should Be Given Land," *New York Times*, July 8, 1980, p. 2.

The United Church of Christ says it this way, in explaining part of its rationale:

> The business system as it exists today has evolved in an endeavor to meet the needs and aspirations of human kind. Those needs and aspirations are ever changing. Over the long run, a business corporation or other organization must serve society and meet the changes desired by society; if the organization does not do so, its business will decline and ultimately it will perish. Thus, every business organization is, or should be, under continuing pressure to assure that what it does is useful and provides effective service to people. This involves a continuing appraisal and reappraisal of objectives, methods and performance. Such an examination of conscience and action will be thoroughgoing only if it is undertaken in the light shed by religious perspectives on all economic activity. Hopefully, Church investors should be able to bring such perspectives to bear on matters that corporate management can influence, and to persuade corporate management to pursue socially desirable policies.[2]

The United Presbyterians say it as follows:

> The reconciliation of man through Jesus Christ makes it plain that enslaving poverty in a world of abundance is an intolerable violation of God's good creation. Because Jesus identified himself with the needy and exploited, the cause of the world's poor is the cause of his disciples. The Church cannot condone poverty, whether it is the product of unjust social structures, exploitation of the defenseless, lack of natural resources, absence of technical understanding, or rapid expansion of populations. The Church calls every person to use his abilities, his possessions, and the fruits of technology as gifts entrusted by God for the maintenance of his family and the advancement of the common welfare. It encourages those forces in human society that raise men's hopes for better conditions and provide them with opportunity for a decent living. A Church that is indifferent to poverty or evades responsibility in economic affairs, or is open to one social class only, or expects gratitude for its beneficence makes a mockery of reconciliation and offers no acceptable worship to God.[3]

---

[2] United Church of Christ, *Report to the Twelfth General Synod of the United Church of Christ on 1977–79 Corporate Social Responsibility Actions*, New York, 1979.

[3] United Presbyterian Church, Committee on Mission Responsibility through Investment, *Mission Responsibility through Investment Manual*, New York, May 1979.

On a more practical note, the church is a shareholder, a partial owner of America's companies. Church endowment programs, pension funds, and other such holdings make the church one of America's significant institutional investors. The United Presbyterian Church pension fund, for example, is worth approximately $500 million; the United Church of Christ pension fund, $300 million; the United Methodist pension fund, over $500 million. Orders and denominations that belong to ICCR probably invest over $6 billion. The churches believe that *ownership demands stewardship.* Thus, they are mandated to look at the social bottom line, as well as the financial return on their investments. We work to end the schizophrenia seen so often in U.S. churches in recent decades, when our stock portfolios were in one pocket, our ethics in another.

Indeed, the church was challenged on many occasions for having passed resolutions condemning discrimination on the basis of race and sex, while our investment managers made decisions for us that totally ignored those concerns. The "twain had to meet"—it is a matter of simple consistency, applying ethics to all levels of our work.

Furthermore, I submit that the church does have considerable expertise. It, too, is a multinational company. (Some would even call it a transterrestial corporation.) As members of a transnational corporation, we get a great deal of feedback from a variety of people in South Africa or Asia, people who are involved in health work in Latin America, or who are experts in the legal field. Gaining expertise is an obligation, not an option. This direct reporting makes a vital contribution to our work.

In short, the investment guidelines developed by the churches over the years, indicate we have a mandate and an obligation to be concerned with the social effects corporations have on our lives.

Involvement of the Church in
Issues of Corporate Responsibility

This conviction has led the Church to some very strange places over the last ten years. In 1971, the first church-sponsored shareholder resolution was filed with General Motors Company, and the presiding bishop of the Episcopal Church attended the stockholders' meeting to present the resolution. At the podium was Chairman James Roche of General Motors, one of the most powerful men in the world; and, at microphone number 1, was Bishop John Hines of the Episcopal Church. They were not debating the reform of the Episcopal prayer book; they were discussing General Motors and its investment in South Africa, the land of apartheid. The Church was debating in the corridors of economic power.

over

63

Another major priority for church bodies concerned about world hunger has been the practices of infant formula companies that market in developing countries. Studies have clearly indicated that mothers who are poor are encouraged by companies to stop breastfeeding and put their children on the bottle. These mothers tend to over-dilute the formula, because they cannot afford to buy adequate amounts. Actually, these mothers too often are preparing a formula for malnutrition and even death, not a formula that feeds and nourishes infants. Clearly the practices of companies—American, Swiss, Japanese, European—that are inappropriately promoting and marketing baby formula overseas must be challenged. This concern has led to long discussions with the management of American Home Products, Abbott, Bristol Meyers, Nestle, and Borden, to name a few. Several years ago, angered and dismayed at a series of clear misstatements in the Bristol Meyers proxy statement made in response to a stockholder resolution, a Roman Catholic order moved into court against the company. The suit, *Sisters of the Precious Blood* v. *Bristol Meyers*, was settled out of court on a mutually agreeable basis.

Other approaches and strategies that the church has used during the 1970s have included engaging in dialogue with corporate executives, representing the church's positions in policy forums, sponsoring stockholder resolutions, reaching out to institutional investors, encouraging constituency education, supporting boycotts, divesting itself of particular stocks to "send a message" to an offending company, and undertaking research into corporate practices. I would like to examine the activities that each of these approaches has generated in some detail.

Dialogue. One of the most important approaches that the church has used in trying to affect corporate decision making is the use of dialogue. This can mean sitting down around the board room table with corporate executives to try to examine the issues and the implications of certain positions on an issue.

The early years of this effort saw many companies engage in such dialogues through their public relations staff. More often than not in the last five years, however, we have actually seen either the chief executive officer or the person who is making the direct decisions about that particular issue.

Those dialogues have been fruitful. I think that companies have seen them as something in which they have a self-interest. Last year, for instance, Thomas Aquinas Murphy, who is the chair of General Motors, called the churches together to discuss the stockholder resolution that was pending on South Africa. At that time he stated that he felt it was important both for General Motors and for the churches to have this dialogue. Perhaps indicating some of the concerns companies have, he said he felt it was not in the best interests of General Motors to appear to be in conflict with the Christian church, and he wanted to work out an agreement instead of creating public conflict.

Policy Forums. A second approach has been the attempt to affect public policy. The church, for example, has sent a delegation to the World Health Organization meetings in Geneva as they debated codes of conduct for the infant formula industry. Church representatives submitted testimony and examples of promotion by the baby formula industry in the third world and called for a code that would prevent abuses by the industry. Similarly, the church has had representatives testifying at the UN or before congressional committees. It has encouraged pension funds at the state and local level to look at the implications of their investments. The church has a voice in the public policy arena which has an effect on the affairs of business.

Stockholder Resolutions. The third approach—which gets a great deal of public attention—is the filing of stockholder resolutions. If the United Presbyterian Church or the Sisters of Mercy or any other group holds stock in a given company, under the Securities Exchange Commission regulations, it can sponsor a resolution that gets sent out to every single stockholder of the company for discussion and vote.

Institutional Investors. I would argue that the church has played an important catalytic role by sponsoring resolutions that ultimately are considered by other institutional investors, such as the State of California or the Ford Foundation, Harvard University or TIAA-CREF (the college teachers' insurance and pension fund), or Connecticut General Life Insurance Company. If the church were not sponsoring these resolutions, the State of California, I would submit, would not aggressively go out and seek an opportunity to address Wells Fargo Bank or Bank of America. An increasing number of institutional investors, moreover, feel that they have an obligation to respond to resolutions that are put before them on the ballot. It is a responsibility of corporate citizenship, if you will. They are participants in the corporate process by being shareholders. They feel an obligation to vote and democratically indicate their wishes to management. Thus by putting a shareholder resolution in front of General Motors or Bristol Meyers, we engage these institutions in an ongoing debate about the approach suggested by a church resolution. We have seen a considerable expansion of that debate going on among institutional investors.

For the 1980s, one of the most exciting trends that we should watch is the increased involvement of trade union pension funds. Hundreds of billions of dollars of wealth are in trade union pension funds, many of them controlled by trustees who have no relation to the trade unions or their members, themselves. We are seeing in the trade union movement an increasing debate about the ways those pension funds could be creatively used for the membership of the unions and about the implicit conflicts in investing in companies, such as J. P. Stevens, that are violently anti-union. And yet, up to now, in most of the trade unions' pension funds, the questions have not been asked. As a result, an investment manager for the United Auto Workers or for the steelworkers, for example, may be innocently investing in J. P. Stevens without even considering what that means for a pension fund of a labor union.

Sponsoring shareholder resolutions, reaching out to institutional investors, soliciting votes, and of course, attending stockholders' meetings are all ways in which the church's voice can be heard. Often, the church's voice is heard most effectively by bringing experts into those meetings, so it is not simply a sister or a priest, a minister or a church bureaucrat, but a professional who speaks with real skill and expertise about the issues.

Constituency Education. I also want to stress the importance of church involvement in constituency education, trying to involve the constituency, across the country, in the work that we are doing on corporate responsibility issues. In the beginning of the whole corporate responsibility effort in the churches, many people in the congregations and around the country were very skeptical of the voice of the church being raised in the economic process. Now, more and more, we hear people saying it is necessary for the church to be speaking out on these issues. They may then hasten to add, "I disagree with what the church has said about South Africa or nuclear power, but I value and cherish their right to be a voice in that arena." I think that is a very important trend that we have seen in the last decade.

Boycotts. Another approach is the boycott or selective purchasing of products. The most prominent example today is a nationwide boycott of Nestle products because of the baby formula issue; we see a very strong outpouring of church support for that boycott. Participating groups range from the Southern Presbyterians, who, in their whole history, have never before endorsed a consumer boycott (and do so now partly on the basis of their mission people from the field who spoke about the abusive practices of Nestle in promoting baby formula), to many Catholic orders and other denominations, as well as an increasing number of trade unions, health groups, and doctors.

That boycott, as well as the J. P. Stevens boycott, takes a good deal of the time and energy of the churches in trying to get the economic message across to those companies that their policies and practices are going to be met with the answer of no by many consumers in the marketplace.

Divestment. Linked to consumer boycotts as a strategy for the church is the divestment of stock, the public sale of stock, to send a message to a company. The American Lutheran Church, for instance, in Minneapolis has been debating this question at great length as it relates to South Africa, and most recently sold $2 million worth of securities in Citibank because it felt Citibank's position on lending to South Africa was unacceptable.

In addition to being a stockholder, the church is a client of numerous banks. In the last several months, we saw an announcement from the United Methodist Church and the National Council of Churches that they were withdrawing $65 million in accounts from Citibank, again because of the South Africa issue. As that withdrawal was announced, the president of the National Council of Churches said that he was attempting to send a message to Citibank—that as long as they did business as usual in South Africa, they could expect that an increasing number of churches and other clients of Citibank would not do business as usual with them.

Research. As a final approach, I want to list the research of churches that are out in the field and that do fact-finding trips on a specific social issue. Our newsletter, for example, is called the *Corporate Examiner.* It tries to do a monthly review of what the churches have been doing to promote corporate responsibility.

Issues for the 1980s

What are the issues that the churches are approaching in the 1980s? What are the questions that they feel the church's voice should be heard on? About a dozen issues will be given the highest priority. These include the energy course that America must take, redlining by banks and insurance companies, and the cost of plant closings and the ethics of making such a decision. I have already mentioned the priority given to the issue of abusive promotion of infant formula in the third world.

Another priority is the issue of alternative investments: where can we put our money to yield the greatest social dividend? We are talking about millions of dollars of church money that have been put into creative institutions, such as the South Shore Bank in Chicago, which is often mentioned as a model in promoting neighborhood development. Such a use of resources is not only a solid and prudent investment, but one that brings a social return, too.

The issues also include a focus on nuclear weapons, the arms race, and disarmament. The United Presbyterian Church, for example, has decided that disarmament and the arms race had to be one of the major priorities for the church in the years ahead. This is, again, a difficult area. The church can question what it means that Bendix, Monsanto, General Electric, DuPont, Union Carbide, and Rockwell are all involved in the active manufacturing of portions of nuclear weapons. Do they have any responsibilities in that area? Is their only responsibility to listen to the government if government approaches them and says, "We want you to bid on a contract"? Is there any ethical decision that they make, themselves, as a corporation, or is the decision basically one of national security, made by the U.S. government alone? These thorny questions definitely involve many companies in which churches own stock.

There is also a good deal of work being done on sexism and racism, not only on equal employment opportunity but other areas as well. Another issue that the church has addressed this year is hazards in the work place, particularly hazards to women who were exposed to certain chemicals and substances on their jobs. Questioning investment and bank loans to South Africa is a priority, as is the expansion of companies in Chile. Yet another issue concerns the labor rights of workers, both in our corporations overseas and in domestic firms such as J. P. Stevens. A final issue that concerns the church increasingly is the question of what do we do with the toxic chemical wastes that surround cities like New York and are creeping into our water system.

Church Actions in the Corporate World

I have outlined some examples of church action, so, as I said before, you can look at the fruits through which ye shall know them. The reader may decide whether they are sweet or not.

Racism in South Africa. One of the major issues that we addressed over the last ten years has been the question of bank loans to the racist regimes in South Africa. That is an issue that was pushed upon the American church agenda by counterparts in South Africa who said, "We want more than your prayers. If you are concerned truly about the situation we face and our struggle for emancipation in our country, then you must look at the policies of your government, you are obligated to look at the policies and practices of your companies, because some of those policies and practices by government and companies help keep us in a state of servitude, and they are not forces for freedom." This injunction forced the U.S. churches to look at their investments, at the leverage they had, and at the voice they could raise to affect government and company decision making.

We have become convinced through research we have done and the U.S. Senate and other groups have done, that the lending by huge banks to the South African government and its agencies is a vote of confidence in white minority rule in South Africa. The evidence shows that loans made directly to the government cannot be controlled, particularly when they are made for balance-of-payments purposes. Such loans, I would argue, undercut the spirit of the arms embargo since they would allow South Africa to buy strategic weapons and armaments.

Loans to the government of South Africa mean that that government knows that it can count on the outside world for support. Especially important for the church is the South African government's definition of itself as part of the white, Christian, anti-Communist West. When the name of Christ is used both by the churches in South Africa and by the ruling party to argue for the right to keep all political and economic power in white minority hands, churches all around the world have a special obligation to act.

I believe that we, in the United States and in the churches, have a special responsibility to say to South Africa that we will not do business as usual. We also feel compelled to raise questions with those U.S. banks that continue lending or leave the door open for lending. And as we do so, we remind those banks that there are others of their colleagues in the banking field that have adopted policies prohibiting lending to the South African government or its agencies because of apartheid, that Chase Manhattan Bank and the Chemical Bank in New York, the Amsterdam-Rotterdam Bank in the Netherlands, and the Midland Bank in Britain have committed themselves to "no loans" policies.

I would argue that, because of our transnational character as a church, we were compelled to listen to our counterparts in South Africa who urged us to act; we were compelled to research and examine the impact of loans by our banks; we were required to look at our relationships both with those banks as their stockholders or clients and with people, particularly bank personnel, in our churches and congregations; and we were required to act, using the variety of approaches and strategies that I mentioned earlier.

There have been numerous banks that have changed their policy

69

on lending in South Africa, either because of the appeal to conscience that churches made in asking them to change, or because of the public pressure the church helped to generate. Any issue in the banking community or the corporate community sometimes needs a little pressure before it gets priority attention. Considering the public opposition and the risk of losing some business as a disincentive, if you will, many banks have seen it as a proper moral judgment and as a good business judgment to say that they will limit certain lendings to South Africa.

Labor Rights in Guatemala. Another case in point, a controversial one for us, related to the involvement of the Coca Cola Company in Guatemala. Our concern comes again as stockholders who care about Coca Cola's corporate responsibility, but also as churches who have heard from our counterparts in Guatemala that we must do more than pray for them in the midst of the repression there.

We discovered that Coke had a franchiser in Guatemala, who had acted in highly questionable ways in trying to break any union organizing effort in the Coke plants in that country. The people who organize in the Coca Cola franchise in Guatemala and who rise to union leadership have been threatened, killed, or thrust into exile. We had increasing evidence that showed that the local franchiser was, indeed, aiding and abetting, if not actively involved, in this kind of effort to break the union and to encourage implicitly, if not explicitly, the violence against union members.

We raised those questions with Coca Cola again and again. We brought as much documentation as we could to bear. The International Food Workers Union became involved in the issue, and then they decided, feeling that they were not getting an adequate response from Coke, that they would stimulate a boycott in five European countries. Coca Cola quickly returned to the bargaining table and has committed itself publicly now to asking their franchiser to sell the company and to seeking a buyer that has some sensitivity to labor issues and to workers' rights.

Energy. A third area where the church has dared to intervene—again, with considerable controversy—has been in the whole energy debate. There have been numerous church statements that pontificate about the energy problem and the direction America's energy future should take. But we saw a number of Roman Catholic orders and Protestant denominations look at their stock portfolios and recognize that they were major stockholders in American utilities. After having done some of the theological reflection on the issue, having developed policy statements within the church, and having drawn on the expertise of clergy and lay people on this issue, the churches approached twelve utility companies through shareholder resolutions, and a simple proposition was put to them: they were asked whether they would agree to put a moratorium on the development of any more nuclear power plants and, instead, to stress the need for alternative energy sources and conservation.

One company in Wisconsin that received a resolution did say that it would drop the plans for building a new nuclear power plant—but not simply because of the resolution. This was a case in which the utilities argued back vehemently and there was tremendous controversy. Still, we feel the church has a special role. When Dayton Power and Light, for example, faced a seventy-five-year-old grandmother, who headed the United Methodist Women in that area and who called for this change of policy at the stockholders' meeting, it was a new infusion of thinking from a different quarter into the debate.

And so we were heartened and surprised at the outpouring of the votes on this issue. On issues of corporate responsibility, we would feel lucky to get 3 to 5 percent of the vote, since most of the major institutional investors automatically vote for management or people send back their proxy cards unmarked and management votes it for themselves automatically. When we got 10 or 12 percent of the vote at some of these utility meetings, it sent a message to management. Individual citizens, I think, were marking their few shares of utility stock to say, "This is an energy future that I want to support." If 10 percent of the company's shares are voted by people who really think and then vote, management must at least be aware that, even among their stockholders, there are serious questions being raised.

Redlining. Under the Home Mortgage Disclosure Act in the United States, banks are required to disclose the geographic areas in which they get their deposits and in which they hold loans. Extension of the Home Mortgage Act has been considered for some time, and the American Bankers Association opposed it, saying that this was another example of more unnecessary paperwork that the federal government was requiring.

As shareholders, we approached a number of banks—among them the Bank of America, some of the Chicago banks, Chemical Bank, and Northwestern Bank in Minneapolis—and said that we believed it was not only in the public interest but, indeed, in the banks' interest, for this reporting to continue. We asked the banks, "How can you internally monitor where your loans are occurring and assure yourselves and the public that you are making an affirmative action effort, and not redlining, unless the data is available?"

To our surprise, the Bank of America agreed, after some consid-

71

erable negotiation, to issue a statement and write the Banking Committee in support of the extension of this act. Since that time, numerous other banks have broken ranks with the American Bankers Association and have either become neutral about the extension of the act or have actually supported it.

Obviously, the effects of bank lending on our cities is critical to their health and development. Redlining is an example of an urban issue in which the church is trying to have an effective voice. Rallying support for the Home Mortgage Disclosure Act may be a small thing, but it is a step in the right direction.

Naturally, all the church's efforts over the last decade have led to controversy, and sometimes angry counterattacks by some sectors of the business community. One corporation chairman has charged the United Church of Christ, and I suppose our center and other churches involved, with being a Marxist-Leninist front organization. *Fortune* magazine of June 16, 1980, had an article entitled, "The Corporation Haters," which said the National Council of Churches was sponsoring a crusade against capitalism, and the Marxists, marching under the banner of Christ, were trying to dismantle the free enterprise system. I think it might be fair to say that we got their attention. In this particular case, we responded that we could not imagine more unfair reporting than characterizing the church's activities as the march of Marxism under the banner of Christ when billions of dollars of church wealth are invested in U.S. companies. Clearly such remarks from the corporate world are not just attacks, they are sometimes concerted campaigns to undermine the credibility of the church in this area.

On the other side, there have been other responses. The chairman of Control Data, who is an active Christian lay person, has encouraged the development of a meaningful relationship between Control Data and a number of churches, including the United Church of Christ. The company and churches have actually consulted on a regular basis about computer sales in South Africa, as a case in point, and they have invested money together in a city venture-investing program in Minneapolis.

Similarly, Thomas Murphy of General Motors recently wrote a letter to the United Presbyterians and to us commending the way in which the church dealt with the issues raised at the General Motors stockholders' meeting. He and others like him would admit the right of the church to be there in the process, as shareholder, as concerned institution, as a voice in the society.

The Effects of Church Activism

I would stress, in closing, that the approaches used by the churches on issues of corporate responsibility integrally involve the concept of dialogue and the appeal to corporate conscience, as well as the exercise of economic pressure. This is true both in the United States and in the World Council of Churches, which spends extensive time in dialogue through a Christian businessmen's organization. I think this combination is based on the Niebuhrian assumption that institutions change when their self-interest is addressed. In the case of many corporations, that self-interest is usually the financial bottom line.

Has the church made any difference? We dare to believe it has. Our victories include the rethinking of policies on bank loans to South Africa, movement toward a code of conduct in infant formula, slightly more open Securities Exchange Commission rules, increased sensitivity to Equal Employment Opportunity reports, expanded debate on energy, greater interest on the part of constituents, and more support on these issues from other institutional investors.

Some would see this whole area as an example of the church's preaching truth to power, raising prophetic questions in America's board rooms. Others would see it as the church's providing an ethical probe, pushing for consideration of social consequences as corporations make very specific decisions in those ethical gray areas where there is no automatic good or bad, right or wrong. In this model, the church's voice simply assists in ensuring that some ethical questions are raised.

What I believe is clear after a decade of active involvement of churches in corporate responsibility work is that we will continue to hear the voice of the church in the marketplace, pointing out the consequences for society of specific corporate decisions. Sometimes that voice will be the mutual voice of dialogue in the board rooms; at other times, the testimony of persons seeking to change public policy; sometimes, a call for selective purchasing; at other times, an insistent voice at stockholders' meetings—but that voice will not go away. It will grow, and, one hopes, it will be heard and heeded when it speaks the truth.

Discussion

QUESTION: Are you concluding now that the application of the Sullivan principles have not achieved the goal that they were intended to achieve?

MR. SMITH: They have not achieved the hopes of Dr. Sullivan to change South African society. Certainly, they have brought about changes in the workplace. In the early 1970s when the churches started this whole effort, one of the things they focused on when they discussed South Africa with Mobil was the workplace and the starvation-level wages that many black employees at Mobil were being paid.

That was news to Mobil. They were not monitoring the workplace, they were monitoring the financial situation. Within two years, every single employee was being paid a living wage or above. Changes in the workplace have occurred because of a variety of forms of pressure including the Sullivan Six Principles.

QUESTION: You referred to educating the churches' constituencies, members of the church. Is there a concomitive commitment of a part of the ICCR to promote individual responsibility in these areas? Does ICCR call upon church members to monitor the investments of their own insurance companies? Do they ask church members to take a look at their own investments? Do they call upon children of church members to refuse scholarships from General Motors and Ford—corporations that have investments in South Africa?

MR. SMITH: You have raised a very important point, and I do think the churches are weak in this area. We have worked, of course, for individual awareness; the United Presbyterian statement or the United Methodist statements, for example, do not just talk about the church's institutional responsibility; they talk about individual Christians and the church, corporately. Letters come from many individuals who say, "I have a few shares of stock in this company," or "I'm in this insurance company. How can I affect its investment portfolio?"

74

QUESTION: I think that the position of ICCR on South Africa is praise-worthy. My fear, however, is that it may excuse members of the church from doing more as individuals and from facing these important kinds of social issues.

MR. SMITH: Yes, it may depend on what the issue is, too. On an issue like South Africa, the handles an individual can use will be limited. If you live in Buffalo or near Niagara Falls and the Love Canal area, you know that churches of all stripes and backgrounds are concerned about toxic waste, and citizens are calling on the national church to raise questions with Occidental Petroleum about Hooker's impact. But they are also organizing on a local level and using a whole variety of approaches to try to save their futures and their health. On certain issues it is much easier to bring together a national-local or national-regional coalition, whose leadership comes from the grass roots. Those are very important models to watch.

QUESTION: Throughout your talk, you mentioned "the church" much more often than you did ICCR. I am a Roman Catholic, and a layman, and I am not a theologian. Most of the people in the Roman Catholic Church would respond when they heard "the church" but, frankly, most of us have never heard of ICCR. And it seems that you are not speaking for "the church" but for ICCR.

Many Roman Catholic dioceses do not belong to ICCR, and some of those dioceses, and some of the orders that do, probably differ with what I call "the church" on such personal moral issues as abortion or such personal doctrinal issues as the ordination of women, on which they want dialogue, even though they take a hard line on social-political questions like the agenda that you listed. Many laymen, in turn, seem to disagree with you and yet would not concede that you represent the Christian position while theirs is the heathen one. In fact, they would say that your bill of particulars differs very little, except in details, from those of Jane Fonda and Tom Hayden or Ralph Nader and Common Cause, and the notion of "church" merely adds an aura of moral superiority to your position that puts you a notch above all the rest of the clamoring interest groups.

How do you respond to those people who claim that your difference is prudential on tactics and strategy or ideological—that is, political and not religious—and how do you address those people who feel that they represent church tradition just as much as or more than you do? Why do you speak for "the church"?

MR. SMITH: Let me be clear that I am not speaking for "the church." The church is a pluralistic institution. If the head of the United Presbyterian Church went to Congress to represent their church and spoke before a committee, he would begin by saying, "I'm not here to speak for all United Presbyterians, but I do wish to represent today what the United Presbyterian position, at its last general assembly, said on this specific issue. That general assembly is a democratically elected body. Here is what it said."

It would be foolishness, of course, for any of us, on any side of any issue, to say that we speak for the whole church. We *can* say that this is the position a church takes at a meeting, this is what the church has done as an investor, this is the study document the church came out with, and we can either commend that document for study or toss it aside.

The reason I am not "speaking for ICCR" is that ICCR is a coalition of church agencies, of 170 orders, including a few dioceses, and 17 Protestant denominations. Those agencies act in their own behalf. ICCR does not speak for them or represent them. What we do is coordinate their work. We are a staff pool on behalf of those agencies that want to work together ecumenically to get a better job done.

Simply stated, I was trying to mirror the trends and thinking and responses of various churches. I believe I have done that accurately.

Obviously, there are members of individual congregations—good Presbyterian lay persons, perhaps—who might disagree on a specific issue or disagree entirely with the whole exercise.

Yet, as the United Presbyterians go back to their General Assembly again and again to test their corporate responsibility, they get increasing support for the church working in this area.

QUESTION: How do you deal with a typical Christian businessman who begs to differ prudentially with your decisions on certain very specific matters, like the propriety or impropriety of redlining authority in making loans?

MR. SMITH: I deal with it by recognizing that Christian persons can have different perspectives, that we are not talking about a lock-step march into the future that everyone agrees on; we are affirming the pluralism that exists in the church and the right to have different opinions and to disagree sometimes, but we are also affirming that the church as an institution, or the church on a local level, or individual Christians, also have the capacity and the power and the obligation to act. There is no way the United Presbyterian Church can be neutral, as a Dow shareholder, for instance, if the issue of Agent Orange and 2-4-5-T comes up. They have to figure out what their position is on that issue and what kind of stand they are going to take.

This does not mean that when the church as investor addresses the top Presbyterian lay people who lead Dow Chemical they are charging those people with individual insensitivity or with not being Christian or with not understanding the issues. I think that the most meaningful resolution in that case would probably be to say that Christians can disagree, as you said, whether it be on a state issue, like that of abortion, or on a corporate issue.

QUESTION: You outlined alternative ways to accomplish your mission. Could you rate these in order of priority?

MR. SMITH: The churches that are part of ICCR usually look at the options and try to decide what combination would be the most effective. Discussion and dialogue are a necessity and will continue. In the near future, shareholder action and resolutions are likely to continue, together with a reaching out to institutional investors to vote. Only on rare occasions when a corporation refuses to respond to dialogue will boycotts happen. Constituency education is a must and will certainly increase.

Another thing that will grow is network-building. We will see, whether on the national or local level, church persons working together with members of other concerned groups on a common issue. On the issue of South Africa, for example, the Black Congressional Caucus, and certain people on the state and local levels have come together with churches and unions. A different network of people exists on the baby formula issue: health professionals and specialists in that area, women's groups, groups concerned about hunger. Whoever the cast of characters, that kind of network-building is bound to increase in the 1980s.

QUESTION: The whole program, or mission, that you feel these churches or church agencies are engaged in seems to come under the rubric of a prophetic type of ministry. I represent a small group that is interested in a different type of approach by a pastoral ministry.

I have been a bureaucrat in the Southern Presbyterian Church, and I know that we almost always affect corporate life from an adversary standpoint. The church people who get involved begin to think of the multinational corporations, of big business in general, as the enemy; yet the enemy is run by our own members. It is inappropriate to act only as an adversary. We must have another approach as well—somebody must care about them as people and give them the message and not preface it by saying, "I am your avowed enemy."

MR. SMITH: I affirm what you are saying; it is an important corrective to some of the things I have said. I do not stand here and define the corporation as the enemy. If we did that, then we would quickly have to say, We have met the enemy and it is us.

It is important not to fall into those traps, to speak of "we," "they," the "good guys," the "bad guys." On specific issues, it is appropriate to say we think that a company has not acted in the most responsible fashion and to call it to account. But it is equally important to use dialogue, to bring some fruitful, quiet remedies to situations. There have been numerous occasions on which those kinds of discussions have been highly productive.

I have heard about a whole new possibility within the church. How do we help people in corporate management, draw them out of the business posture they are in and put them at ease? In a neutral place like the church, perhaps, a discussion can take place that is not on the record and not adversarial, but provides an occasion to examine the ethical and social dimensions of what we do.

How do we help Christians in business make decisions? I do not mean help in a paternalistic way, or that the church has the answer— but how do we allow people to talk to each other so that they can share how they grapple with those issues and make decisions? How does the church play a role in this process? The best examples I have seen have occurred mostly at the local level, in congregations where creative pastors have set up those kinds of dialogue sessions on ethics in business.

QUESTION: You—the ICCR and its affiliated churches, at least—have been working on the assumption that we are part of the system. We own these shares, so we are part of the system. In one sense, this can be our burden, too, as a church.

For example, a group of us were talking earlier about Douglas Fraser, the union leader who is now part of the board of Chrysler. There is a terrific conflict of interests for Fraser and the union, and this will become clear in the coming months.

At what point, when the church holds shares in the companies, are we ourselves faced with a conflict of interests and rendered, therefore, unable to think as straight as we might wish? Perhaps there really are not two different consciences that are in adversary roles or in conflict; perhaps we are often just playing a game of rhetoric with these shareholder resolutions and are not really as conscientious as we ought to be, because we are a part of the system.

Furthermore, since there is pluralism within the corporation just as there is pluralism within the church, who really articulates the conscience of the corporation?

MR. SMITH: I do not know whether, in the 1980s, we will be able to identify one, or even two or three, loci of conscience. It seems to me that many voices will be raised, from many quarters. Certainly, the people who were affected at Love Canal are a voice of conscience for Hooker Chemical right now. Certainly, the church, as shareholder, can play a role. Perhaps government can, too, on certain occasions.

I want to stress that the church is a transnational corporation. The way in which we mirror what we are hearing in certain third world nations is very important—as is the ability of a trade union to say, "Listen, a company is acting irresponsibly in Taiwan by using young female laborers, burning them out in three years, then throwing them out of work." We have all heard such stories.

I think we must be clear about identifying where the voices of conscience are leading us; it probably will not be one or even a few centralized places.

The question of conflict of interests because of the church's involvement in the system is a very provocative question. At a meeting of the United Presbyterians or the United Methodists, for instance, if the question comes up whether a foundation of the church should take a slightly lower return in income to make an investment that they believe will pay a social dividend, what follows will not be an easy discussion; the "prudent men" in that room will argue that the church has an obligation to maximize their return, just as any other financial investing institution does. Then someone else will say, "Well, the church has got to march to a different drummer. We have the right to risk capital for a social gain, as long as we are not throwing it away, not making a totally imprudent investment."

That, I think, is a clear example of how the fact that the church can be locked in to the system sometimes does prevent it from acting creatively. Despite attempts to try to overcome them, the restraints are very real—legal restraints, fiscal considerations, prudent people saying, "Let's not put our money into a vulnerable place, no matter what the positive social benefit might be."

QUESTION: What were some of your general impressions of Dr. McCracken's concept of the role of the corporation in society, as he expressed them earlier?

MR. SMITH: We have heard before, from many other quarters, that we should get the government out of the task of planning the economy, or controlling the economy, or regulating a company. I do not want to overstate the implications of this position. Dr. McCracken also said that there is a role for government—I heard that, loud and clear.

79

I was not sure, however, what remedies he would suggest if a company did not act responsibly. He said that a company needed to serve society or it would go out of business; that is probably true as a general theme. But what if a company, as it is serving society, does one thing that is irresponsible and harms a sector of society? What are the remedies that we are free to call upon? It is not my position, nor that of most of the groups that are part of ICCR, immediately to run and ask big government to do the job.

In a strange way, the corporate responsibility movement is quite conservative in that it asks the corporation to police itself, monitor itself, and change its own practices before it asks for codes or government laws; as a last resort, it may be necessary for society to set up incentives or penalties through government.

I also reacted to the objection that government tries to plan the economy without understanding that we already have a planning process in the economy, that the corporations are involved in making the plans and that these plans and designs have consequences for us all.

When U.S. Steel decides to close down some steel plants in Youngstown, Ohio, there are social consequences. That was a plan. U.S. Steel had it, not the U.S. government. I am not saying that the U.S. government should have been the planner but we should not assume that the government is the only agent involved in economic planning. The corporation obviously makes economic plans that affect all our lives.

QUESTION: Specifically, didn't Dr. McCracken say, in effect, that K-Mart had perhaps contributed most to society and to business by being the best kind of K-Mart it could be?

MR. SMITH: I have no problem with that as a concept, but how can you ensure K-Mart is the best kind of K-Mart it can be, maximizes the social contribution it makes, and minimizes social injury? I felt that Dr. McCracken did not adequately address the question of minimizing the social injury a company might cause as it goes about its work of providing goods and services. How do we ensure, for example, as K-Mart tries to be the best kind of K-Mart it can be in a business sense, that it really takes seriously its affirmative action program for women and minorities, which is being the best K-Mart in a much larger sense? It is clear to me that as K-Mart, or any other company, goes about its business, it does not automatically deal in a creative way with things like affirmative action. Perhaps the majority of American companies would automatically do it. But there are too many cases in which it is not well done, or in which we have to catch up with history. I think, therefore, that we have got to think of a different dynamic to make the company accountable.

QUESTION: First, when you speak, discuss, or engage in shareholder resolutions, do you use the language of a particular revelation or tradition, or some kind of language of the common good or the human condition?

Secondly, in the utilization of that language, I notice that in your areas of concern, there is nothing, for example, about the decrease in the productivity of the American corporation and the American worker, or the decline of efficiency in the American workplace. Is the language concerned with this kind of a problem?

MR. SMITH: Since we are a coalition, the answers to your question about language and how things are expressed will vary widely. A Sister of Mercy, standing up at a stockholders' meeting, might take the opportunity to explain that she sees her participation as a mission responsibility and that it comes out of her Christian commitment. She might speak of the gospels and feel comfortable doing that.

An Episcopalian might not feel so comfortable speaking that way at a meeting, preferring to speak about the common good or trying to speak in a logical secular way, saying, "We believe this is a logical approach. We are convinced that this is the proper route." But they would then reach out and try to convince people of the logic of their position.

They might also argue, if we went back to the South African issue, that a company about to put $100 million in a new business venture might well look twice to see if the venture was prudent, because it might be highly risky in the long run.

So different voices are heard. In discussing the resolutions themselves, more likely than not a church will refer to a policy authorizing the resolution, but basically this is not a process of evangelization in a Christian sense. Rather, it is an attempt to reach out, in the language that people can understand best, to those who will be voting on a resolution, and to argue a case in the most credible way.

As to your second question, it has been an issue. Certainly we hear from corporate executives a concern not only about productivity but also about what Reginald Jones has written of many times, the lack of inventiveness and what is happening to our ability to create and make new things happen in American society.

This is not an issue that the churches have addressed at great length. They have talked, in times past, about the quality of the workplace. In particular, I can remember times in the 1960s when people were talking about how to make the workplace a more human or creative environment, an environment that would relate to productivity. General Motors is talking about how to make Lordstown a more creative workplace, not simply because they are concerned about the psyche of the people who work there, but for the sake of creativity and productivity. If people feel good about their work, they will obviously work more efficiently and more effectively.

The Third World, Foreign Aid, and Global Redistribution

P. T. Bauer

The Third World As a Creation of Aid

The third world, or the South, is the collection of countries whose governments, with the odd exception, demand and receive official Western aid. The concept of the third world and the policy of official aid are inseparable. The third world or the South is a product of official Western foreign aid; without foreign aid there is no third world, there is no South. The primary significance of foreign aid lies in its role in having brought about the third world as a collectivity united solely in demanding, expecting, and receiving official aid from the West.

The third world and foreign aid were even born together when President Truman in his Point Four Program, in January 1949, advocated official aid to improve conditions in the less developed world (now the third world), where, so he said, over one half of mankind was living in misery and despair. This was the beginning of the practice of lumping into one category the vast number of widely different societies of Asia, Africa, and Latin America.

What else but foreign aid do the countries of the third world— India and Botswana, Singapore and Ecuador, Thailand and Honduras, for example—have in common? It is not stagnation: many third world countries have progressed much more rapidly in recent decades than the United States or Britain. Nor is it poverty, as many third world societies, especially in Southeast Asia and Latin America, are richer than large groups in the West. Nor is it a sense of brotherhood, as is evident from hostility or even conflict between aid recipients, such as India and Pakistan, Morocco and Algeria, Ethiopia and Somalia, and many others.

It is widely believed that foreign aid is an instrument for placating the South in a North-South economic conflict that has replaced an East-West political conflict. This is not so. The West has created a South hostile to itself. Individual third world countries are often neutral or even friendly to the West. But the organized and articulate third world is always hostile. The East-West political conflict has not been laid to rest. The East has been reinforced by a South created by the West. The emergence of the South has served only to tilt the conflict against the West. This has been evident since at least the mid-1950s.

Besides the creation of the third world, or the South, a further important political result of aid has been that it has contributed to the politicization of life in the third world. This politicization, assisted by official aid, has led to conflict and tension in many third world countries. It has also helped to bring to the fore governments more sympathetic to the Soviet bloc than to the market societies of the West.

It is often suggested that aid is mere peanuts and therefore not worth discussing. This is plainly unfounded in view of the wide political repercussions of official aid. But even the economic implications of aid in the West are far from negligible. Although small relative to the national income of the donors, aid is often substantial in relation to their payments deficits or budget deficits. Thus, in 1978, U.S. foreign economic aid was about one half the current accounts deficit. In that year the weakness of the dollar, the world's principal reserve currency, was a major international concern, and Western governments persistently chided the United States for the slide of the dollar. At the same time they pressed the United States to provide more economic aid to the third world. In recent years U.S. economic aid has also amounted to around one-sixth or so of the federal deficit. The economic implications in the West of continued foreign aid are therefore not negligible. Its primary significance, however, lies in the wide political consequences just noted.

Aid and Development

Who can be against aid to the less fortunate? This would be like being against motherhood. Foreign aid is the transfer of billions of dollars of Western taxpayers' money to distant governments and to the official international organizations. To call this aid simultaneously disarms criticisms, prejudges the effects, and obscures the realities of the policy.

The case for aid is widely taken for granted. This has permitted major anomalies. Much Western aid has gone to oil-rich OPEC countries. It has also often been granted to both sides in a war—India and Pakistan, Ethiopia and Somalia, Tanzania and Uganda, Algeria and Morocco. Large-scale aid still goes to governments whose policies directly impoverish their subjects, for instance, by forcible collectivization of farming, expulsion of the most productive groups, suppression of private trade and industry, and restriction on the inflow of capital.

Although the case for these wealth transfers, which are termed aid, is usually taken for granted, various arguments and rationalizations in their support are often heard. The most durable of these has been that official aid is indispensable for reasonable third world progress. Yet many countries in Southeast Asia, Africa, and Latin America progressed rapidly long before official aid. This particular argument patronizes third world citizens by saying that they crave material progress but, unlike the West, cannot achieve it without external doles.

Foreign aid cannot promote appreciably the growth of the national income. It is far more likely to retard it. Countries where government or business can use funds productively can borrow abroad. The maximum contribution of foreign aid to development in the sense of the growth of the national income cannot therefore exceed the avoided cost of borrowing.

An example may help here. According to the official statistics, external aid to India in the late 1970s was around 3 percent of GNP. If the cost of capital is put as high as 20 percent per year, then the avoided cost of borrowing in this case is 0.6 percent of the officially estimated GNP, provided that aid is a free and untied grant. It is less because some aid is tied and some of it is repayable. The maximum contribution to development turns out to be even smaller when it is remembered that the actual GNP of a country like India much exceeds (probably by a factor of about three) the official estimate when expressed on a basis comparable to that of the United States.[1]

Any tiny, marginal benefit from the reduction of the cost of investible funds is likely to be more than offset by the adverse repercussions of official aid. These adverse effects are asymmetrical with the possible maximum benefit in two ways. First, they are brought about by amounts of aid, which, while small in relation to the national income, are nevertheless large compared with government revenues or foreign exchange earnings in the recipient countries. These are the relevant magnitudes, because aid is concentrated on governments. Second, the tiny maximum benefit results from a reduction in the cost of investible funds. But the volume of these funds is not a major factor in economic development. The basic determinants are personal, social, and political factors. The adverse repercussions operate on these basic determinants.

Official aid increases the money, patronage, and power of the recipient governments and thereby their grip over the rest of society. It thus promotes the disastrous politicization of life in the third world and intensifies the struggle for power. This result increases conflict, especially in the multiracial societies of most third world countries. This

---

[1] Cf., for instance, the comparison of real and nominal GDP per capita for India (and many other third world countries) in Irving B. Kravis, Alan W. Heston, and Robert Summers, "Real GDP per Capita for More than 100 Countries," *Economic Journal,* vol. 88 (June 1979), especially table 4.

sequence diverts energy and attention from productive activity to the political arena, because people's livelihood or even their economic and physical survival come to depend on political and administrative decisions.

Foreign aid promotes state-controlled economies in various other ways as well. State economic controls again lead to politicization, restrict external contacts and domestic mobility, and retard the spread of new ideas and methods.

Official aid often impairs the international economic position of the recipients by driving up the rate of exchange, helping to maintain overvalued exchange rates, or increasing the money supply. It tends also to encourage imprudent financial policies, because external payments difficulties are an effective ground for appeal for aid. Aid reinforces the widely prevalent idea that third world betterment depends on outside factors. It also biases development policy toward unsuitable external models—witness official airlines in countries whose citizens normally do not travel and rarely use these airlines.

Thus foreign aid cannot advance significantly the material progress of the recipient countries. This is so because the maximum benefit to development is the avoided cost of borrowing, that is, the reduced cost of some investible funds. The volume of these funds is not a basic determinant of economic advance. Reduction in the cost of these funds, which represents a small proportion of the national income, cannot possibly promote progress significantly, even in the most favorable circumstances. And because the major adverse effects of official aid operate on the basic determinants of progress, the presumption of the outcome of aid for development must be negative. That is, it is more likely to obstruct than promote material progress, and even when it does promote it, the contribution must be minimal.

Counsel has been darkened in this field by the familiar references to Marshall aid given by the United States to Western Europe after the war. The analogy between Marshall aid and official transfers to the third world fails completely. In post-war Europe the task was not development but reconstruction. People's faculties, institutions, and political arrangements were appropriate to sustained prosperity, as was evident from pre-war experience. This is why Marshall aid could be terminated in four years, and West Germany could become an exporter of capital soon afterwards. Contrast this with the advocacy of indefinite wealth transfers to the third world, and with the difficulties of many aid recipients to service even very soft loans.

The conclusion that, even in the most favorable circumstances, the contribution of aid to third world development cannot be significant follows from evidence, from inference about the availability of capital when it can be used productively, and from the pertinent magnitudes, that is, the avoided cost of capital and the amount of aid as a percentage of national incomes.

The adverse presumption about the effects of aid on development is supported by evidence of various kinds. For instance, many third world governments have found it difficult to service their obligations, even very soft loans, the modest burden of which has been largely reduced by inflation and by numerous earlier write-offs. The many examples include Ghana, which, in spite of earlier substantial aid and large earnings from cocoa, defaulted repeatedly in the 1960s and 1970s.

The adverse presumption is strengthened by the conditions that obtained in many recipient countries after decades of aid—very low living standards, recurrent famine, breakdown of the exchange economy and of public security and health (sometimes aptly termed disdevelopment). It is also supported by the shift in the advocacy of aid from development to other objectives.

It is often thought that the effects of aid could be established from empirical evidence with the help of statistical analysis. This is not so. As it happens, the statistical evidence is conflicting. Some studies have found significant correlation between aid received and the growth of national income. Others, including those of the Pearson Commission, have found no such correlation.

But even if there were a consistently high correlation between aid and development (which there is not), this would show at most that capital could be used productively in the recipient countries. (At most, because it is impossible to isolate the effects of the inflow of investable funds from the many other factors that affect development, all of which operate with different time lags; and also because of the huge margins of error in the estimates of third world incomes.) Even if it were established, which is in practice impossible, that aid funds over a period proved highly productive in their overall effects, the maximum contribution of aid to development would still be restricted to the avoided cost of borrowing, since the funds could have been obtained commercially from abroad. Large-scale regression analyses, which have at times been undertaken to establish the contribution of aid to development, are thus irrelevant.

Relief of Poverty

Relief of poverty is now a much-canvassed objective of aid, and one with obvious moral overtones. But official aid does not go to poor people, to the skeletal figures of aid propaganda; it goes to their rulers, whose spending policies are determined by their own personal and political interests, among which the position of the poorest has very low priority. Indeed, to support rulers on the basis of the poverty of their subjects is more likely to encourage policies of impoverishment than to deter them. Many third world governments have persecuted and even expelled the most productive groups, such as ethnic minorities—the Chinese in Vietnam and Indonesia, and Asians in East Africa, for example. On the criterion of poverty, such governments qualify for more aid because incomes in their countries have been reduced. Official Western aid to third world governments, especially in Asia and Africa, has extensively supported brutal, inhuman policies, which have greatly aggravated the lot of the poorest.

Poverty as measured by per capita income as the criterion of aid also involves other major anomalies. For instance, if more of the poor died as a result of disease, this would raise per capita incomes and provide an evidently perverse reason for reducing aid. Again, the meaning of riches and poverty depends crucially on people's requirements, and thus on physical and social living conditions. This is obvious for physical conditions, notably climate. But it applies also to social conditions, including customs and values. If, for instance, as a result of changes in mores or official policies, women are discouraged from taking paid work, this would register as a fall in income even though it would not indicate impoverishment as commonly understood; nor should it serve as an appropriate ground for more aid. Such anomalies could readily be multiplied.

Attempts to avoid some of these anomalies by trying to give official aid directly to the poorest, or by prescribing the policies of the recipient governments, would be resisted and sabotaged by third world governments. If this resistance could be overcome, other intractable problems would arise.

The poorest, whether entire societies or the poorest groups within one society, are unlikely to possess aptitudes and motivations for economic achievement to the same extent as those who are more prosperous. This is why relief of poverty and promotion of development differ radically as objectives of aid. They are indeed largely at variance, differing in much the same way as alms to a beggar differ from scholarships to promising students, or as assistance to an invalid differs from loans to young people to establish themselves in business.

The poorest groups in third world countries tend to be materially unambitious. Official handouts to improve their economic conditions will have to be continued indefinitely if the beneficiaries are not to relapse into their original poverty. Poor people can therefore be turned into paupers; whole societies can be pauperized in this way. The Navajo Indians, heavily subsidized by the U.S. government for many decades, are a familiar example. A less familiar but informative and pertinent recent example is that of the large-scale pauperization in the United States trust territory of Micronesia in the Pacific, described in a lively and informative report in the *Washington Post*, July 27, 1978. Many Micronesians have abandoned productive economic activity, such as agriculture and fishing on a large scale, because they can live comfortably on the handouts supplied by the U.S. administration. These results of aid discourage attitudes and skills necessary for economic achievement. They amount to what has been termed *disdevelopment*, the deskilling of people who will subsequently have to reacquire the faculties required for economic achievement.

Aid to relieve poverty thus readily becomes worldwide outdoor relief. The outcome of pauperization is persistent poverty, which in turn rationalizes indefinite aid.

Intervention by the donors to avert pauperization by instilling in the recipients the requirements of economic achievement is not feasible. In many societies of the third world such attempts would require wholesale reforms of local beliefs and values, including some of those most deeply felt. Such attempts would involve far-reaching coercion of the supposed beneficiaries. These realities are obscured in such ambiguous phrases as the need to modernize agriculture or to reform institutions. But what is envisaged is not the reform and modernization of a sector or of an activity, but of the people engaged in them, not of beliefs and values, but of those who hold them, and not of institutions, but of those who participate in them. What is to be transformed is people, that is, persons and groups of persons, not abstract entities such as activities, sectors, and institutions.

Many aid recipient governments, as well as their populations at large, would refuse aid if it meant coercive transformation of values and attitudes. Such policies are much more likely to aggravate poverty than to relieve it, because they would set up determined resistance, which could be overcome, if at all, only at the cost of turning the population into an apathetic mass incapable of effort and enterprise. It is therefore just as well that in practice official aid stops short of such drastic attempts purporting to relieve poverty.

Aid and Employment

Aid is often advocated on the ground that it provides employment by promoting exports. This is like saying that it benefits a shopkeeper to be burgled if the burglar spends part of the loot in the shop. Aid-financed exports are bought with taxpayers' money. Taxpayers therefore have less to spend at home. Direct domestic employment subsidies would be cheaper and more effective and would make the process clearer.

According to another version of this argument, aid benefits the donor economies and sustains employment by promoting long-term development of the recipients. By assuming without question that aid is necessarily effective, this argument prejudges the issue. It also ignores the alternative and more productive uses of the capital represented by aid.

It is often said that official Western aid is indispensable to prevent the third world from drifting into the Soviet orbit. A large and growing volume of Western official aid is multilateral, that is, it is channeled through international agencies. In the allocation of aid these agencies are not permitted to take into account the political interests of the donors. Moreover, the Soviet bloc is represented in these international agencies and can therefore influence the allocation of multilateral aid, even though its financial contribution to aid is small. But Western political interests are also largely ignored in bilateral aid, which is given regardless both of the conduct of the recipients and of their political significance. Many recipients insult and thwart the Western donors as best as they can.

Redistribution and Restitution

Aid is often envisaged as an instrument of global redistribution. But foreign aid differs radically from domestic redistribution, whatever the case for the latter. Foreign aid goes from government to government and is not adjusted to the personal circumstances of taxpayers and recipients. Many taxpayers in donor countries are far poorer than many people in recipient countries, where, moreover, aid mainly benefits the relatively well off. Again, redistributive taxation postulates a basic similarity of conditions, and therefore of requirements, within its area of operation. Globally, however, these requirements differ widely. This is obvious for physical requirements dictated by climate; but it applies also to political and social considerations. Should Americans be taxed for the benefit of governments whose policies directly reduce incomes in their countries, or whose citizens refuse to kill animals, as in India, or who refuse to let women take paid work, as in many Moslem countries?

Further, because international income differences reflect people's qualities, mores, institutions, and political arrangements, any reduction in income differences must be temporary, because the basic factors behind them soon reassert themselves. The process of politically organized redistribution would therefore have to be continued indefinitely.

The policy also implies transfers from more productive to less productive people and thereby reduces the overall productivity of resources.

Another much-canvassed argument is that aid represents restitution for Western misconduct, past or present. This argument is the reverse of the truth. So far from the West having caused the poverty of the third world, contact with the West has been the principal agent of material progress there. The materially most advanced societies and regions of the third world are those with which the West established the most numerous, diversified, and extensive contacts: the cash-crop-producing areas and entrepôt ports of Southeast Asia, West Africa, and Latin America; the mineral-producing areas of Africa and the Middle East; and cities and ports throughout Asia, Africa, the Caribbean, and Latin America. The level of material achievement usually diminishes as one moves away from the foci of Western impact; the poorest and most backward are the populations with few or no external contacts, the aborigines being the limiting case.

The West was materially far ahead of the present third world countries when it established extensive diversified economic contacts with them in the nineteenth and twentieth centuries. It was through these contacts that human and material resources, skills, capital, and new ideas, including the idea of material progress itself, flowed from the West to the third world.

In recent times the role of external contacts in promoting economic advance in the third world has been much more significant than that of similar contacts in the earlier history of Europe.

To begin with, as just noted, the very idea of material progress in the sense of sustained, steady, and increasing control over man's environment is a Western concept. People in the third world did not think in these terms before the advent of Western man. Scholars of widely different philosophical and political persuasions, for instance, J. B. Bury and Christopher Dawson, have long recognized the Western origin of the idea of material progress.

In the nineteenth and twentieth centuries, when the West developed multifarious commercial contacts with the present third world, the gap in economic attainment between the West and these regions was very wide, much wider than such gaps in the past. Thus, the establishment of contacts offered correspondingly greater potentialities, which were further enhanced by the great improvements in transport and communications over the last two hundred years or so.

Since the middle of the nineteenth century, commercial contacts established by the West have improved material conditions out of all recognition over much of the third world, notably Southeast Asia; parts of the Middle East; much of Africa, especially West Africa and parts of

Eastern and Southern Africa; and very large parts of Latin America, including Mexico, Guatemala, Venezuela, Colombia, Peru, Chile, Brazil, Uruguay, and Argentina.

I need not labor further the argument that the West has not caused the poverty of the third world, but has promoted progress there. But it may be useful to supplement the argument by a few observations pertinent to the idea of restitution. It is often urged that Western colonialism has caused third world backwardness. In fact, many of the most backward third world countries never were Western colonies, for example, Tibet and Liberia. Many of the most prosperous countries of the West never had any colonies or were even themselves colonies of other countries, for example, the United States, Canada, and Australia. However, while the idea that Western colonialism has caused third world poverty is demonstrably unfounded, there have been many victims of colonialism in history, people killed or maimed in colonial wars and tribal farmers dispossessed by colonialists. These people are by now dead and cannot be helped even by the World Bank.[2] Their descendants have gained from being born into the colonial or postcolonial world, rather than into the circumstances of precolonial Africa and Asia, where epidemic and endemic disease, tribal warfare, and lack of public security were widespread, if not universal. Indeed, millions of people who would otherwise have died survived because of Western techniques and ideas, notably the medicine and public security that came with colonial rule.

Even if it could be established that colonialism was on balance harmful to the colonized, this would still not provide an argument for Western aid generally. Major aid donors never had any colonies or dependencies of significance. Even in the case of colonial powers whose predecessors may have inflicted damage on certain groups, any theory of restitution would still fail. Except over very short periods, historical wrongs cannot be put right. For example, what date would we fix after which the crimes would be considered as justifying compensation? How far back in history should we go—a hundred years, a thousand years, or longer? How would we identify the descendants of the criminals and of the victims? And would all historical crimes be invoked or only those perpetrated by the West? Or, more precisely, by the supposed forebears of people living in the West against the supposed forebears of some third world peoples?

Should Outer Mongolia (or its actual masters) pay compensation

---

[2] It is doubtful whether the rest would have preferred the short span of life, poverty, disease, and incessant tribal wars in order to retain control of their countries, the resources of which they were unable to develop.

to Poland, Hungary, and Turkey, and several OPEC countries for the depredations of the Mongols many centuries ago, because the Mongols came from Central Asia? Should the Soviet Union compensate the descendants of the people displaced or killed in the Russian colonization of Siberia in past centuries? Should the United States pay compensation to some African countries for the activities of some nineteenth-century American slavers, even if this involved taxing American Negroes for the benefit of present African governments? Should present-day Americans be taxed to make amends to American Indians when most of the taxpayers are descended from immigrants who entered the country long after the time of any wrongs perpetrated against the ancestors of the Indians? A statute of limitations on historical wrongs is more than just; it is unavoidable.

Reform of Aid

Nonsense is rarely harmless, particularly in public discussion. It is, therefore, a worthwhile exercise to try to expose widely held misconceptions. I want, however, to say something about what I think the West should do to help people in the third world. In particular, I want to address what the West can do to relieve poverty and promote economic advancement in the third world. Official aid as it has operated so far has obstructed rather than promoted these objectives.

Relief of need should be left to voluntary agencies, notably to nonpoliticized, religious, and medical charities. Many of them already operate successfully in the South. They could do much more if it were recognized that relief of need belongs to their sphere and that it is not the task of official transfers, which in this realm should be restricted to disaster relief.

There are significant advantages in leaving the relief of need to charities, particularly those charities that are not largely politicized.[3] They know far more than Western governments about local conditions in distant societies, where circumstances differ greatly from country to country, as well as from Western conditions. Genuine charities are also usually more interested in assisting the poorest and most distressed than are third world rulers. Nor do the activities of charities directly promote the politicization of life, or increase the prizes of political power, or exacerbate political tension, or sustain the pursuit of harmful, oppressive, or inhuman policies. Indeed, insofar as voluntary agencies provide

---

[3] Some *soi-disant* charities now have primarily political aims, such as international redistribution or so-called liberation; they are thus best regarded as political parties or front organizations.

an alternative source of help to third world people, their activities may even marginally reduce the power of the rulers over their subjects. Further, voluntary aid is financed by people who give freely to help their fellow man. Official aid, in contrast, is tax money, which has to be paid. Many third world people sense this difference, and are suspicious of claims that aid is inspired by charitable and disinterested motives. Many citizens in the West also seem aware of the difference.

A specific example is pertinent. In June 1976 a referendum was held on a Swiss government proposal to provide the official International Development Association with substantial funds for contributions to third world governments. The proposal was supported unanimously by the media and by churches, universities, and schools. For constitutional reasons, it had to be tested in a referendum. In this referendum—the first popular vote ever taken in the West on foreign aid—the proposal was heavily defeated. At the same time the Swiss voluntarily contributed large sums to a fund for the victims of an earthquake in Italy, as well as to many third world charities. The public can distinguish official aid from voluntary charity. Voluntary donations serve also to refute the claims of third world leaders that aid is a matter of right, not of charity.

Voluntary charity for helping the poor in the third world, though greatly preferable to official aid, also needs to be administered with considerable care if it is not to bring about untoward results. If it is envisaged as a long-term process of giving out alms, rather than as disaster relief, it can easily lead to permanent pauperization. It is also likely to encourage feelings of superiority in the donors and of dependence in the recipients, as often happens under official aid as well.

To turn now to development, the West can best promote third world development by reducing its often severe barriers to imports from poor countries. These inhibit development, investment, and employment and therefore reduce the benefit that the South derives from external contacts. Foreign trade has transformed economic life in much of the South, notably the Far East, Southeast Asia, parts of Africa, and Latin America. Relaxation of trade restrictions could extend and accelerate this process. External trade is an effective stimulus to economic progress. The people and the finance involved in it are far more responsive and better adjusted to local realities than are official transfers and their dispensers. Commercial contacts are not only economically more effective but also much less likely to provoke social and political upheaval than are attempts at forcible modernization or large-scale confiscations, so often supported by official transfers and their advocates. External trade also brings to the fore local traders, entrepreneurs, and other self-reliant groups interested in improvement through market processes. They are far more likely to be friendly to the West than the rulers of socialist economies or of other closely controlled economies encouraged by official transfers.

Reduction of trade barriers is apt to be resisted by those threatened by it. Some aid funds might be diverted to compensate those who are threatened by such measures. This measure, too, is open to various objections. But if practicable, it might be the lesser of evils compared with ever-increasing trade barriers coupled with continuing or even increasing transfers.

Official transfers are, however, certain to continue. How could they be reformed? To begin with, they should take the form that would make it possible to identify their costs and benefits. This rules out indirect methods of resource transfers such as commodity agreements. Not only are their results perverse, but their overall impact cannot be assessed. Nor are such schemes subject to any form of congressional or parliamentary control. The transfers should be untied cash grants. Tied aid confuses subsidies to exporters and gifts to the recipients, besides suggesting that they are instruments for dumping otherwise unsalable goods. Soft loans conceal their usually very large grant element, confusing investment and handouts. Again, the donors are apt to see them as gifts, while the recipients see them as burdens. Cash grants should be bilateral, to enable a modicum of control by the elected representatives of the taxpayers, that is, the real donors. Inhuman policies or policies utterly hostile to the donors can also be checked somewhat more easily under a bilateral system.

It should also be made clear that the grants are in effect straight gifts from the Western donors to the recipient governments, not restitution for past or present wrongs or instruments of global egalitarianism. Unless restitution or redistribution are specifically rejected, the West will find it is subject to indefinite blackmail.

The transfers should go only to governments that are genuinely interested in the welfare of their subjects and that promote it by effective administration, the performance of the essential tasks of government, and the pursuit of liberal economic policies. This would reduce the effect of aid in politicizing life and would be more likely to promote prosperity and reduce conflict.

Unless reformed along these lines, international wealth transfers will continue to promote totalitarian systems in Asia, Africa, and Latin America. They will continue to disappoint and to frustrate many generous and compassionate supporters of aid to the less fortunate.

Discussion

QUESTION: Do your arguments against foreign aid apply to the OPEC countries making their oil wealth available to the third world?

PROFESSOR BAUER: If the Arab countries decide to give money to third world governments this is up to them. It will not promote the material progress of the peoples of the recipient countries. I think the OPEC rulers pursue this policy primarily in order to buy votes at the United Nations. It is also a form of risk diversification on the part of Arab rulers. They want to hold some of their assets in U.S. dollars, some in pounds sterling, some in real estate, and also some in what they think is political goodwill of the governments to which they give some of their surpluses.

QUESTION: Many illustrations you give of aid or development seem unhappy. I gather, from something else you wrote, that you might offer Hong Kong as a positive example of how development can take place properly. If that is true, will you explain how and why development worked there and whether there are any useful lessons to be learned from this case?

PROFESSOR BAUER: Hong Kong is of interest as a limiting case of a consideration that applies widely. Material progress does not depend on natural resources or on external donations. It depends on the personal, social, and political determinants of development, that is, on people's attributes, motivations, mores, and on the policies of their governments. This is evident on the contemporary scene and evident also from many examples in history. I mentioned Hong Kong as an extreme and striking example.

QUESTION: Moving into the area of myth and the persistence of myth, I recall a National Council of Churches pronouncement that attributed poverty in the third world to three systemic causes: colonialism, neo-colonialism, and multinational corporations.

The empirical evidence that this statement was wrong on all three counts seems not to have sunk in. How do you account for this gullibility of intellectuals and other well-minded people?

PROFESSOR BAUER: Throughout the third world the poorest countries and societies are those with the fewest external contacts. Peaceful external contacts extend people's opportunities and promote material progress. Throughout the less developed world the level of economic achievement declines as we move away from the impact of Western contacts. To say that the multinational corporations have exploited the Pygmies or the desert folk or the aborigines is patently untrue. Further, the poorest countries of the third world have never been colonies: witness Nepal, Bhutan, Tibet, Liberia, Ethiopia. Many colonies progressed rapidly while they were still colonies: for example, Malaya, the Gold Coast (now Ghana), Nigeria, and many others. Nor should we forget that the United States, Canada, Australia and New Zealand were colonies and were prosperous under colonialism.

QUESTION: Why has religion declined in the National Council of Churches?

PROFESSOR BAUER: They have lost their nerve—which seems amazing, in a way, at a time when the troubles of the age are clearly in the spiritual field, material prosperity having exceeded all expectations. Even in wretched England, poor England, there are 1½ television sets per family. People in England think of ghastly economic depression and slump, even though the country is more prosperous than ever. Yet they feel terribly uneasy.

The answer is, of course, that material prosperity has not brought about the results expected from it. And the churches, instead of saying that the troubles of the age are spiritual troubles, adopt the opposite spirit, and try to compete with the labor bureaus and employment exchanges and welfare agencies, because they, themselves, have lost their self-assurance.

QUESTION: Do you see any major impediment to applying your analysis of foreign aid to the domestic welfare state that exists in the United States and Great Britain?

PROFESSOR BAUER: There are certain obvious similarities between domestic welfare programs and foreign aid. For instance, those who run these programs are major beneficiaries. But I think there are also fundamental differences. In domestic welfare programs the payments go to individuals and families, while under foreign aid they go to governments. Again, domestic welfare programs operate in particular countries where physical conditions, notably climatic conditions, and social mores are broadly uniform. Globally, there are wide differences in climatic conditions and mores and, therefore, differences in people's requirements.

QUESTION: I was reading over some reports on Pope John Paul II's visit to Brazil. An economist writing in the *Washington Post* said that 80 percent of the population are poor, and their earning power has decreased since the multinationals went in, while the remaining 20 percent have less earning power or buying power. The report cited inflation brought about by the multinationals' presence as the cause.

PROFESSOR BAUER: First of all, mass consumption on a per capita basis has increased enormously in Brazil over the last twelve years. Second, it is probably true that income distribution in Brazil may well have become less equal over the last twelve years than it had been—although I believe it is practically unchanged—for the simple reason that there has been a fall in the mortality of the poor; in particular there has been a tremendous decline in infant and child mortality.

In discussions of income, factors such as life expectancy, the possession of children, and health are not regarded as components of income or of welfare. This means that the most important components of welfare are excluded, and we have the anomalous effect in all these statistics, that the survival of a child registers as a deterioration in per capita income, but the survival of a cow registers as an improvement. It is impossible to make sense of the matter. Suppose it is true that income distribution has "worsened" because more poor people have survived? Is this an improvement or a deterioration?

The population growth in Brazil is phenomenally rapid because of the fall in mortality. The Western media are full of stories about the Brazilian Northeast, about the shantytowns. Shantytowns are the places where people congregate when they go from the countryside to the city. Often, these so-called shantytowns are very stable communities.

The Northeast is over 90 percent black, but are you surprised that they are relatively poor compared with Europeans, the Portuguese descendants, the Japanese, the Lebanese? Brazil is full of Central European and Japanese immigrants who come in with nothing and have become prosperous. They did not take from the poor.

What this discussion somehow implies is that the incomes of the prosperous have been taken from the poor, whether in South Africa, Western Europe, Brazil or wherever; that somehow the poor have been exploited.

I think the proper way to look at the situation is to see that poverty is a natural state, a condition from which various people have emerged in varying degree. Some have emerged sooner or to a greater extent or more rapidly than others. But that has not obstructed the development of those others at all. It has promoted it.

QUESTION: I have two interrelated questions. One has to do with your suggestion about charitable organizations that administer foreign aid. I am assuming that if people were not taxed to provide aid to other countries, they would be relieved of their tax burden and could contribute more to charitable organizations than they can now afford. Do you think it is realistic to expect that people would freely give to charitable organizations in the volume that would be necessary to help third world countries?

Second, are you basically optimistic or pessimistic about the human condition?

PROFESSOR BAUER: As for the volume from charities financed by private donation, I gave the example of very large sums of money, though not very large on a per capita basis, that were given freely by the Swiss for disaster relief. Of course, much depends on what you mean by enough, and for what purpose. Official donations, for the reasons I suggested to you, do nothing to relieve poverty. They are simply wealth transfers from the American taxpayer to the government of the third world country.

Operations by nonpoliticized charities would, to a much greater extent, help relieve poverty directly. But this, too, is full of pitfalls. The thrust behind your question seems to be that if only we could somehow manage to divest ourselves of resources on a substantial scale, we would be doing good. I am not interested primarily in the mental state of the giver, but in what the giving does for the recipients.

As to whether I am pessimistic or optimistic about the human condition, one thing I am absolutely certain of is that the human condition is a complex problem, and it will not be greatly affected if incomes in the third world increase by 2 or 3 percent per year.

I have no doubt that if the people of India voluntarily changed their attitude to taking animal life, this could greatly promote material progress. Equally, I have no doubt that if we went around slaughtering animals in India, it would lead to spiritual collapse.

These are multidimensional questions, and I am certainly not prepared to answer them, but I feel very strongly that the correct answer lies with the philosopher and theologian, not the economist.

QUESTION: You alluded to spiritual vibrancy in India. Could you comment on the impact of foreign aid on the religious convictions of recipients or on the religious life of the recipient country?

PROFESSOR BAUER: The effect of foreign aid on religious attitudes has been negligible. What aid has done is to promote the politicization of life, which exacerbates political tension and leads to conflict.

QUESTION: You commented about the reality factor that must change, for political reasons if not for a social or economic development reason. In the last week, we have seen Secretary of State Muskie call for aid to Nicaragua, for political reasons, to try to show the good faith of the United States of America.

Equally, we have heard people in Congress call for immediate aid to Zimbabwe, for like reasons. I wonder if political motivation did not have a role in the construct you have built, or do you think that there is a necessity or any legitimacy in giving aid primarily for a political reason?

PROFESSOR BAUER: The claim that foreign aid is an instrument of American political strategy is simply a device to sell this policy to the U.S. public. The advocates of aid suggest that aid promotes U.S. political interests. If aid were to serve this purpose, it would have to be bilateral and not multilateral, and it would have to be geared to the conduct of the recipients and to their political and military significance. Nothing of this sort has happened. Large scale bilateral and multilateral aid has gone to many third world governments that have insulted and thwarted the United States as best as they could.

QUESTION: I would like to go back to a question you raised with respect to the decline of religion, and this might have something to do with the willingness of intellectuals to believe patent nonsense.

In the last ten years, the United States has been obsessed with civil rights, and also with economic justice, the redistribution of wealth and incomes, and so on.

Do you think this phenomenon has anything to do with the decline of religion? Does this obsession, in a time of great prosperity, with the subject of wealth and income redistribution indicate a form of idolatry? Is this something that has become a god in lieu of the true God?

Second, assuming one is still a pious, believing Christian, is it appropriate to be actively interested in the subject of economic justice, so as to provide a remedy for the degree of inequality in our society?

PROFESSOR BAUER: These are very broad questions.

There is a passage in Pascal's *Pensées* which goes something like this: "Travaillons donc à bien penser: voilà le principe de la morale"— Let us work then, to think well; this is the principle of morality. This whole area of discourse is pervaded by what I call intellectual sloth. Let me try to clarify some of the issues.

Take the word *inequality*. I have drilled myself never to talk about inequality, but about income differences, because *difference* is a neutral term. The moment you talk about inequality, you have implicitly prejudged the issue, particularly since people now use *inequality* almost interchangeably with *inequity*.

Second, *redistribution* is also a treacherous concept, although harder to avoid, for various reasons. There is no distribution of income apart from its production, with negligible exception not directly relevant to our discourse. What is called your income has not been distributed to you; you generated it, you produced it. There is no distribution of income separate from its production.

What is called redistribution is the confiscation of part of people's income and its transfer to other groups, chiefly to some people who are less well off than either those whose income has been confiscated or the advocates and administrators of transfer.

If we bear in mind that this is what is meant by redistribution, we can start to say something. I see no reason at all why economic or social justice should be taken to mean equal incomes, equal conventionally measured incomes. Yet social justice has now come to mean equal incomes. How is it unequal that those who have contributed less to the flow of income should have less income than those that have contributed more? What I am saying is so simple that I blush to say it. Yet it strikes people as paradoxical.

QUESTION: Arthur Okun advocates that no one should receive less than one-half of the average annual income. Many people advocate just a little less difference in incomes.

PROFESSOR BAUER: Why should those who have more than 60 percent of the average be taxed to bring up others to whatever it is, 40 percent of the average? I see absolutely no reason for this. I see a great many reasons for trying to help those who are really poor, for whatever reason; I think we have a moral duty to help them.

But this has nothing at all to do with equalizing income or reducing income differences. In fact, because the systematic, politically organized redistribution transfers resources from those who can use it more effectively to others who can use it less effectively, the process also has a whole range of other costs. The reduction of income differences and the relief of poverty are completely different and conflicting objectives of policy.

The Okun formula is altogether arbitrary. If people today were not bemused by the latest news item and statistics, but had a modicum of culture, they would know that Tocqueville had already addressed himself to this issue 150 years ago. In *L'Ancien Regime*, chapter 2, he pointed out that when social and economic differences are reduced, the remaining ones are seen as particularly irksome. The idea that by reducing income difference a little bit you will appease discontent or unhappiness is a complete myth.

QUESTION: You said that unofficial, voluntary aid is okay, so I am motivated to go back to my church people and say, "Let's give more, this is all right." You also said that official aid is not okay. But when I consider all the reasons why official aid is not okay, I can apply those same reasons to unofficial aid, because unofficial aid can politicize people at the grass roots—the church people we are working with—as much as official aid can.

You also said that poverty is our natural state, but it seems to me that poverty is our unnatural state; in one sense, we are all at the edge of a precipice, if you will, and we are trying not to fall down into it. In one sense, all of us in the world are immigrants, and some of our forebears have given us a better start than others; some of us are nearer the edge of that precipice than others.

PROFESSOR BAUER: I used an infelicitous term; you are quite right and I accept your correction. Instead of saying "natural," I should have said "original" or "starting point." What I want to get at is the idea that some people being better off than others in no way prejudices the prospect of those who are less well off. There is an ocean of poverty from which some have emerged to a greater extent than have others, but the earlier or greater emergence of some in no way precludes the emergence of others.

I did not say that voluntary aid is okay and official aid is not okay, because I do not think the categories are as simple as that. I said that, for the achievement of the declared objectives of wealth transfers, namely, relief of poverty, voluntary aid has certain advantages compared with official aid, but it is not without its own very grave problems. It certainly does not go directly from government to government and does not immediately and directly strengthen the grip of the rulers over their subjects and increase the stakes in the fight for political power in the recipient countries the way official aid does. It can be adjusted far more to suit the circumstances of the recipients.

QUESTION: You began by saying that the third world was really born with foreign aid. Later, you argued that the addition of wealth in poor areas of the world was advanced by contacts with the West. Are you saying that there has not been a general increase of wealth among all people, but only in some kind of aggregate of people in certain areas, many of them colonies, because of contacts with the West?

Earlier you said that one of the disadvantages of direct aid is that it goes to governments of countries and will never reach the poor, that there is a distance between governments and many of the poor people in those countries.

I wonder if there is any connection between the kinds of contacts the West had with the rest of the world before World War II, between the middle of the nineteenth and the middle of the twentieth centuries, and the conditions of those countries now, in which the governments apparently have such an attitude to their poor people that even aid from the West does not filter down to them?

PROFESSOR BAUER: In what are now Ghana and Nigeria, there was not a single cocoa tree till the late 1880s. Every single cocoa tree in Ghana and Nigeria has been planted, owned, and operated by Africans. In response to the activities of the merchants who bolstered output and sold consumer goods, this has transformed this area.

Similarly, in Southeast Asia there was not a single rubber tree in the whole of that vast area, from what is now Sri Lanka to Indonesia, until the second half of the nineteenth century. The botanical name of the rubber tree is *Hevea brasiliensis*. It comes from Latin America. Well, over one-half of an area planted in rubber in Southeast Asia is Malayan and Chinese, the people's response to a commercial demand.

What has that to do with foreign aid? These are commercial contacts, adjusted to people's circumstances, institutions, mores, productive resources. And throughout the third world, the most advanced and advancing areas are those with the most extensive commercial contacts to the West.

Western Guilt and Third World Poverty

P. T. Bauer

Come, fix upon me that accusing eye.
I thirst for accusation.

—W. B. YEATS

Guilt in the West

Yeats's words might indeed have been written to describe the wide, even welcome, acceptance by the West of the accusation that it is responsible for the poverty of the third world—that is, most of Asia, Africa, and Latin America.

Western responsibility for third world backwardness is a persistent theme of the United Nations and its many affiliates. It has been welcomed by spokesmen of the third world and of the Communist bloc, notably so at international gatherings, where it is often endorsed by official representatives of the West, especially the United States. It is also widely canvassed in the universities, the churches, and the media the world over.

Acceptance of emphatic, routine allegations that the West is responsible for third world poverty reflects and reinforces Western feelings of guilt. It has enfeebled Western diplomacy, both toward the ideologically much more aggressive Soviet bloc and toward the third world, and the West has come to abase itself before countries with negligible resources and no real power. Yet the allegations can be shown to be without foundation. They are readily accepted in the West partly because the Western public has little firsthand knowledge of the third world, and partly because of widespread feelings of guilt in the more prosperous West.

NOTE: In current usage, the third world means most of Asia, except Japan and Israel; most of Africa, except white southern Africa; and Latin America. Classification of the oil-producing countries is often vague—sometimes they are included in the third world, sometimes not.

Western Responsibility and Third World Poverty

A few characteristic examples will illustrate the general theme of Western responsibility. I shall begin with academic writers.

The late Paul A. Baran, professor of economics at Stanford, was a highly regarded development economist; he contributed the chapter on economic development to the *Survey of Contemporary Economics* published by the American Economic Association. He was a prominent and influential exponent of Western guilt in the early days of contemporary development economics. In his widely prescribed university textbook, Baran wrote:

> To the dead weight of stagnation characteristic of pre-industrial society was added the entire restrictive impact of monopoly capitalism. The economic surplus appropriated in lavish amounts by monopolistic concerns in backward countries is not employed for productive purposes. It is neither plowed back into their own enterprises nor does it serve to develop others.[1]

This categorical statement is wholly and obviously untrue because, throughout the underdeveloped world, large agricultural, mineral, commercial, and industrial complexes have been built up through profits that have been reinvested locally.

Professor Peter Townsend of Essex University, perhaps the most prominent British academic writer on poverty, wrote:

> I argued that the poverty of deprived nations is comprehensible only if we attribute it substantially to the existence of a system of international social stratification, a hierarchy of societies with vastly different resources in which the wealth of some is linked historically and contemporaneously to the poverty of others. This system operated crudely in the era of colonial domination, and continues to operate today, though more subtly, through systems of trade, education, political relations, military alliances, and industrial corporations.[2]

This again cannot be so. The poorest and most backward countries have until recently had no external economic contacts and often have never been Western colonies, so their backwardness cannot be explained by colonial domination or international social stratification. And industrial corporations are not notable for their presence in the least developed countries of the third world (the so-called fourth world), such as Afghanistan, Chad, Bhutan, Burundi, Nepal, and Sikkim.

---

[1] Paul A. Baran, *The Political Economy of Growth* (New York: Monthly Review Press), 1957, p. 177.

[2] *Concepts of Poverty* (New York: Elsevier, 1970), pp. 41–42.

In this realm of discourse university students echo what they have learned from their mentors. About ten years ago a student group at Cambridge published a pamphlet on the third world. The following was its key passage: "We took the rubber from Malaya, the tea from India, raw materials from all over the world and gave almost nothing in return."

This is as nearly the opposite of the truth as one can find. The British took the rubber *to* Malaya and the tea *to* India. There were no rubber trees in Malaya or anywhere in Asia until about one hundred years ago, when the British took the first rubber seeds there out of the Amazon jungle. From these sprang the huge rubber industry—now very largely Asian-owned. Tea plants were brought to India by the British somewhat earlier; their origin is shown in the botanical name *Camellia sinensis*, as well as in the phrase "all the tea in China."

Charles Clarke, a former president of the National Union of Students, said in his presidential address, delivered in December 1976, that "for over a hundred years British industry has been draining wealth away from those countries." So far from draining wealth from the less developed countries, British industry helped to create it there, as external commerce promoted economic advance in large areas of the third world, where there was no wealth to be drained.

Western churches and charities are riding the same bandwagon. Professor Ronald J. Sider is a prominent American churchman. In an article in an influential evangelical magazine, he wrote about the "stranglehold which the developed West has kept on the economic throats of the third world" and then went on to say: "It would be wrong to suggest that 210 million Americans bear sole responsibility for all the hunger and injustice in today's world. All the rich developed countries are directly involved . . . we are participants in a system that dooms even more people to agony and death than the slave system did."[3] These are evident fantasies. Famines occur in third world countries largely isolated from the West. So far from condemning third world people to death, Western contacts have been behind the large increase in life expectancy in the third world, so often deplored as the population explosion by the same critics.

Many charities have come to think it advantageous to play on the theme of Western responsibility. According to a widely publicized Oxfam advertisement of 1972:

Coffee is grown in poor developing countries like Brazil, Colombia and Uganda. But that does not stop rich countries like Britain exploiting their economic weakness by paying as

---

[3] "How We Oppress the Poor," *Christianity Today*, July 16, 1976.

little for their raw coffee as we can get away with. On top of this, we keep charging more and more for the manufactured goods they need to buy from us. So? We get richer at their expense. Business is Business.

A similar advertisement was run about cocoa. Both advertisements were subsequently dropped in the face of protests by actual and potential subscribers. The allegations in them are largely meaningless, and they are also unrelated to reality. The world prices of coffee and cocoa, which, as it happens, were very high in the 1970s, are determined by market forces and not prescribed by the West. On the other hand, the farmers in many of the exporting countries receive far less than the market prices, because they are subject to very high export taxes and similar government levies. The insistence on the allegedly low prices paid by the West to the producers and the lack of any reference to the penal taxation of local producers are but two examples of the concern of guilt literature with the flagellation of the West rather than with the condition of the local population.

The intellectuals outside the academies and churches are also well to the fore. Cyril Connolly wrote in an article entitled "Black Man's Burden":

It is a wonder that the white man is not more thoroughly detested than he is. . . . In our dealings with every single country, greed, masked by hypocrisy, led to unscrupulous coercion of the native inhabitants. . . . Cruelty, greed and arrogance . . . characterised what can be summed up in one word, exploitation.[4]

If this were true, third world countries would now be poorer than they were before Western contacts. In fact, they are generally much better off.

Insistence that the West has caused third world poverty is collective self-accusation. The notion itself originated in the West. For instance, Marxism is a Western ideology, as is the belief that economic differences are anomalous and unjust and that they reflect exploitation. People in the third world, however, especially articulate people with contacts with the West, readily believed what they were told by prominent academics and other intellectuals, the more so because the idea accorded with their interests and inclinations.

Inspired by the West, third world politicians have come habitually to insist that the West has exploited and still exploits their countries. This stance is indeed a routine tool of their trade. Kwame Nkrumah, a

---

[4] *Sunday Times* (London), February 23, 1969.

major third world figure of the 1950s and the 1960s, was a well-known exponent of this view. He described Western capitalism as "a world system of financial enslavement and colonial operation and exploitation of a vast majority of the population of the earth by a handful of the so-called civilized nations."[5]

In fact, until the advent of Dr. Nkrumah, Ghana (the former Gold Coast) was a prosperous country as a result of cocoa exports to the West, with the cocoa farmers the most prosperous and the subsistence producers the poorest groups there.

Dr. Nyerere, president of Tanzania, said, in the course of a state visit to London in 1975, that "if the rich nations go on getting richer and richer at the expense of the poor, the poor of the world must demand a change." When the West established substantial contact with Tanganyika, effectively the present Tanzania, in the nineteenth century, this was an empty region, thinly populated with tribal people exposed to Arab slavers. Its relatively modest progress since then has been the work of Asians and Europeans. Dr. Nyerere is a highly regarded, almost venerated, world figure, especially in Britain and America. His frequent moralizing diatribes, drawing on the staple allegations of Western responsibility for the poverty of Tanzania and other third world countries, strike a responsive chord in the guilty conscience of the Western liberal intelligentsia; this is doubtless one reason for the prestige he enjoys.[6]

The notion of Western exploitation of the third world is standard in publications and statements emanating from the Soviet Union and other Communist countries. The late Soviet academican I. Potekhin, a prominent Soviet authority on Africa, is worth quoting because Soviet economic writings are taken seriously in Western universities. "Why is there little capital in Africa? The reply is evident. A considerable part of the national income which is supposed to make up the accumulation fund and to serve as the material basis of progress is exported outside Africa without any equivalent."[7] There are no remittances abroad from much of Africa and none from the poorest parts, so they cannot explain the low level of capital. Such remittances as there are represent returns for resources supplied. In Africa, as elsewhere in the third world, the most prosperous areas in the third world are those with the most commercial contacts with the West.

---

[5] Kwame Nkrumah, *Towards Colonial Freedom* (London: Heinemann, 1962), p. 40.

[6] In an adulatory profile in the London *Observer,* Nyerere was cozily referred to as "St. Julius." An article in the *Financial Times* (August 11, 1975) described him as "Africa's senior statesman and a man of formidable intellect."

[7] I. Potekhin, *Problems of Economic Independence of African Countries* (Moscow: Academy of Sciences, 1962), pp. 14–15.

The West and Third World Progress

The transformation of Malaya (the present Malaysia) illustrates the influence Western contact has had on third world countries. In the 1890s it was a sparsely populated area of Malay hamlets and fishing villages. By the 1930s the country had become the hub of the world's rubber and tin industries, with large cities and excellent communications, a country where millions of Malays, Chinese, and Indians lived much longer and better than they had formerly done, either in their countries of origin or in Malaya.

Large parts of West Africa were also transformed over roughly the same period as a result of Western contacts. Before 1890 there was no cocoa production in the Gold Coast or Nigeria, only very small production of cotton and groundnuts, and small exports of palm oil and palm kernels. By the 1950s all these had become staples of world trade, all produced by Africans, but originally made possible by Westerners, who established public security and introduced modern methods of transport and communications. Over this period imports both of capital goods and of mass consumer goods for African use also rose from insignificant amounts to huge volumes. The changes were reflected in government revenues, literacy rates, school attendance, public health, life expectancy, infant mortality, and in many other indicators.

Statistics by themselves can hardly convey the far-reaching transformation that took place over this period in West Africa and elsewhere in the third world. For instance, in West Africa slave trading and slavery were still widespread at the end of the nineteenth century; they had practically disappeared by the end of World War I. Many of the worst endemic and epidemic diseases for which West Africa was notorious throughout the nineteenth century had disappeared by the time of World War II. External contacts also brought about similar far-reaching changes over much of Latin America.

The role of Western contacts in the material progress of Black Africa deserves further notice. All the foundations and ingredients of modern social and economic life present there today were brought by Westerners, during the nineteenth and twentieth centuries. This is true of such fundamentals as public security and law and order; wheeled traffic and mechanical transport (transport powered by steam or gasoline instead of muscle—almost entirely human muscle in Black Africa); roads, railways, and manmade ports; the application of science and technology to economic activity; towns with substantial buildings, regular supplies of clean water, and sewerage; public health, hospitals and the control of endemic and epidemic diseases; and formal education.

These advances resulted from peaceful external contacts. An

important by-product of the establishment of these commercial contacts was that they made easier the elimination of the Atlantic slave trade, the virtual elimination of the slave trade from Africa to the Middle East, and also of slavery within Africa. Although the peaceful commercial contacts with which this essay is concerned had nothing to do with the Atlantic slave trade, in the contemporary climate it is impossible not to refer to that trade in an essay on Western responsibility for third world poverty.

Horrible and destructive as was the Atlantic slave trade, it cannot be claimed legitimately as a cause of African backwardness, still less of third world poverty. Asia was altogether untouched by it. The most backward parts of Africa, such as the interior of Central and Southern Africa and most of East Africa, were largely unaffected by it. It is notable that the areas most involved in the Atlantic slave trade, particularly West Africa, have in recent decades been economically the most advanced areas in Black Africa. A recent study of precolonial southeastern Nigeria examines and illustrates the economic development that was promoted by the slave trade. In particular, it is shown that the "slave trade . . . led to sufficient economic development of the region" to enable the profitable trade in palm oil to burgeon in the early nineteenth century.[8]

It is pertinent to recent and current political discussions on Western guilt that the slave trade between Africa and the Middle East antedated the Atlantic slave trade by centuries and far outlasted it. It is also pertinent that slavery was endemic over much of Africa long before the Atlantic slave trade began and that it was eventually stamped out by the West. Arabs and Africans appear not to feel guilty about slavery and the slave trade, but Western Europeans and Americans often do and are made to do so; guilt is almost exclusively a prerogative of the West.

Western activities, supplemented at times by the activities of non-Western immigrants—notably Chinese, Indians, and Levantines, whose large-scale migration was, however, made possible by Western initiative —have thus transformed material conditions in many parts of the third world.

All this is not to say that over the past hundred years there has been uniformly substantial material advance throughout the third world. Large areas, especially in the interior of the third world, have had few contacts with the West. Also, in much of the third world the political, social, and personal determinants of economic performance are often uncongenial to economic achievement. The policies of many governments obstruct economic achievement and progress. Moreover, people

---

[8] David Northrup, *Trade Without Rulers: Pre-colonial Economic Development in South-Eastern Asia* (Oxford: Clarendon Press, 1978), p. 176.

often refuse to abandon attitudes and mores which obstruct economic performance and which they willingly prefer to other forms of conduct, forms that would be conducive to greater material comfort; this is a preference that is neither unjustified nor reprehensible. But such considerations in no way warrant the allegations that Western contacts have obstructed or retarded third world progress or caused third world poverty. The poorest and most backward countries are those with no such contacts. Wherever local conditions have permitted it, commercial contacts with the West, and generally established by the West, have eliminated the worst diseases, reduced and eliminated famine, extended life expectancy, and improved living standards.

Prosperity and Poverty

Many of the assertions of Western responsibility for third world poverty reflect or express the belief that the prosperity of relatively well-to-do persons, groups, and societies is always achieved at the expense of the less well-off, that is, that the incomes of the relatively prosperous are not produced by those who earn them, but have somehow been taken from others. In fact, with a few clearly definable exceptions (which do not apply to the relations between the West and the third world), incomes are earned—produced—by the recipients and not acquired by exploitation—by depriving others of what they had or could have had. This simple consideration is obscured by the practice, which owes much to American usage, of referring to the poorer as deprived, even if nothing has ever been taken from them. How could the incomes of, say, Americans or Swiss have been taken from, say, the aborigines of Papua or the desert people or Pygmies of Africa? Indeed, who deprived these groups, and of what?

In Asia and Africa it is an article of faith of the most influential and articulate groups that their societies have been exploited by the West, by locally resident Western expatriates and by ethnic minorities, notably including those who had risen from poverty to a relative prosperity, like the Chinese in Southeast Asia, the Asians in East Africa, and the Levantines in West Africa. The appeal of these misconceptions is all too familiar. They are especially useful to politicians who have promised a prosperity they cannot deliver. They are also often useful to other influential local groups who expect to benefit from policies inspired by these ideas, especially from the expropriation or destruction of prosperous minorities.

In recent decades the notion that relative prosperity implies exploitation has been reinforced by two streams of influence whose impact in this area has been cumulative. The first is Marxist-Leninist ideology.

The second is the spurious belief that the capacities and motivations of people are the same everywhere, a belief that is influential in the advocacy of enforced egalitarianism.

In Marxist-Leninist ideology any return on private capital implies exploitation, and service industries are regarded as unproductive. Thus, earnings of foreign capital and the incomes of foreigners or ethnic minorities in the service industries become forms of exploitation. Further, neo-Marxist literature has extended the concept of the proletariat—which is exploited by definition and is poor because it is exploited—to the peoples of the third world, most of whom are in fact small-scale cultivators.[9]

The belief in a universal, basic equality of economic capacities and motivations has also promoted the idea of Western responsibility. For if human habits and motivations are everywhere the same and yet some societies are richer than others, this suggests that the more prosperous have exploited the rest. Because the public in the West has little direct contact with the third world, it is easier to put across the notion that the West has caused third world poverty. This is an area where the familiar observation applies only too well, that our trouble is not ignorance but rather that we know so many things that are not true. The upsurge of egalitarianism helps the idea of Western exploitation. The idea receives a further helping hand from the practice I have already noted, namely, describing poor or backward societies as deprived or underprivileged.

Colonialism and Poverty

The principal assumption behind the idea of Western responsibility for third world poverty is that prosperity generally reflects exploitation. Some variants or derivatives of this theme are often heard, usually geared to particular audiences. One of these variants is that colonialism has caused the poverty of Asia and Africa. It has particular appeal in the United States, where hostility to colonialism is traditional. For a different, and indeed opposite, reason, it is at times effective in stirring up guilt in Britain, the foremost excolonial power.

Whatever one thinks of colonialism, it cannot be held responsible for third world poverty. Some of the most backward countries never were

---

[9] This extension of Marxist-Leninist ideology is reflected, for instance, in the passage from the Soviet academician Potekhin (see p. 108). Marxist-Leninist statements are apt to be designed for political purposes. Thus, in Potekhin's small book, the passage I have quoted is immediately followed by the injunction that Western enterprises in Africa should be expropriated and economic activity collectivized—an injunction now accepted by a number of African states.

colonies: Afghanistan, Tibet, Nepal, and Liberia, for instance. Ethiopia is perhaps an even more telling example (it was an Italian colony for only six years in its long history). Again, many of the Asian and African colonies progressed very rapidly during colonial rule, much more so than the independent countries in the same area. At present, one of the few European colonies is Hong Kong—whose prosperity and progress are, or shall be, familiar.

Nor is the prosperity of the West the result of colonialism. The richest and most advanced countries, Switzerland and the Scandinavian countries, for example, never had colonies, and some were colonies of others and were already very prosperous as colonies, such as North America and Australasia. The prosperity of the West was generated by its own peoples, not taken from others; the European countries were already far ahead of the areas where they established colonies.

In recent years the charges that colonialism has caused third world poverty have expanded to cover "colonialism in all its forms." The terms *economic colonialism* and *neocolonialism* have sprung up to cover external private investment, the activities of multinational companies, and indeed almost any form of economic relationship between relatively rich and relatively poor regions or groups. This terminology has become common currency in both academic literature and the media. It regularly confuses poverty with colonial status, a concept that has normally meant lack of political sovereignty. References to "colonialism in all its forms" as a cause of third world poverty is a major theme at UNCTAD meetings.

One unusually direct formulation of these ideas (which are normally expressed in much more convoluted form in the academic and official literature) was provided in an editorial in the June 1978 issue of *Poverty and Power*, published by War on Want, a British charity: "We see poverty in the third world as a result of colonial looting in the past and neocolonial exploitation in the present."

The shift to neocolonialism and economic colonialism in the allegations of exploitation of the third world by the West reflects Leninist doctrine, in which colonial status and foreign investment are by definition evidence of exploitation. This, for instance, is the principal theme of the publication by academician Potekhin that I have already quoted. A more important factor behind the shift has presumably been the demise of political colonialism and the consequent need of accusers of the West, and especially of the United States, to find new ground for their accusations, while simultaneously retaining the benefits of the older terminology.

Foreign private investment and the activities of the multinational companies have expanded opportunities and raised incomes and government revenues in the third world. References to economic colonialism and neocolonialism both debase the language and distort the truth.[10]

External Contacts and Third World Advance

The operation of international trade is alleged to be manipulated by the West and to damage the third world, primarily because the terms of trade of the third world are adverse and also deteriorate persistently, which, among other untoward results, is said to explain the third world's declining share of global trade, as well as its large external debt. These allegations are irrelevant, unfounded, and often the opposite of the truth.

The terms of trade have little or nothing to do with third world poverty; the poorest areas have no external trade. Their condition shows both that the causes of backwardness are domestic and that external commercial contacts are beneficial. Even if the terms of trade of the third world were a significant factor behind prosperity or the lack of it, and if they were unfavorable or deteriorating (which they are not), this would not mean that external trade is damaging to the third world, but only that it is not quite as beneficial as it would be under more favorable terms of trade. Third world countries would be even worse off if there were no external trade to have terms about.

As the third world comprises most of the world, the aggregation of the terms of trade of all its countries has a very limited meaning. The terms of trade of some third world countries and groups of countries operate differently and often in opposite directions to those of others; the effect of the OPEC price increases on many third world countries is only one recent and familiar example. Again, except over very short periods, changes in the terms of trade as conventionally measured have little significance for welfare without reference to changes in the cost of production of exports, the range and quality of imports, and the volume of trade.

Insofar as changes in the terms of trade do affect development and welfare, what matters is the amount of imports that can be purchased with a unit of domestic resources, and this cannot be inferred from the ratio of import and export prices. (In technical language, the comparisons relevant to economic welfare and development are the factoral terms of trade and not the crude commodity terms.) Further, expressions such as "unfavorable terms of trade" are meaningless except by refer-

---

[10] A convenient recent example is a statement by the Ayatollah Khomeini in January 1979: "Our people are weary of it [colonial domination]. Following their example other countries will free themselves from the colonial grip." *Daily Telegraph*, January 10, 1979. In its long history Iran never was a Western colony.

ence to a base period. In recent decades, however, even the crude commodity terms of trade of third world countries have been exceptionally favorable. When changes in the cost of production, the great improvement in the range and quality of imports, and the huge increase in the volume of trade are taken into account, the external purchasing power of the exports of the third world in the aggregate is now very favorable, probably more so than ever before. This in turn has made it easier for governments to retain a larger proportion of export earnings through major increases in royalty rates, export taxes, and corporation taxes. These severe taxes in many third world countries, often increased when prices have risen, make clear that the terms of trade of a country are not the sole determinants of the people's ability to buy imports (which is the purpose of external trade), let alone of their living standards. It is also of some interest that the arguments that the terms of trade of the third world deteriorate persistently do not usually specify either why or how this should come about, or over what period this condition is supposed to continue, since it must presumably come to an end before they decline to zero.[11]

A reduction in the share of a country or group of countries in global trade has by itself no adverse economic implications whatsoever because it often reflects the expansion of economic activity and trade elsewhere, which normally does not damage, but benefits, those whose relative share has declined. For instance, since the 1950s the large increase in the foreign trade of Japan, the reconstruction of Europe, and the liberalization of intra-European trade have brought about a decline in the share of other groups in world trade, including that of the United States and the United Kingdom. Furthermore, domestic developments and policies unrelated to external circumstances—such as increased domestic use of previously exported products, domestic inflation, special taxation of exporters, or the intensification of protectionist policies—frequently reduce the share of a country or group of countries in world trade. (In recent decades the third world's share of total world trade has in fact increased greatly compared with earlier periods; and of course it has increased hugely under Western influence in modern times, as before then the areas forming the present third world had little external trade.) Of course, if international trade harmed the peoples of the third world, then a decline in the share of the third world in this trade would be beneficial, with the ultimate economic bliss attained when the third

---

[11] When some ostensible evidence is produced in support of these allegations, it usually turns out to involve shifts in base periods or in the aggregates under discussion. I have examined these matters in some detail in *Dissent on Development*, chapter 6, "A Critique of UNCTAD."

world no longer had external economic relations, at any rate with the West.

The external debts of the third world reflect resources supplied to it. Indeed, much of the current indebtedness of third world governments consists of soft loans, often very soft loans, under various aid agreements, frequently supplemented by outright grants. With the worldwide rise in prices, including those of third world exports, the cost of even these soft loans has diminished greatly. Any difficulties in servicing these loans do not reflect external exploitation or unfavorable terms of trade, but either wasteful use of the capital supplied or inappropriate monetary and fiscal policies. The persistent balance of payments deficits of some third world countries do not mean that they are being exploited or impoverished by the West. Such deficits are inevitable if the government of a country, whether rich or poor, advancing or stagnating, lives beyond its resources and pursues inflationary policies, while attempting to maintain overvalued exchange rates.

The decline of particular economic activities—of the Indian textile industry in the eighteenth century, for instance—as a result of competition from cheap imports is sometimes cited as an example of harmful external trade and thus of Western responsibility. This argument identifies the decline of one activity with the decline of the economy as a whole. Cheap imports extend the range of choice and of economic opportunities of people in poor countries. They are usually accompanied by the development and expansion of other activities. If this were not so, the population would be unable to pay for these imports.

The so-called brain drain, the migration of qualified personnel, from the third world to the West is often instanced as an example of Western responsibility for third world poverty or stagnation. This is a somewhat more complex issue than those noted so far, but it certainly does not substantiate the familiar accusation. The training of many of the emigrants was financed by the West. Again, formal education is not an indispensable instrument, or even a major instrument, of emergence from personal poverty or economic backwardness—witness the rapid progress to prosperity of untrained or even illiterate people in many third world countries. The enforced exodus or outright expulsion of many enterprising and skilled people (including many formally educated people with economically valuable qualifications) from many third world countries, the discrimination of many third world governments against ethnic minorities or tribal groups, and their refusal to employ foreigners, are much more damaging to development than voluntary departures under the brain drain. Moreover, many of these emigrants leave because their own governments cannot or will not use their services. So it is not they but their governments that deprive the society of productive resources.[12]

The West is said also to have damaged the third world by ethnic discrimination. The very countries in which such discrimination by Westerners occurred, however, were those where material progress had been initiated or promoted by contact with the West. The most backward groups in the third world (aborigines, desert peoples, nomads, and other tribesfolk) were quite unaffected by ethnic discrimination on the part of Europeans. Many communities against which discrimination was often practiced—the Chinese in Southeast Asia, Indians in parts of Southeast Asia, Asians in Africa, and others—have progressed greatly. In any case, discrimination on the basis of color or race is not a European invention, but has been endemic in much of Africa and Asia, notably in India, for many centuries or even millennia. Any ethnic discrimination by Europeans was negligible compared with the massive and sometimes brutal persecution of ethnic and tribal groups systematically practiced by the governments of many independent Asian and African states.

It is anomalous, even perverse, to suggest that external commercial relations are damaging to development or to the living standards of the people of the third world. These relations benefit people by opening up markets for exports, by providing a large and diverse source of imports, and by acting as channels for the flow of human and financial resources and for new ideas, methods, and crops. Because of the vast expansion of world trade in recent decades and the development of technology in the West, the material advantages from external contacts are now greater than ever before. The suggestion that these relations are detrimental is not only unfounded but also damaging because it serves as a specious justification for official restrictions on their volume or diversity.

The basic realities of the economic relations between the West and the third world are obfuscated by the practice—rife in the contemporary

---

[12] It was clearly implied in an article in the London *Observer* of July 22, 1979—"The boat people's 'brain drain' punishes Vietnam"—that the refugees from Vietnam left for the selfish and unpatriotic reasons that they could not adapt to the new socialist order, that they could earn more elsewhere, for example, in the United States, and that their voluntary departure, an example of the brain drain, deprived their country of much-needed skills, including medical skills. In describing what was in reality a brutal mass expulsion, the article uses the terms *exodus* and *loss*—a revealing misuse of language.

But if the refugees were attracted simply by higher incomes abroad, they could have left much earlier, and at no risk. In fact, there were hundreds of thousands of these refugees; the massive persecution in Vietnam has been well documented and even admitted by the government; and a large proportion of the refugees perished in the course of their escape. Thus, the implication in the *Observer* article was not only specious but especially callous as well. Incidentally, most of the medical education in the former Indochina was organized or provided by the French.

development literature—of confusing governments or elites (especially so-called progressive governments or elites) with the population at large. Many third world governments and their local allies do indeed often benefit from restricting the external commercial contacts of the population, and more generally from the imposition of state economic controls. For instance, restrictions on external commerce enable governments to control their subjects more closely, a situation from which the rulers benefit politically and materially. Articulate and influential local groups also benefit politically and financially from organizing or administering third world economic controls. These realities are concealed in certain allegations, for instance, that the West has forced imports on third world countries. It is, of course, the rulers who object to the imports desired by their subjects.

The allegations that external trade, and especially imports from the West, are damaging reveal a barely disguised condescension toward the ordinary people in the third world, even a contempt for them. The people, of course, want imports. If they did not want the imports, the goods could not be sold. Moreover, the people are prepared to produce for export; if they did not, they could not pay for the imports. To say that this is damaging is to suggest that people's preferences are of no account in organizing their own lives.

The Impact of Western Activities

The mere existence and day-to-day activities of the peoples of the West are by themselves said to harm the third world, and often extremely so.

Cheap consumer goods developed and used in the West, but available also in the third world, are said to obstruct development there by encouraging spending through the so-called international demonstration effect. This contention disregards the level of consumption and the extension of choice as criteria of development. Yet these are what economic development is about. The notion of a damaging international demonstration effect also ignores the role of external contacts as an instrument of development; it overlooks the need to pay for the new consumer goods, and this usually requires improved economic performance, such as more work, additional saving and investment, and readiness to produce for sale. In short, it overlooks the obvious consideration that a higher and more varied level of consumption is both the principal justification and even the meaning of material progress, and also an inducement to further economic advance.[13]

---

[13] At the official level, a damaging international demonstration effect may indeed operate by encouraging the adoption of show projects and unsuitable technologies financed with public funds. This is not, however, what the exponents of the in-

An updated version of the international demonstration effect proposes that the eager acceptance of Western consumer goods in the third world is a form of cultural dependence engendered by Western business. The implication here is that the peoples of the third world have no independent minds, that they are incapable of deciding how best to spend their incomes, and that they are mere puppets manipulated by foreigners at will. In fact, however, Western goods have been accepted selectively and not indiscriminately in the third world, where they have been of massive benefit to millions of people.

It is a further anomaly that the charge of cultural dependence often accompanies the charge that, by means of its patent laws, the West damages the third world by obstructing the spread of Western technology. Thus both the supplying of Western goods and also the alleged withholding of Western goods are said to be damaging.

As is not surprising, allegedly lavish consumption habits and the pollution and plunder of the environment in the West have also been pressed into ideological service. A standard formulation is that per capita consumption of food and energy in the United States is many times that in India, so that the American consumer despoils his Indian opposite number on a large scale. For instance, Professor Tibor Mende, a prominent figure in development circles, has written that, "according to one estimate, each American has twenty-five times the impact on the environment—as a consumer and polluter—as an Indian."[14]

Even babies are drafted into the campaign to promote Western guilt. There are the familiar pictures of babies with distended bellies. An article entitled "The Greed of the Super Rich" in the London *Sunday Times* opens as follows: "One American baby consumes fifty times more of the world's resources than an Indian baby. . . . The wheat need of the people in Africa's Sahel region could have been met by a twentieth of the wheat European countries use each year to feed cattle."[15]

The West has now even come to be accused of mass cannibalism. According to Professor René Dumont, widely known French agronomist and consultant to international organizations, "in over-consuming meat, which wasted the cereals which could have saved them, we ate the little children of Sahel, of Ethiopia, and of Bangladesh."[16] This grotesque

---

ternational demonstration effect usually have in mind. Nor is it appropriate to blame the West for the policies of third world governments in adopting unsuitable external models.

[14] *Newsweek*, October 23, 1972. Note the reference to each American as consumer and polluter, but not as producer. According to *Newsweek*, Professor Mende is "one of the world's foremost authorities on developing countries."

[15] August 20, 1978.

[16] Quoted by Daniel P. Moynihan, "The United States in Opposition," *Commentary*, March 1975.

allegation has come to be widely echoed in the West. According to Jill Tweedie, a prominent editorial writer for the *Guardian*: "a quarter of the world's population lives, quite literally, by killing the other three-quarters."[17] Another article prominently featured in the *Guardian* referred to the "social cannibalism which has reduced over three quarters of mankind to beggary, poverty and death, not because they don't work, but because their wealth goes to feed, clothe, and shelter a few idle classes in America, Europe, and Japan . . . money-mongers in London and New York and in other Western seats of barons living on profit snatched from the peasants and workers of the world."[18] Such ridiculous statements could be multiplied many times over. Their expression by prominent academics and by journalists in the so-called quality press tells much about the contemporary intellectual scene.

The West has not caused the famines in the third world. These have occurred in backward regions that have practically no external commerce. The absence of external trading links is often one aspect of the backwardness of these regions. At times it reflects the policies of rulers who are hostile to traders, especially to nonindigenous traders, and often even to private property. As a matter of interest, it has proved difficult to get emergency supplies to some of the Sahelian areas because of poor communications and official apathy or hostility.[19]

The various allegations and accusations noted in this section over-look the fact that Western consumption has been more than paid for by Western production, which finances not only this consumption but also domestic and foreign investment as well as foreign aid. Both production and consumption per head are higher in the West than in most third world countries. The higher level of consumption is not achieved by depriving others of what they have produced.

Politicization of the Third World

The West has indeed contributed to third world poverty in one sense, but in a way radically different from the familiar assertions.

Western activities since World War II have done much to politicize economic life in the third world. In the terminal years of British colonial rule, the traditional policy of relatively limited government was aban-

---

[17] January 3, 1977.

[18] June 11, 1979. The article, written by Ngugi wa Thiang'o, opened a special survey of Kenya.

[19] If the West is to attempt permanently to support the population of these areas, this would preclude any prospect of the development of viable agriculture there, quite apart from the cost to Western consumers and taxpayers and from their reaction to it.

doned in favor of close official economic controls. As a result of this change of policy in most British colonies outside the Far East and Southeast Asia, a ready-made framework for state-controlled economies or even for totalitarian states was presented to the incoming independent governments. The operation of official Western aid to third world governments, reinforced by certain strands in its advocacy and by the criteria of its allocation, has also served to politicize life in the third world.

These controls have wasted resources, restricted social and economic mobility and also external contacts, and provoked fierce political and social strife. These consequences in turn have brought about poverty and even large-scale suffering.

Many independent third world governments would presumably have attempted in any case to politicize their economies extensively, because this greatly enhances the power of the rulers. But they would have been unlikely to have gone so far as they have in recent years, or to have succeeded in their attempts, without Western influence and assistance. All this, however, does not validate the position of the exponents of Western guilt. The most vocal and influential critics both of colonial rule and of Western contacts with the third world have emphatically urged large-scale economic controls and other forms of politicization of life in the third world. Indeed, they have blamed colonial governments and Western influence for not promoting such policies sooner and more vigorously.

Condescension toward the Third World

The persistent, though unfounded, harping on Western responsibility for third world poverty has been effective. Its efficacy helps to explain why Western governments support and endorse baseless and offensive statements by third world politicians, and why the West so often abases itself before governments, usually unrepresentative governments, whose countries are sparsely populated by relatively small numbers of backward people. The insistence on Western responsibility and guilt is often closely related to condescension toward the third world. This condescension manifests itself in many different ways.

The image of the third world as a uniform stagnant mass devoid of distinctive character is one aspect of this condescension. It reflects a stereotype that denies identity, character, personality, and responsibility to the individuals and societies of the third world. Because the third world is defined as a world other than the West and a handful of Westernized societies such as Japan and South Africa, it is regarded as if it were all much of a muchness. Time and again the guilt merchants envisage the third world as an undifferentiated, passive entity helplessly at the mercy of its environment and of the powerful West. Cyril Connolly, in the article from which I have already quoted, implies that Asia, including the Far East, and Africa as well, are all populated by black men exploited by the West. Such lumping together is offensive to millions of people, and especially to the great majority of Indians, Chinese, and Arabs.

The Cambridge pamphlet, which I have also quoted, says that "half the world's people never had any education at all. That means they are largely unfit for anything except scratching a living from the earth." According to this ridiculous and patronizing statement, the only worthwhile education is formal Western education. Without it, people are uncivilized and without economic hope. So much for the culture of China and India, or the progress of people without Western education in many third world countries.

The third world is a vast and diverse collection of societies which differ widely in religion, culture, social institutions, personal characteristics and motivations, political arrangements, economic attitudes, material achievements, rates of progress, and many other aspects. In material achievement they range from Pygmies and desert people in Africa to rich entrepreneurs in Asia and sophisticated industrialists in Latin America, and in culture from Stone Age people in Papua and aborigines in many countries to representatives of ancient civilizations in Asia and the Middle East. It is a patronizing travesty to lump together Chinese merchants of Southeast Asia, Indonesian peasants, Indian villagers, tribal societies of Africa, oil-rich Arabs of the Middle East, aborigines and desert peoples, and inhabitants of huge cities in India, Africa, and Latin America.

The exponents of Western guilt further patronize the third world by suggesting that its economic fortunes, past, present, and prospective, are determined by the West; that past exploitation by the West explains third world backwardness; that manipulation of international trade by the West and other forms of Western misconduct account for continuing and deepening poverty; and that the economic future of the third world depends largely on Western donations. Whatever happens to the third world is largely our doing, which makes us feel superior even while we beat our breasts.

A curious mixture of guilt and condescension is also discernible behind the toleration or even support of brutal policies of many third world governments. Third world rulers are not really guilty because they only follow examples set by the West. In this scheme of things neither third world rulers nor their peoples have minds or wills of their own: they are envisaged as creatures molded by the West or, at best, as being at the mercy of their own environment. Moreover, like children, they are not altogether responsible for what they do. In any case, we must support them to atone for the alleged wrongs our supposed ancestors perpetrated on their supposed ancestors. Economic aid is also necessary to help the children grow up. Similarly, the most offensive and baseless utterances of third world spokesmen need not be taken seriously, because they are only third world statements (a license which has been extended to their supporters in the West).

Insistence on Western foreign aid is a major theme of the recent literature of Western guilt. But whether or not linked to patronization (and it is usually so linked), Western responsibility is a singularly inappropriate argument for aid, quite apart from being unfounded. It leads to a disregard of the effects of aid in the recipient countries and of the conduct of the recipient governments. It discourages even cursory examination of the likely political, social, and economic results of these Western aims. The concern is with divesting the West of resources, not with the effects of these donations.

Such results of the harping on Western guilt are not surprising. A feeling of guilt has nothing to do with a sense of responsibility. Exponents of guilt are concerned with their own emotional state and that of their fellow citizens, not with the results of the policies inspired by such sentiments. The principal idea behind Western guilt, namely, that the West has prospered at the expense of the third world, is nonsense. And, especially in public affairs, nonsense is rarely harmless.

Discussion

QUESTION: Despite your comments that erosion of religion in modern society has resulted in an inability to think coherently and to make logical connections, I strongly suspect that many people here have by now made some connection between your comments about foreign aid and domestic aid to "underprivileged minorities," that is to say, welfare for the poor. Would you apply your principles and comments across the board to the domestic scene?

PROFESSOR BAUER: Not across the board. There are certainly many similarities between foreign aid and domestic welfare programs. But there are also certain differences.

The welfare recipients and the taxpayers in the United States do live in broadly similar physical and social environments. Also, foreign aid does not go to individuals. If it is handled through intergovernmental transfers, it goes to foreign governments. Welfare payments go to welfare recipients.

The differences are important. For example, I asked earlier if there is any justification in taxing American men and women for the benefit of governments who expel their most productive citizens or who rule over societies in which women are strongly discouraged from taking paid work or in which the great majority of people are reluctant to take sanctioned animal life. The sanctity of the cow in India is only the limiting case.

There are such enormous differences, on a worldwide basis, in social, political, and physical conditions, and therefore in requirements, that we cannot regard foreign aid simply as a worldwide extension of the welfare system, although it does have that element in it.

QUESTION: May I qualify my question? You said that foreign aid drives up the rate of exchange and contributes to inflation; that it leads toward statism; that it fosters a greater amount of control by the government over its people. With regard to the domestic scene, does not welfare, if

124

you want to call it that, or aid to the underprivileged, drive up inflation and increase a statist control?

PROFESSOR BAUER: It does. Here again, there are evident similarities, but there are also differences. For example, on the domestic scene, there is no such thing as a rate of exchange with the outside world. Taxes are collected in dollars, and welfare recipients are paid in dollars or food stamps. The problem of currency exchange does not arise. But there is no doubt that these large welfare payments are an important contributory cause of inflation.

QUESTION: Your focus on absolute wealth and poverty in the world and, therefore, your point that the West does not cause poverty in the third world—because if one looks at the third world before contact with the West and afterwards, one sees that it is actually better off—seems to me to end up being an abstraction that takes our mind off the reality of the situation in which the criticisms are now being made.

Let me give an analogy that you can perhaps comment upon. It could be argued that the American Indian is better off today in terms of economic opportunity than he was before the arrival of the European, measured against the zero starting point or the relative starting point of the Indian. Such a position does not take into account that there is a whole new structure of North American life which transforms the existing situation.

Your argument also sounds very much like the argument of the Afrikaner in South Africa, namely, that South African blacks are better off—and I think that can be demonstrated—than blacks in most of the rest of Africa, relatively speaking, because of job opportunities, health care, housing, and so forth.

The problem is, the American Indian and the South African black does not compare himself either to his former starting point of zero, or to the other blacks in the rest of Africa. Therefore, he does not feel thankful for his relatively advanced economic position over Indians in his grandfather's day, or over blacks outside of South Africa, but are, rather, in the situation where the economic structures and his own relative positions are controlled by the wealthy of the world. Isn't justice and injustice relative to other peoples ignored by your argument about absolute poverty?

PROFESSOR BAUER: I addressed myself to the question whether or not contacts with the West have impoverished the peoples of the third world. Many people, notably including clerics, say that Western contacts have impoverished the peoples of the third world and have obstructed their material progress. I have argued that this is demonstrably untrue. It is, incidentally, also condescending toward the people of the third world because the argument suggests that the people there do not know what they are doing when they buy Western goods or produce for export to the West.

Ordinary people in the third world do not resent the prosperity of the West. It is intellectuals and politicians in the third world who blame the West. This argument suits their political purposes.

The difference in prosperity between, say, Americans and Amazonian Indians, is enormous. But where is the injustice? The Amazonian Indian lives in a different world from ours. Why isn't there a range of choice? Some of those people would like to join our system, to trade with us; it is difficult, looking at it from the outside, to determine who would like to trade with us and gradually join the Western commercial system, and who would not.

Few people could have foreseen in the 1880s that after the planting of the first cocoa tree in the Gold Coast, within a few decades Africans would plant millions of acres of cocoa trees in the West African colonies. A cocoa tree takes six years to grow to maturity, so whoever plants a cocoa can plan at least six years ahead. Yet many Westerners think of Africans as being children of nature, incapable of looking forward, of taking a long view.

QUESTION: I like what you just said because it reminded me of some theology of Karl Rahner that I read recently regarding more legitimate uses and less legitimate uses of power. The arbitrary limitation of human choice is a less legitimate use.

I'd like to relate. that, and what you said earlier about how colonialism can affect situations, with the particular case of a multinational corporation in the Dominican Republic, namely, Gulf & Western Industries.

Our order had been active in the Dominican Republic since the 1940s, and when Gulf & Western began to become a dominant presence there, some of the people with whom we were acquainted grew apprehensive.

Because of the colonial history, Gulf & Western came on the scene under less than optimal circumstances. Many people considered the government in power to be autocratic and oppressive. Now, that government and Gulf & Western entered into certain liaisons, which were seen by some seriously to limit the freedom of the people who did not enjoy as many economic advantages as others. For example, Gulf & Western was permitted to repatriate only a certain amount of its capital investment. That left it free to invest heavily on the island. But because

Gulf & Western is so large in relation to the economy of the Dominican Republic, the sheer investment of that capital seemed to depress indigenous business initiatives that might otherwise have flourished there.

Then there were other problems, such as land use, and cash crops, and sugar cane that might have gone to food consumption. The peasant in South Africa who raises his cocoa tree and trades with the West is employed by somebody; he deals through that brokerage mechanism. The peasants of the Dominican Republic were employed by Gulf & Western, even perhaps lived in its houses, traded at its stores, and so forth.

Now, because of the situation that prevails, because of the timing, multinationals by their very presence can inhibit the freedom of people at the bottom of the economic ladder. Add to that the interiorization of poverty. You mentioned earlier that people who are poor do not have the economic drive and initiative to succeed. Often, that is because they feel that they are somehow unworthy and incompetent. In the Dominican Republic, some of the people I met thought they could succeed in only one of two ways, either by winning the lottery or by winning the favor of the dictator in power.

How, then, does the multinational corporation behave in this kind of milieu?

PROFESSOR BAUER: People in many third world countries produce cash crops for sale instead of food crops for their own use for the same reason that I teach at a university instead of growing my own food. I am better off by earning a salary, even if it is only a pittance, and buying food in the shops rather than trying to grow it myself. The cocoa producers of West Africa and the rubber producers of Southeast Asia are much better off by producing these crops than if they were engaged in subsistence cultivation.

Do you think that people in the Dominican Republic would be freer and have wider horizons if Gulf & Western had never operated there?

QUESTION: My question has to do with the susceptibility of the West to arguments that generate or, perhaps better, reflect profound guilt feelings. I am struck by the continuity of that theme in your comments, and I wonder what that says about American culture and, indeed, about Americans as religious people.

It has often been remarked that among the world's religions Christianity seems particularly attuned to guilt and profound feelings of guilt. Might it be that our susceptibility to rationalizations, as you choose to call them, is a response to a profound and deep residual religiosity that is being touched in ways that are quite irrelevant to the factuality of the appeals that are being made?

PROFESSOR BAUER: I think that these matters are related to the decline of the sense of personal responsibility and personal sin. Collective guilt and the plainly insubstantial rationalizations of this sentiment have stepped into the vacuum brought about by the decline in the sense of personal responsibility for one's conduct.

QUESTION: Do you think that multinational corporations have been as imaginative as they might have been with respect to the development of strategies toward dealing with more oppressive local governments, in both developing their own advantage and, at the same time, increasing the freedom of opportunity for people?

PROFESSOR BAUER: The big multinationals try not to interfere in local politics. They are quite right in this as it is not their task to engage in such activity. Were they to do so, they would be accused of improper political interference. Your question and the charge behind it are examples that the multinationals are nowadays always in the dock. They are accused of misconduct if they take a hand in politics and also if they stay outside it.

The Transnational Enterprise and World Economic Development

Reginald H. Jones

As an active Christian layman of the Congregationalist persuasion, I have sought to express religious values in life and vocation. I am sure that I have not always succeeded, but the effort has been sincere. And as a corporate executive, I have been the target of outspoken religious groups who seem to resent business people as a class and big business people in particular. Some of these spokesmen have been awesome in their self-righteousness, with no forgiveness in their souls. So I have a double reason—as a churchman and as a church target—to join in this discussion of the modern corporation from a moral or religious point of view.

Is Business Satanic?

Everyone has heard about the inscription on an ancient tombstone in a rural English cemetery that simply said, "I told you I was sick." That rueful epitaph may well describe the state of the relationship between some members of the church hierarchy and many big business executives. As an example, the other day I saw a news report out of Indianapolis, dated April 17, 1980. The Methodist Church was holding its General Conference, and Bishop Dale White saw fit to make the following statement to a press conference.

> All of us, really, are hostages, those in the developed countries as well as those in developing nations. Hostages to a vast political economic system of cruelty structures which are pre-ordaining that the rich get richer and the poor get poorer. . . . These systems are so pervasive, so corrupting of the good intentions of decent people, so powerful, so destructive of human well being, so intractable and self-defensive, that perhaps the word which Khomeini uses for them, the word "satanic," is the only word which is aptly descriptive.

Statements like that—and we hear them oh-so-frequently from the church hierarchy, echoing the "liberation theology" of the World Council of Churches—leave me stunned. I am not sure whether the bishop includes the Soviet totalitarian system or the Cuban system or the systems of the Russian colonies in Eastern Europe and Afghanistan in his condemnation; but since he has no constituency or following there, I can only believe he is referring to the comparatively free and economically productive system here in the United States, and perhaps in the liberal democracies of Western Europe, Canada, and so on. We are told that our business and political institutions are so corrupt, so cruel, that we and all our works stand condemned as the creatures of Satan.

Now, I am puzzled as to where or how one starts to reason with a prejudice of such profound character. What does one say to people who ask, "Can a person be a Christian and still work for a corporation?"

If I may witness from my own experience of forty-one years working in a large corporation, the General Electric Company, I must confess that we are imperfect human beings operating in an imperfect environment, and we have made mistakes and committed sins along the way; but I will not accept that our work has been the work of Satan.

We have been inventing and manufacturing useful products, good ones, with an excellent reputation for quality, that help to make life more enjoyable and more productive for people everywhere.

We are providing jobs that most employees deem satisfying and fulfilling, jobs that grant a good measure of economic security to about 400,000 families—300,000 here in the United States and 100,000 in other countries.

We have also been bearing our share of civic duties in any community where we have operations, not only through the taxes we pay and the charitable contributions we make, but more importantly, through the offering of our time and talents.

I cannot bring myself to believe that these activities—the main activities to which I and my 400,000 associates have devoted our lives—are satanic, cruel, or destructive, that they reduce standards of living or make the poor poorer. Nor am I willing to see the rest of our economic and political institutions in that bitter light. There is some basic misapprehension at work here, some misunderstanding of the real world as it is experienced by most of our church congregations.

Sociologists have observed that criticism of business increases in direct proportion to the distance people have from the business process. People actually engaged in business see it in the most positive light. Union leaders, government officials, people in the business schools—those who have some regular contact with the business world—are more critical, but basically supportive. The really intransigent criticism of business comes primarily from the academic and religious communities, which have little contact with business and little opportunity to know what actually goes on there.

To those whose minds are closed by prejudice, ideological commitments, or peer-group pressures, there is little we can say. I have learned that such persons prefer to be adversaries, and I conclude they do not want to understand. For the vast majority of people in academic and religious communities, however, people whose minds *are* open to evidence and experience, what really seems to be needed is a greater exposure to business people and a better sense of their motivations and values. We may represent different subcultures, but it is not all that hard to build two-way bridges of understanding.

My work in recent years has involved quite a bit of bridge-building —between business and government, business and the union movement, business and academia, business and the media. But instead of speaking in generalities, perhaps I can be most useful here by discussing the company I know best, having been associated with it for forty-one years. I will discuss particularly its relationships with the less developed countries, as a multinational or transnational enterprise.

The General Electric Company

First, a few words about General Electric. Most people know us for our consumer products—refrigerators and light bulbs and other electrical appliances. These products, however, make up less than a quarter of our sales. In fact, all our electrical and electronic businesses put together compose less than half of our company. We are involved in the materials business, both manmade and natural resources. We provide a wide range of services and many forms of transportation equipment. We are a major source of capital goods for industry. Roughly a third of our business is international in character, with exports of almost $3 billion from our U.S. factories making us one of the biggest aids in the U.S. government's struggle with balance of payments problems. We are a diversified company whose main mission has been, since the days of Thomas Edison, to bring technology to the uses of society, largely for infrastructures so vital to the standard of living.

Most of our first century as a company, since 1878, was spent in helping the United States to electrify and industrialize. Now, as many other nations decide on the course of industrialization and economic development, our main opportunities and responsibilities lie in helping them to achieve *their* objectives—in competition with other high-technology companies based in Japan, West Germany, England, France, and other developed countries.

Big as we are, we do not have unlimited resources and cannot do everything we would like to do. We have to direct our sales efforts and our investments to those countries with a measure of stability which seem to have the greatest need for our products and services and which will accord us fair and equitable treatment, because that is where our efforts are most likely to succeed.

The image presented in television shows and books like *Global Reach*, of titans of industry sitting in their towers in New York or Tokyo or London and deciding to dump their products on helpless little countries that are defenseless against the corporate giants, is just so much rubbish. That approach to business, if anyone is so foolish as to try it, is a sure formula for failure.

The Basic Formula for Business Success

We have found over many years that the key to business success in any country is to consult with the people who are there, both the officials in charge of economic policy and the private sector people who have a sense of the people's wants and needs. Find out what they are trying to do—discover their priorities, their plans for the nation, their most urgent needs, their rules for participation in the local economy. Then figure out the best way to make your capabilities and products and services fit those needs and regulations. If a company takes the trouble to do this groundwork, the odds will favor business success, because both parties—the company and the host country—want the venture to succeed.

Relationships between companies and countries do not develop suddenly, on the whim of some corporate titan who suddenly decides he has to have a big operation in Lower Slobovia. It is usually an evolving process.

Characteristically, the first contact is made through a local agent helping us to develop some export business. General Electric's main exports are products that help a country build up its economic infrastructure—that supportive, fundamental part of the economy below the more visible consumer structure. We provide equipment for electric power systems, transportation systems, communication systems, and health-care systems. Our first sales to a developing country are usually of high-technology equipment and construction services that help that nation lay its economic foundations.

After we have developed such an export relationship with a country, the need arises for people and facilities to service our equipment. So we establish an international network of service and repair facilities, which also involves training foreign nationals in the maintenance of such equipment—an early form of technology transfer.

The pressures then build up for us to establish manufacturing facilities in the country. Many countries establish "local content" laws, requiring that at least part of a product they are going to import, such as locomotives, be assembled in local factories. These factories in turn become the basis of their own export industries. We cannot establish such production facilities in all countries, of course, but where there is enough political stability to assure that the investment has a good chance of surviving and prospering, we set up the facility—often in a joint venture with local partners, since that is what most countries want these days.

There are, of course, many other factors involved in such decisions—competitive factors, market opportunities, financial incentives and disincentives, attitudes of the local government and people toward outsiders, and so on. Against this background, let me describe some of General Electric's present involvement with less developed countries—LDCs—around the world.

GE in Latin America

Some of our oldest and most productive connections are in Latin America. Our Brazilian affiliate, General Electric do Brasil, with major manufacturing facilities in Campinas, Rio de Janeiro, and São Paulo, has been an important supplier of heavy apparatus to the country's infrastructure. Large industrial motors, controls, switchgear, generators, and complete industrial drive systems are supplied to the nation's utility system and its basic industries. We also produce a range of consumer goods for the growing Brazilian market. In the past, we exported quite a few locomotives to Brazil. But when the government there passed local-content laws requiring that locomotives for the Brazilian railway system be assembled in Brazil, we worked out an arrangement by which our locomotive plant in Erie, Pennsylvania, continues to provide the high-technology parts, which are then assembled with simpler components in our Brazilian plants. Brazil is anxious to build up its own export industries, so we recently signed an agreement with the government to expand several of our operations there—including the locomotive operations—which will provide about $700 million in export business for Brazil, mostly to Latin American markets, over the next twelve years. This will assist Brazil with its awesome problem of paying for imported oil.

The contribution that a transnational enterprise like General Electric can make in a developing country was summarized in a report by the National Planning Association here in the United States. It said:

> Among the foreign enterprises that have contributed importantly to Brazilian advancement . . . the General Electric Company has been outstanding. It was the first to establish in Brazil a manufacturing operation of significant size in an industry other than textiles and food processing. It has always been the leader not only in training and education of Brazilians in modern industrial skills and management techniques but also in promoting Brazilians to the highest positions of managerial and technical responsibility once they have attained the required qualifications. And the diversification and expansion of its own manufacturing, marketing, and engineering activities over nearly half a century have both stimulated and been stimulated by the corresponding diversification and expansion of the Brazilian economy as a whole.[1]

That study was published in 1961, almost twenty years ago. It sums up the continuing goals of General Electric do Brasil. I could go on with descriptions of our activities to help Brazil develop its exciting potential, including a hugely expensive and imaginative project we have completed, in partnership with a Brazilian mining company (they own 51 percent of the venture), to develop iron ore resources in a remote area where the ore is moved by pipeline over the mountains to a newly built port some two hundred miles away.

Another country important to General Electric and to the United States is our neighbor to the south, Mexico. GE's operations have been a part of Mexico since 1896. Today GE-Mexico is the country's leading electrical manufacturer, producing lamps, consumer appliances, electrical and electronic industrial components, and electrical power-line equipment. This is a strongly Mexican operation. With more than five thousand employees, less than half of one percent are Americans. This is characteristic of U.S. multinational corporations, by the way, in contrast to European companies. We move as fast as we can toward putting the business in the hands of foreign nationals, which means bringing people to the United States for training and also conducting many training courses in foreign countries.

Smaller affiliates are located in Venezuela, Argentina, Uruguay, Chile, and Colombia, and where we do not have manufacturing operations of our own, we license technology to local manufacturers—for products ranging from television receivers in Costa Rica, Guatemala, and Peru, to distribution transformers in Chile, and washing machines in Ecuador and El Salvador. We are highly flexible in our business arrangements, depending on local circumstances and desires.

---

[1] Theodore Geiger, *General Electric Company in Brazil* (Washington, D.C.: National Planning Association, 1961).

We are not so flexible, however, that we lose sight of our own standards and principles. In some Latin American countries, for example, the institutions of graft and kickbacks are so deeply ingrained that it is impossible to do business in accordance with our own policies and principles of attracting business on the merits of our products and prices. This is especially true in construction work, for example. So we have simply closed down our construction businesses in some locations and decided to forgo the business. There are plenty of other opportunities. I must add, though, that many of our foreign competitors do not have the same compunctions, figuring that "When in Rome, do as the Romans do." So far, I have not seen other governments rush to bring legal pressures to bear on the subjects of questionable payments, human rights, or environmental concerns.

Rural Electrification

As an illustration of the role that a transnational company can play in a very poor country, consider GE's experience in helping to bring electricity to rural villages in the Dominican Republic.

In the little Dominican town of Laguña de Nisibon in the early 1970s, farmers dried their rice crops by setting them out in the sun, and workers produced concrete blocks with a primitive manual press. Electricity had still not reached this town, which was typical of 160 such unelectrified rural villages in the country. In 1971, the Dominican government embarked on an ambitious rural electrification plan. On the basis of previous experience with General Electric in electrification work, the Dominican government gave us a contract to expand their steam power generation facilities, and our Italian construction company, Sade/Sadelmi, was hired to do the arduous work of stringing miles of lines from the power plant through swamps and timberland and across mountains to some of the villages involved. The work was completed, and on the basis of our performance, we have received contracts for more work of the same kind.

Electrification has wrought dramatic changes in the village of Laguña de Nisibon. An electric concrete-block maker now churns out building blocks for homes. Electric grain-driers prepare rice for storage in the town's food co-op. GE mercury lamps light the main street. Young workers attend evening classes at the electrically lit one-room school. Television brings news of the outside world, and refrigerators keep food and antibiotics from spoiling.

The U.S. Rural Electrification Administration estimates that, with the exception of two countries in Latin America—Nicaragua and Costa Rica—only 5 percent of the rural homes in this part of the world have electricity. Worldwide, nearly one billion people in rural areas are living without electricity. Laguña de Nisibon is a positive example of what can be accomplished, and we aim to be part of the process. Some of us are old enough to remember when rural electrification was a major development objective in the United States, and just as General Electric benefited from the extension of power lines to all parts of the country back in the 1930s and 1940s, so we now see benefits and opportunities in bringing electrification to many other nations of the world.

Africa and Asia

There is so much to consider that I will have to skip over our work with developing countries on other continents. I can assure you, however, that GE has provided much of the economic infrastructure to African nations such as Nigeria, Ghana, and Egypt. In Asia we have been involved with the successes of Singapore, South Korea, and Taiwan. But the real message from these three Asian countries is that nations that make themselves attractive to industry and that encourage their own entrepreneurs can, with the help of transnational suppliers, turn economic miracles. Tom Snedeker, manager of our Korea Liaison Office, says, "Current headlines don't tell the real story here. Much more important over the long run is the rise of Korea from near-destruction twenty years ago to one of the world's fastest-growing economies, with a solid GNP of $25 billion in 1977, and with a steadily growing middle class. Two decades ago, people were eating the bark off trees to keep from starving. Many of these skyscraper-lined streets in Seoul were mud lanes. Today, Korea's 10% to 11% annual real growth rate is the envy of other countries."

Similar comments can be made about Taiwan and Singapore, whose progress stands in such stark contrast to that of the rest of Southeast Asia. While India stagnates in a socialist muddle and Vietnam and Cambodia are being destroyed by Communist governments gone berserk, Korea, Taiwan, and Singapore have come, in a relatively short time, from economic obscurity and poverty into the front rank of the world's trading nations. And they have done it despite severely limited supplies of both fuels and raw materials.

How have they done it? They have developed effective "value-added" economies, importing natural resources and then converting them into finished products for export at highly competitive prices. To manage this neat economic trick, they each draw on literate, educated people with keen entrepreneurial and managerial skills—mostly expatriate Chinese who chose not to stay in Communist China. They have people with disciplined work habits, and all three nations have plowed back a high percentage of their incomes as investments in advanced technologies.

There is another common denominator that we would hope is not lost on other developing nations: each of these three countries, in varying degrees, demonstrates the vitality of private enterprise and individual initiative. There is in each country more centralized control than Americans are used to, or believe in, but underneath this outer shell of authoritarian government there is ample room for the innovator and entrepreneur, and this flexibility has been a powerful factor in the economic success these nations enjoy.

This is an all too brief picture of how one company, General Electric, has been able to participate significantly in the development of nations on all continents. Our strategy is basically to learn what nations need and want, what *their* plans and priorities are, what rules and regulations they have for participating in their local economy, and then be flexible enough and creative enough to match our business strategies to their perceived needs and desires. This is a far cry from the imperial multinational corporations of popular fiction and Marxist caricature. And I hope it demonstrates that large business firms can and do operate in such a way as to help the people of the world achieve their legitimate aspirations for a better life.

The World of Work

One often hears the charge, from our socialist brethren, that the multinational companies move into an underdeveloped country and exploit the workers there with low wages and sweatshop working conditions. That may be true of some fly-by-night outfits, but it is not true of the large established concerns like General Electric. We bring stateside working conditions to our plants in other countries, as the pride and enthusiasm of our employees reflects.

For example, GE established several manufacturing plants in Puerto Rico back in the 1950s, and we are now the largest employer on the island. Like other companies, we were orginally attracted by the tax incentives; but as the tax incentives ran out, we stayed in Puerto Rico because we were pleased with the performance of our people and the general success of those operations.

When we first put in a plant to make household wiring devices at Juana Dìaz, we put in a paved parking lot. I remember noticing just five or six cars in the lot. Two years later, I saw an appropriation request to enlarge the parking lot substantially. Remembering those lonely five or six cars, I questioned the request. But on my next trip to Juana

Diaz I was amazed to see the lot full and employees' cars parked all over the place. We enlarged the parking lot, and I think that example demonstrates that we are not underpaying or exploiting our employees.

Another example in Puerto Rico: another company had to vacate a plant it had built at Vega Alta—the operation ran into some kind of financial difficulty, and I arranged for General Electric to take it over. It was something of a mess by our standards, so we installed new lighting, air-conditioning, and better equipment and gave the place a fresh coat of paint—dark green up to waist height, and a lovely soft green from there to the ceiling. A couple of months after the plant opening, a deputation from the employees came in to our employee relations manager and asked if the company had any objection to the women employees wearing uniforms. We said we had nothing against uniforms, but because we did not think that they were necessary, we did not want to go to the expense of buying them. The young lady who was the spokesperson said, oh no, she did not expect us to pay for them, she just wanted to know if we had any objections. So the women went to San Juan and bought some cloth and made skirts to match the dark green and blouses to match the soft green. The attitude of those employees speaks volumes. It gives me a lift to see those women wearing their handmade uniforms, clearly so proud of themselves and their bright and cool workplace.

Leafing through a recent publication produced under a grant from the Episcopal Church Publishing House and advocating class war and a rejection of capitalism, I noticed a headline that said, "To most people, the world of work is a place of crucifixion." I wondered what the author would think if he could see that plant in Puerto Rico and sense the pride, the sociability, the feeling of status and personal fulfillment that work has brought to those women. For most people, work is not a crucifixion; it is a salvation. It is when people have to retire that they get sick and depressed and lonely; that is why retired people forced the Congress to outlaw mandatory retirement. I have no patience with people who deliberately destroy the morale of working people by telling them that they are being exploited when they are not. That is irresponsible and unchristian.

People Want Material Progress

There is one strain of thought in current fashion—Herbert Stein calls it the Woodstock school of economics—that derides material progress. We are urged to abandon high technology and return to a pastoral style of life. This is a false ideal. The poor may be blessed, but they do not like poverty. The "poor but happy" society does not exist anywhere.

About four years ago, George Gallup reported on the largest opinion survey ever conducted, a worldwide project covering nearly seventy nations on six continents. Fundamental questions were asked about attitudes and expectations in life, and the most important finding was the huge discrepancy, in terms of human happiness, between the technologically developed and the underdeveloped nations. Says Mr. Gallup, "On the average, people in the richest countries—those who live in North America, Australia, and Western Europe—report themselves as being far happier, find their lives more interesting, worry less, and would like few, if any changes in their own existences. They are also more content with their family life, their countries, their communities, their education, and with themselves. By stark contrast, only 28 percent of the Latin Americans, 8 percent of the Africans, and a mere 6 percent of the Indians surveyed consider themselves fully satisfied with their lives." Do these unhappy people reject industrial society? On the contrary, they want it desperately. As Gallup says—and this is an overwhelmingly important finding—"The inhabitants of the Third World want more industry in their countries by ratios exceeding 20 to 1."[2] The only question is how to get it, and that is largely a political and social question.

I have noted that church leaders tend to emphasize the redistribution of wealth, but that is not really the key to the problem. Most of human history is a history of redistributions of wealth, as one group after another has moved into power; but none of these redistributions changed the fundamental human condition of scarcity and poverty. It is the *creation* of wealth—the creation of a civilizing surplus—that is the key to a better life for all people. As John Kennedy said, "A rising tide lifts all boats."

Poverty is the plight of all primitive or traditional peoples; not until the rise of industrial capitalism did any society have the capability to eliminate stark poverty. It is ironic that industrial capitalism, which owes so much to the Protestant work ethic and to Judeo-Christian respect for personal stewardship, has now become the favorite whipping boy for the adherents of "liberation theology."

If the churches are sincerely interested in helping to bring a better life to the peoples of the world—and I certainly agree that this is one of our religious obligations—then they might do well to set aside their preoccupation with theoretical socialism and look at the real world, which offers many examples of the results of capitalism and socialism as actually applied. Sixty years after the great Soviet Socialist Revolu-

---

[2] George H. Gallup, "What Mankind Thinks about Itself," *Reader's Digest* (October, 1976), pp. 132–136.

tion, Russia is still unable to feed itself, and its economic progress—even with the most ruthless controls over its work force—is not very impressive compared with the economic and social progress of the nations that have adopted democratic capitalism, in Europe, Asia, and North America. Among the developing nations, even those with authoritarian governments, the record is clear: those that encourage entrepreneurship and private enterprise have surged ahead, and those that adopted the socialist road have found their progress frustrated. Transnational companies must necessarily deal with the world as it is and adapt to a very broad spectrum of economic and political systems in their commercial transactions; but their catalytic role seems to be most effective in those countries that are sympathetic to the principles of private enterprise.

The Public Franchise

One reason for my participation in this seminar is my awareness, like that of many other corporate executives these days, of our public franchise. While we are directly accountable to our Boards of Directors and share owners, we also recognize an accountability to the public. Through the marketplace, law, and the pressures of public opinion, the public decides whether a company will succeed or fail. We know that we have obligations over and above economic performance; we must meet public expectations in terms of moral values and social responsibilities.

As I said to our managers at the first management conference after I had become chairman of General Electric, in January, 1973, we are stewards for some of the most valuable resources of the nation, or of the world. General Electric is a unique configuration of assets, one of the most productive enterprises on the globe. Those assets are truly significant to the progress of humankind, and must not be squandered, mismanaged, or directed toward socially destructive ends. So we recognize our public franchise, and how easily it could be lost.

Our religious institutions feel accountable to a Higher Authority, but they, too, must be concerned with questions of legitimacy and public accountability. They also have a public franchise. A church cannot long survive if its people follow other leaders. I notice that the denominations most closely associated with left-wing activism are losing members and that the evangelistic denominations, with their emphasis on personal faith and more traditionally defined social action, are growing vigorously. I wonder if this trend does not suggest that the church leaders associated with the National and World Councils may have drifted off course—lost touch with their congregations, lost touch with the felt needs of those they serve? Perhaps they have been so carried away with their prophetic and revolutionary roles that they have lost sight of their rabbinical function—the conserving, caring, nurturing function that means so much to ordinary men and women. As James Gustafson put it at a recent Notre Dame seminar, churches have been, and ought to be, communities of moral formation. He suggests that some may be failing in that function.

Just as some corporate executives have felt that the attitudes of the public are not really very important (these are the Neanderthals among the corporate executives), so one also detects a certain contempt for common opinion, a little impatience with the backwardness of congregations, among some church leaders and some of the church professionals at the Interfaith Center at 475 Riverside Drive in New York.

We in business only occasionally hear a kind word from those quarters. Rather, almost everything that is said about business, particularly big business, seems to emphasize its well-publicized sins and errors. The millennium is not at hand, and we in business have not reached chiliastic standards of perfection. We have our sinners and backsliders. But it does seem unfair, and perhaps a bit hypocritical, for the religious leaders to hold business to a standard of perfection that is not universally observed even in the house of religion.

Forbes magazine, in an article on the electronic church, reported that the electronic evangelists grossed $600 million last year, twelve times as much as a decade ago. Some may regard that as merely a successful growth business, but most electronic evangelism exhibits a crassness that would embarrass most of us in the business community. Yet its notable success may suggest a failing on the part of the established churches to satisfy deep religious needs of our people. And in the other wing—the far left wing—we have people who are so filled with hatred for our system of democratic capitalism, so intent on defaming the achievements of the many parishioners who work in the large corporations, that we must wonder how Christian motives could produce such violent hatred. They claim good intentions, but the road to hell is paved with good intentions. A passionate intensity that would sacrifice our freedoms, that helps the totalitarians stretch their grim reach around the globe—and that is what the liberation theologians and their supporters seem to be doing—is to me a sinful error.

Perhaps the situation calls for a little more humility all around. We are all trying our best, but even that best will not go far without the grace of God. If we extend a bridge of understanding to each other, and let the Holy Spirit work its way, who knows what could come of it? Not perfection, but perhaps a little more movement toward the Kingdom of God.

Discussion

QUESTION: You have spoken of your concern with corporate obligations over and above fiscal performance, and you mentioned that an international corporation, when it goes into a foreign country, rightly looks for stability. Repressive government often goes with stability, unfortunately, as in Brazil. What kinds of conversations go on at GE about the connection between stability and profitability?

MR. JONES: That is a good question. It comes down to a question of accountability and looking at a particular LDC. One of the criteria for investment is stability of government, and I think the questioner is saying that a corporation would not invest in a country whose government was so unstable that the investment might be lost the next day. But many of the stable LDCs have authoritarian governments—Brazil was cited as a specific example—and the question was asked, what conversations go on at General Electric when the company is considering making an investment in a nation ruled by a relatively authoritarian government such as Brazil's.

I have come to the conclusion, based on pragmatic observations over many years of travel around this globe, that there is no way that an underdeveloped, illiterate society can move from a form of colonialism—feudalism, if you want to call it that—directly to a democratic system. It just does not seem to happen. You have to have an electorate that is capable of informed voting before you can have a real democracy. If a nation is in an authoritarian period in which there is a reasonable recognition of the rights of individuals, I believe that we should invest in such a nation.

Singapore, under Lee Kuan Yew, has about as authoritarian a form of government as can be found anywhere in the world, and yet the natives of Singapore are, by and large, happy with their station in life. These people have a life today they never thought possible.

Now, let us consider Brazil, which presents a specific problem. I have traveled extensively in Brazil, particularly in the back country, and in my opinion many of the people of Brazil are not ready for a democratic society at this stage. In Rio, São Paulo, and Belo Horizonte, a large middle class is developing—educated, literate, very articulate people, good, sound businessmen and good, sound academicians; there is growth, at long last, of democracy. It is coming slowly, but it is coming.

We had our first strike in São Paulo a couple of months ago. By government decree, strikes have never been allowed. It was interesting. The people said to me, "We don't want to strike General Electric, but this guy down the street is not being fair with his people, and we have been pulled out." All the São Paulo metal-working industries were pulled out because of two or three bad employers. Our workers went to great lengths to explain to us that they were not unhappy with General Electric.

I was asked at a press conference in São Paulo, "Isn't it awful that you have a strike. What are you going to do, pull out?" And I said, "We have strikes in factories all over the world. We are used to dealing with this sort of a problem. Of course, we aren't going to pull out." In fact, while I was there I announced the new $700 million export program that I mentioned earlier, a program involving very substantial investments.

I am sensitive to the problem of human rights. I am also sensitive to the awful poverty that exists in a nation like Brazil, and it is terribly important that we alleviate that poverty as quickly as possible. We are going to do that more effectively by being there than by not being there.

One of my associates, the night before the strike, was walking on the main street of São Paulo, when three youths came up, knocked him down, and took his wallet. People stood by and watched what happened. Crime is rampant. Why? Poverty. The more people there are to build a sound economic structure, the less poverty there will be. And the faster we can get movement on human rights, the faster we will get movement on democracy.

President Figueiredo asked me, when I was in Brasilia, about the problem of the strikes and how we felt about them. I told him I thought that, in allowing workers to strike, Brazil was moving in the right direction.

QUESTION: I hear the passion, the commitment, in what you are saying. But I am having trouble understanding whether you are really responding objectively to the question that was asked. It was not a loaded question. How do you face the charge, which I am sure you hear frequently, of a kind of imperialism?

MR. JONES: I believe in democratic capitalism, but I have tried to explain that in a society that has not developed as the United States has, the people are less interested in democracy than in a good job and in raising their economic standards. They do not care who is running their nation—and I must say, when 50 percent of our young people don't even go to the polls, I am afraid we are in serious trouble ourselves.

But if we can get capitalism going, if the government is stable enough to permit us to start raising the economic standards, then I think that, in nation after nation, we have a good chance of fostering the kind of democracy with which we are familiar.

QUESTION: What can a company like General Electric do about the violations of human rights that often accompany these stable but repressive governments?

MR. JONES: I do not think the answer is for us to pull out of Brazil because of violations there of our principles of human rights. The way to help solve that problem is, I think, to be there and to help develop a middle class. Workers who have high enough standards of living send their children to colleges and to universities; those children become an informed electorate.

QUESTION: I accept the idea of staying there and working to build a better reality, but whose values are being inculcated?

MR. JONES: The people in any country will develop their own sets of values, but I think we can help them. The church is there to help them, and our businesses are there to help them. We in the United States have a political structure, we have an economic structure, and we have a cultural or moral structure. There are bridges between all three of these structures, but do not allow one structure to dominate the other two. There has got to be a certain amount of independence. Our job, as I see it, is not to transport abroad our total set of values and moral standards. That is what we tried to do with legislation such as the Fair Practices Act. It was a mistake. People abroad will not accept it.

Let us help countries build their economic structures, and as that is done in nation after nation, the moral and the political structures will follow, and they will be built along lines compatible with ours, because capitalism flourishes in a democratic society, not in a socialist society.

QUESTION: You mentioned the degree of personal commitment required for a society to achieve a form of democratic capitalism. It seems that personality requires a social structure to support its growth and development in the direction of the responsible exercise of power. Is not such a structure equally a matter of character in the fabric of the life of the society, as is the structure of the human soul perhaps a matter of character in the fabric of the invisible life?

If you will admit that, how does a corporation go beyond the reasoning of its economic impetus, beyond the romance that sustains its cohesion and its passions, and beyond the products that flow from its "imagineering" into the realization of the character of the new society?

MR. JONES: You have brought up a very vital ingredient: character. Let me say that I have come to one very interesting conclusion as a result of my forty-one years of corporate life, and that is, simply put, that every major corporation in the United States has its own culture, and no two are alike. I have often wondered what causes this culture to develop in a company. It isn't the existence of a set of policies; every company has a set of policies, and in essence, they all say the same kinds of things.

What does cause a corporation to develop its own character, its own unique culture? Why does it have a grain? As every carpenter knows, you can do certain things if you work with the grain, but the minute you try to work against the grain, you are in trouble. I have come to the conclusion that the culture of a corporation is developed by its senior management, and that deals directly with the point of character. And it is interesting to note that the culture evolves. It is dynamic, not in any revolutionary way, but it is not static.

Let me give you an anecdote that tells the point. In the middle of the 1950s, General Electric Company used to have an island in the Thousand Islands called Association Island, and all the senior managers of the company could be gathered together there. Our chief executive officer was Charlie Wilson, a Sunday school teacher, not a college graduate, who came up through the ranks, a highly religious man. At a meeting on Association Island, Charlie Wilson read that a Westinghouse executive had said that Westinghouse was going to increase to a size that would eclipse General Electric, which was then about twice the size of Westinghouse. Wilson thundered from the podium, "They should live so long! Their children should live so long! Their grandchildren should live so long!" Then the band played "Onward Christian Soldiers," and we got up out of our seats and marched to the flagpole. The American flag went up, followed by the General Electric flag. And, by God, there wasn't a dry eye in the house.

Now, can you imagine me, thirty years later, behaving in such a way with the senior management, which now comes together once a year, at a very large hotel?

I tell that story repeatedly to managers at General Electric. I say,

"You know, you are so sophisticated that you would laugh at me if I did that to you." But there isn't anyone in that audience who does not understand what I am talking about.

We talk stewardship with our people. We talk character. We tell our managers that they are responsible for the economic lives of their employees. This is not paternalism. An employee is making a significant contribution to the company through his time and talents, and we have to be equally concerned about his economic life—his income, his job satisfaction, and all the rest.

Nor is it just the economic life of the employee; it's the inner fulfillment he achieves. And our people understand; they respond. What we are really talking about, even if indirectly, is character. In our opinion, what distinguishes our company, what we feel is so significant in our company culture, is our concern for each other.

QUESTION: You may not rail at the audience and have people marching around the flag with tears falling from their eyes, but I have a feeling that you would be happy to stand upon the mountain and point in twelve directions and utter the first benediction. The rabbinical role is key here. Do you think, as I do, that in some respects this says a lot about the character of General Electric? That is a compliment.

MR. JONES: Yes, I do, and thank you. I appreciate it.

QUESTION: I would like to pursue that notion of character as a central element of your discussion, because our culture seems to have certain characteristics—commitment, honor, a sort of good will, a character in general—yet some of the detractors of capitalism think and claim that capitalism, and specifically multinational corporations arriving in a heretofore uncapitalistic territory, encourage such things as greed, selfishness, and materialism, in the personal culture, the family culture, and eventually the whole culture they bring with them.

I wonder, in this regard, if there is such a thing as the separation of church and business, because we have seen in the United States in the last thirty years the kind of separation of church and state whereby officially religious sentiments are almost not allowed in the public enterprise. Have you noticed the same thing in the corporate enterprise? Can you appeal, as a businessman, privately but as a corporate representative, to certain religious sentiments and values among your constituents?

MR. JONES: I cannot do it from the podium, as you recognized when you said that I could perhaps do it privately.

Long ago, in our New Orleans office, a Cajun regional manager used to open every sales meeting with a prayer and close every one with a benediction. He really played on the emotions of his salesmen. He played on them marvelously. One cannot do that today—not from the podium. There is that separation to which you have alluded. But certainly in private conversations and in discussions, our concern for standards and for each other can play through.

Just about every day I write—longhand—one or two letters to bereaved wives of employees I have known, or to employees whose wives or children have died, and in each letter my religious convictions come through—because they are right there. I can talk about the only source of solace and comfort, about keeping these people in my prayers. There isn't a manager in General Electric who doesn't know that my family and I have been involved in religious activities all our lives.

QUESTION: In answering a previous question, you mentioned the need for "a certain amount of independence" in the economic sector. Could you expand on that?

MR. JONES: When we talk democracy, we are talking about a system of government in which the electorate elects the representatives who will head the government and who will, therefore, serve them.

When we talk capitalism, we are talking about an economic system that is built on the principle of private ownership of property and the entitlement of the rewards from such ownership. It is not too difficult to differentiate that from socialism, for in socialism the productive means are owned or controlled not by private individuals, but by the state. And I think that we are in danger of turning toward statism, that is, a condition in which the state has increasingly gained control not solely of the political system but of the economic system as well.

I have grave concern that when this happens, it will not be long before the state becomes involved in the cultural/moral system, just as it is in Communist countries. Once the state starts to invade your religious area, you religionists are going to get considerably exercised.

Academicians were generally complacent about the trend toward statism until they began to experience the kind of federal regulations we have been living with in business. Now they are up in arms about the intrusion of government in academic life.

QUESTION: In general, why does socialism have so much more appeal than capitalism for academicians and students?

MR. JONES: For several years I have been saying that the reason we have difficulty selling capitalism to youth is that we have no theology for capitalism. Youth are attracted to socialism because socialists talk about doing so many good things for so many people: from each according to his ability, to each according to his need.

We have no theology. Adam Smith started to write *The Theory of Moral Sentiments* before he started to write *The Wealth of Nations*. He finished the latter but never really finished the first. We have been trying desperately to find somebody with the capability of writing a theology for capitalism—one that would be attractive to youth.

QUESTION: I wonder if you are not falling into some of the same errors that you charged the critics of the corporations with. I think you characterized the critics of American corporate affairs in an uncharitable way: they are all "liberation" theologians and revolutionaries. Yet, as you know, some of the churches are multimillion-dollar shareholders in General Electric or General Motors or Exxon. It is, therefore, somewhat unfair to pretend, in a way that can be damaging to the dialogue, that all church critics are trying to throw over that enterprise system and put in another. There is a pluralism within the church just as there is in the corporate sector.

MR. JONES: In my defense, I do this on purpose. It's hyperbole. It has to be done because hyperbole is dealt in by the other side, and unless I can have my innings, as it were, I don't think we are going to find a common ground for informed dialogue. Some very violent things *are* being said about capitalism by official church groups and spokesmen, and somebody has to call them to task.

I do not stand before you and say that I am speaking for corporate America. I speak for a man named Jones who works for General Electric Company. What disturbs me is that these spokesmen say they speak for the church, and they do not. They speak for a church hierarchy, not for the membership of the church.

QUESTION: We should continue to argue this point on the basis of the many people in the business community, some of whom would say that apartheid in South Africa is a great idea and that the United States should recognize South Africa and build a bond of allegiance with it. It would be unfair for me to quote somebody from Allegheny Ludlum or Hewlett-Packard and say that all of American business wants to back South Africa.

I think we both agree that the ambiguity of the middle ground must be recognized; the gray areas need to be discussed. Those are where the thorny questions come up and where the hard business decisions, as well as the hard moral decisions, must be made. I am calling, as you are, for some dialogue in that middle ground.

MR. JONES: And you know we have always been willing to have that dialogue.

QUESTION: Yes, we have appreciated those sessions. GE has always had its door open to any church investor who wants to come in.

In your earlier remarks you clearly indicated that the goal of General Electric in its business overseas, as well as to make a profit, is to try to help in the social and economic development process. I heard you say that was a goal, and I heard you tell a number of success stories.

I wonder if you can recall cases in which GE has invested overseas and made a profit, has been fair to its employees and done a good job for them, but has not been able to help in the social and economic development process. The kind of electrification example you gave was a dramatic one, in which the common good was greatly served by GE's involvement. But are there some cases where your hands are really tied as you go into a developing country?

MR. JONES: Yes. We were kicked out of Cuba, our properties taken over by Castro. We were kicked out of China under the earlier Mao government, our properties confiscated; we are just now receiving some compensation. In these cases we have been pushed right out of the economy and have been unable to be a factor in it.

QUESTION: Are there cases where you have been in a country for ten or twenty years and made a profit and done a good job for your employees, but because of the social structure of that country, you did not feel comfortable with the contribution you were able to make?

MR. JONES: Yes, I will give you an example. Last week, after great deliberation, we finally closed our Tehran office, which is staffed totally by Iranian nationals. We have been paying those people for many months with absolutely no prospect of any business, and we finally decided that we could not continue to do so. That was a tough decision to have to make, because I do not know what those people are going to do for a livelihood.

QUESTION: Has GE been able to help out in India?

MR. JONES: We have tried for some fifty or sixty years to find a way to operate in India. In the early days, when India was a colony of Great Britain under the viceroy, we had some very small sales operations there. Following Britain's withdrawal and the development of

149

India's own government, we opened up two factories. Government rules and regulations became so onerous, however, that we closed first one plant, then the second one. Today, we are effectively out of business in India. There just does not seem to be any way that we can work there, although we have tried hard to do so. We lost a considerable amount of money in our Indian operations and were willing to work at it for a long time. But it became harder instead of easier and we have given up.

QUESTION: What are your views on the growing movement to invite the federal government and sometimes the state government to shore up failing industry in the United States? What is your view of the potential impact of that movement on democratic capitalism here at home?

MR. JONES: I am firmly opposed to government moving in to shore up a sick industry. Under the capitalistic system, you have the freedom to succeed. You should also have the freedom to fail. GE has failed in some businesses, and so we just got out of those businesses.

It would be much less expensive for the United States, and, therefore, for you and me, and much more productive for our economy, if Chrysler, for example, were allowed to go through bankruptcy. What would happen?

We have a legal mechanism that provides for a series of steps. Frankly, I think you would find that Chrysler's newer, more efficient plants would be acquired by foreign manufacturers, and that these plants would be more successful than they had been under Chrysler management, and would wind up having more and better satisfied employees. Other parts of Chrysler, perhaps their marine divisions and a few others, would go right on under some form of a reconstituted Chrysler Corporation.

You would also see the demise of obsolete, antiquated facilities such as those in Hamtramck. It would be much cheaper to develop retraining methods, perhaps even move some families to other areas, even if it meant keeping them on some form of compensation for an indefinite period, than try to maintain the whole superstructure of the Chrysler Corporation which, in spite of its valiant management, is a sick company.

I feel the same way about any industry or company that is in trouble.

In meeting foreign competition, the United States has the problem of operating on the principle of comparative advantage and believing in free fair trade, and many other nations do not.

The unions, which were once the bastion of free trade, have now become the dominant force for protectionism. Lane Kirkland once asked some West German labor leaders how they defined free trade. "Oh, easy," they said, "an open United States market." Kirkland insisted that the openness had to be reciprocal and he's right.

The nontariff barriers by which other countries close their markets to our products are a real problem. Now, after the Tokyo round, we are developing codes of conduct. We are going to have to monitor compliance, and if we do not get free and fair trade, I suspect we will have no choice but to teach a lesson and perhaps go to some form of retaliation. But I resist protectionism. Once we start down the road of protectionism in international trade, we are all going to be a lot poorer.

QUESTION: What is the role of the business leader today?

MR. JONES: Not to be an apologist for business, but to be a fighter for business, because business is in the interests of the people of this country. I spend half of my time on what I call the externalities, because I do not believe there will be a General Electric Company if Americans do not understand General Electric and do not want it to exist.

The power of public opinion is enormous, and our public franchise is our greatest asset. We try to maintain and enhance it by turning out good values, products that people want to buy. But that is not enough. Increasingly, we have to communicate our views and our purposes to the public and to our representatives in Washington. We have to take a constructive part in the formation of public policy affecting business.

I think we have to do this. We are not going to maintain this system unless we take the time to explain it to people. I spend a fair amount of time on campuses, which are so different now than they were in the 1960s. There are some open minds out there now. I also spend a lot of time in Washington. And I think that over time, if you build your credibility by delivering on your promises and by having the facts, you get the audience. It is our only hope for maintaining this system.

QUESTION: Personally, I do not see business as being in a Catch-22, no-win situation. We live in a sort of win-lose world; we give a little and we take a little. In that context, if we really want to have dialogue and credibility, it is necessary for us to develop some kind of blue-ribbon respectability on both sides.

Why not found, for example, an institute on business and religion, which could be co-sponsored, as it were, by the National Council of Churches and the Conference Board or the Business Round Table. This would provide a respectable network, which would diminish suspicion and enable us, when we come together, to ask ourselves some of the important questions as to who, really, is the enemy.

Although individual missionaries to the campuses will do some good, unless we set up a responsive network, we aren't going to save any systems. An institute on business and religion could be involved in strategic planning on the part of those who are concerned. We could begin to ask such basic questions as, What does it mean to have Christian behavior? What is a Christian?

As you said, every corporation has a personality, and the senior management of that corporation, to a large extent, sets the tone. Now, I suspect that long before you became Chairman of GE, your moral formation had already begun. You had confrontations, and your moral development, in a Christian context, came along. From that moral development, you developed a sense of wanting to achieve. Economic development followed, and you also saw the checks and balances of American political life.

Now, you seemed to indicate that in overseas operations we will come in and foster economic development, which will lead, in time, to political development.

MR. JONES: Third World countries have their own culture, their own moralities. Recently, in Riyadh, I spoke at length with Minister Yahmani. We discussed cultures and religions, and it really came home to me that we, as religious people, do not understand the Muslims and their culture and their religion.

It came home to me in meetings with Jordanians and Palestinians and Egyptians. I was very happy when President Carter told Muslim leaders that Americans appreciate differences in religion, that we all worship God through different disciples and in different ways and different means, but that in no sense is the United States concerned with a holy war or with any attempt to export our religion or to conflict in any way on religious matters.

But I think we can go to another country, and help with the development of its economic system. A literate class develops, and the political system changes. You see it happening in nation after nation. Look at Venezuela, right now having the discipline to go through a recession, tightening the money supply to bring down the inflation and get the economy on a sounder footing with a democratic government.

But I draw the line at bringing in our moral and cultural system. Other nationals can see how we operate, but they have to develop their own way, within their own religion and their own culture.

Now, to your other point, I would want to think about that institute. It may well have merit. My concern is that when informal dialogue is institutionalized, it sometimes becomes suspect, because of the pro-liferation of procedures and agendas. We lose some meaning along the way. I would want to think about it.

QUESTION: What is GE doing, as a corporation, to build bridges?

MR. JONES: I am not the only one in General Electric that is out there on the campus tour. We encourage all of our managers to get out and spend time on campuses. And we periodically bring groups of professors to our own educational facility in Crotonville, N.Y. One week it might be faculties in a given engineering field. The next week it might be faculties in the humanities. When academics come in, we have an opportunity to discuss some of our concerns with them and to get some advice and counsel from them.

The other thing we do is contribute money. Private universities, particularly, are in dire financial straits—although we give money to public institutions as well. We have steadily been increasing our con-tributions from the General Electric Foundation. There are so many worthwhile programs in academia that we would like to support.

I will admit there is one area where we are very self-serving. We have one program that is concerned with the defense of America's economic system, a program to support academics who are doing the research that we think will provide the foundation on which we can build a fuller understanding of the system. They are not just in eco-nomics; some are in political science, sociology, the humanities, and so on. We have been very active in making corporate America understand that these people need help and support.

QUESTION: What do you think about proposals that members of labor unions and representatives of the general public serve on corporation boards?

MR. JONES: We wrote an issue of our annual report on the subject of corporate governance. I have fairly strong feelings on the subject. I do not believe that a corporate board is improved by the presence on it of representatives of special interests. I believe that the members of a board of directors should be responsive and accountable to all the shareowners of the corporation, not just to a select special interest group.

I have great difficulty, frankly, with the idea of Doug Fraser, whom I know well, sitting on the board of Chrysler. He has been very honest, asserting that he intends to protect the interests of the workers. I do not think that his presence is going to lead to particularly productive dis-cussions at board meetings.

Our board of directors is an eclectic group, comprising big bankers and big businessmen, small businessmen, the president of Rensselaer Polytechnic Institute, a retired head of one of the big eight accounting firms, a brilliant woman, a black former judge, and a former assistant secretary of the Treasury. They work harmoniously and constructively together. They bring varying viewpoints to the discussions and are certainly not monolithic in their approach to problems. Very independent and very intelligent people, all of them recognize that they represent all the shareowners of the company, and not a special interest.

I think one of the great problems with Washington today is the demise of a strong two-party system and the development of special interest politics. We have so many splinter groups on the Hill today, all out for some particular special interest, that we cannot get any meaningful legislation passed. Congress adjourned last week, recessed, will not be back for another ten days, and never even passed the appropriation for the Export-Import Bank. Nine and one-half months into the fiscal year, and the Ex-Im Bank still does not have its appropriation for fiscal 1980. Why? A lack of discipline on the Hill. Now if we move that same special interest approach over to the corporation, there will be a power battle. Corporations will be much less effective performing their duties than they are today. And don't think for one moment that corporations are not thin-skinned, perceptive, and very interested in what the special interest groups think; they are.

If we do not know what the church groups and the environmentalists and the consumerists are saying, we are in deep trouble. We know what they are saying, and we do not need a representative on the board to tell us that. In fact, I think a director representing a special interest would not think he was serving his constituency unless he became adversarial. Ours is an advocacy society, an adversarial society. Whoever has 51 percent is in the majority and says so. In Japan, which has a consensus society, the consensus develops slowly, not through the battle of special interests.

Big corporations are not as adversarial as our political system is. They have more of a consensus society than anyone outside them believes.

I cannot sit in my office and dictate, willy-nilly, what General Electric is going to do. I could do it for two or three months, perhaps, then the board of directors, hearing from my associates, as they would, would say, "Jones, you had better straighten up and fly right or you are out."

Now, with a few exceptions, firings that take place at the top of corporations are written up to suggest that the incumbent resigned for personal reasons or because he wanted to pursue other interests. But don't kid yourself; he has been booted right out. The turnover at the top of large corporations is much higher than anybody appreciates; that is one of the reasons for the consensual approach—the mutual forebearance and the search for agreement—in big companies. People do not fully appreciate that the greatest constraint on a corporate executive is peer approval.

The Socialist Critique
of the Corporation

Bernard Murchland

Everything ideal has a material base and everything material has an ideal fulfillment.

GEORGE SANTAYANA

The main character in Walker Percy's *The Moviegoer* used to go to the local library to read the journals whenever he felt depressed. First he would read all the liberal journals. Then he would read all the conservative journals. The liveliness of the debate between the two and the animosity they bore one another never failed to cheer him up. It was, he reflected, one of the few remaining signs of life in an otherwise dead world. I have something of that attitude toward the socialist-capitalist controversy. It is, to say the very least, a wondrous spectacle of vitality. But, more than that, I believe it is one of the crucial arguments of our time.

I want to enter the fray here in three ways. First, I want to present a pastiche of socialist arguments against capitalism in general and the corporation in particular. Second, I want to criticize those arguments. And third, I want to make some suggestions about how we might talk about the reality of modern corporations in philosophico-theological terms.

Religious Socialists

The socialist animus against capitalism is by now so well articulated and so prominent a feature of our intellectual landscape that it probably calls for little elaboration here. Certainly we need not run through the fundamentals of Marxism yet one more time. Since we are talking in this conference about the theology of the corporation, I will restrict my sampling to "religious socialists." A significant portion of religious thinkers in the twentieth century have favored socialism. In England that tradition runs back to the mid-nineteenth century, to Frederick Maurice, an Anglican clergyman, Charles Kingsley (the novelist and also an Anglican clergyman), and John Ludlow, who claimed that "so-

156

cialism was the true character of the great Christian revolution of the 19th century."[1] They were moved by the sufferings of the poor, which they blamed on the self-interest and competition of laissez faire capitalism. They set the tone for the many socialist organizations that subsequently came into being.

In 1908 William Temple, later to become Archbishop of Canterbury, wrote an article in the *Economic Review* in which he proclaimed:

> In the epistle to the Ephesians, where St. Paul achieves the completion of his doctrine, he preaches the fullest scheme of evolutionary socialism, so far as all fundamental points are concerned, that has yet been conceived by man. Socialism is the economic realization of the Christian Gospel. . . . The alternative stands before us—Socialism or Heresy; we are involved in one or the other.[2]

In the 1930s the Free Church Christian Left, under the leadership of the philosopher John MacMurray, asserted that it was "the religious mission of the working class to achieve Socialism."[3]

In the *Slant Manifesto*, published in 1966, the thesis that "Christian commitment carries with it an obligation to be Socialist" was further argued.[4] The Slant writers accused capitalism of "being an assault on the essential communal nature of human life" (p. 23), of ignoring "the human feeling and energy which find expression in the arts" (p. 32), and of alienating labor, brutalizing culture, and other related charges. One writer referred to the church as "the sacrament of a socialist society" (p. 148).

In America the religious socialist tradition dates from about the same period. In 1849 Henry James, Sr., identified the aims of Christianity and socialism. In 1851, a Philadelphia businessman named Stephen Colwell wrote a book called *New Themes for the Protestant Clergy* in which he said: "We look upon the whole socialist movement as one of the greatest events of this age. . . . The works of socialists have exposed the hideous skeleton of selfishness in capitalism; they have pursued it with unfaltering hatred and this constitutes our main obligation to them."[5] After the Civil War socialist activity on the part of the clergy-

---

[1] Charles Luther Adams, "Christian Socialism," *Encyclopaedia Britannica*, 1972, p. 701.

[2] Quoted in *Marxism and Christianity*, ed. Herbert Aptheker (New York: Humanities Press, 1968), p. 203.

[3] Adams, "Christian Socialism," p. 702.

[4] Adrian Cunningham et al., *Catholics and the Left* (Springfield, Ill.: Templegate, 1966).

[5] Catherine R. Harris, "Religion and the Socialist Movement in the United States," in Aptheker, ed., *Marxism and Christianity*, p. 221.

men intensified. Prominent among these clerics was George D. Herron, a Congregationalist minister who has been called "the most influential and dramatic character in the Christian socialist movement and the intellectual leader of social Christianity during the last decade of the 19th century."[6]

Later Walter Rauschenbusch (whom Reinhold Niebuhr somewhat misleadingly called the "real founder of Social Christianity" in America) preached "a new order that would rest on the Christian principles of equal rights and democratic distribution of economic power." Niebuhr, much influenced by Rauschenbusch in the 1930s and 1940s, was the leader of the Fellowship of Christian Socialists. He called himself a "Christian Marxist" and spoke against the centralized power entailed by private ownership, believing it to be "an invitation to injustice" that diminished the possibilities of democracy. But Niebuhr was critical of Marxism and saw no easy solution in the socialization of property. For him, the problem with all forms of property was power, and power is intrinsically corruptive. Eventually he abandoned socialism.

Another prominent member of the Fellowship of Christian Socialists was Paul Tillich, who had become a socialist in Germany after World War I. Tillich maintained that "religious socialism stands fundamentally on the ground of Marx's analysis of capitalistic society."[7] Casting his critique in a Biblical idiom, he called the capitalistic system demonic: "The effect of the capitalist system upon society and upon every individual in it takes the typical form of possession, that is, of being possessed; its character is demonic."[8] Socialism, on the other hand, is rooted in prophetic expectation. It looks to the new being beyond the tribulations of history. "Both prophetic and socialist expectation are a witness of life to its fundamental openness. They are a protest of life against false concepts of transcendence."[9] (Martin Buber in *Paths in Utopia* and other writings adapts a somewhat similar position. Buber's socialism was based on the I-Thou dialogue, which was incompatible with the I-It posture of capitalism.) Tillich concluded his *Socialist Decision*, as might be expected, on a prophetic note.

> The salvation of European society from a return to barbarism lies in the hands of socialism. Only socialism can make certain that the unlimited possibilities for technical domination of the world that have been created in the bourgeois period will

---

[6] Ibid., p. 223.

[7] Paul Tillich, *Political Expectation* (New York: Harper and Row, 1971), p. 48.

[8] Ibid., p. 50.

[9] Paul Tillich, *The Socialist Decision* (New York: Harper and Row, 1971), p. 111. Although written in 1933, this book was not translated until 1977. It articulates perhaps the best developed position of any religious socialist.

remain under human control and will be employed for the service of humanity. Only socialism can prevent these possibilities from becoming the means of their own self destruction and that of the very society that wrested them from nature.[10]

Tillich is perhaps the most intellectually acute of the religious socialists, even though in later years he lost confidence in socialism. Latter-day voices, it seems to me, are largely echoes of his thinking. Thus Harvey Cox invokes the prophet Amos: "Let justice surge like water and goodness flow like an unfailing stream."[11] Thus Robert Bellah, in *The Broken Covenant*, welds a moral vision to socialist goals and criticizes corporate values as a kind of "crude social Darwinism" that "negates community concern."[12] Thus Rosemary Reuther excoriates the "currently regnant capitalism that controls the political order for the sake of the few, a system that organizes a maldistribution of wealth, of social decision, and services." She demands "an economic democracy— a system that is democratically owned, democratically controlled, democratically planned, democratically shared, a system organized around the needs of the whole rather than the profits of the rich."[13] Thus Peter Steinfels: "Socialism is the substitution of democratic, conscious choice for class rule. . . . [Socialism] is the promise of public life in which all individuals would exercise, as social and communal creatures, their capacity for making the decisions that heretofore were reserved for a class or a class determined system."[14] Thus Dorothee Sölle: "Christian faith grasps the world as unliberated but aimed at liberation. Faith means insistence on a radical and comprehensive regeneration in contrast to all naturalistic interpretations of life."[15] Thus the Latin American theologian José Bonino, for whom socialism is the means by which "the ultimate and engaged character of love" is to be realized.[16] Thus John Cort, editor of *Religious Socialism*, who says that

> the ownership and control of the means of production mainly by those who place profits and power first in their scale of values has produced . . . alienation and such highly empirical phenomena as inflation, unemployment, shocking contrasts

---

[10] Ibid., p. 161.

[11] In *Religious Socialism*, vol. 3, no. 2, p. 11.

[12] See the review of *The Broken Covenant* by Morris Bernstein in *Religious Socialism*, vol. 2, no. i, p. 8.

[13] In *Religious Socialism*, vol. 1, no. 2, p. 15.

[14] In *Religious Socialism*, vol. 3, no. 2, p. 3.

[15] In *Religious Socialism*, vol. 2, no. 3, p. 1.

[16] José Bonino, *Christians and Marxists* (Grand Rapids, Mich.: Eerdmans, 1976), p. 105 and *passim*. See also Harvey Cox's review of this book in *Religious Socialism*, vol. 1, no. 2, pp. 111–112.

of wealth and poverty not only as between rich and poor nations but as between rich and poor citizens of our own country. These things are awkward to reconcile with a concern for peace and justice, not to mention the Judeo-Christian values which command at least lip service in our society.[17]

An excellent summary of socialist criticisms of capitalism and the corporation can be found in *Marxism: An American Christian Perspective* by Arthur McGovern, S.J.[18] Like Tillich, McGovern takes his stand on the side of Marxism. Modern corporations, he contends, are monopolistic. Fewer than a thousand persons are the principal decision makers in the top 200 corporations and the twenty largest banks. They control most of the nation's wealth and plan what is best for society. Secondly, the corporations are imperialistic, deriving much of their profits from foreign expansion. As a consequence, corporations are exploitive (especially of the third world) and exercise undue control over the state, especially in the area of foreign policy. "Military spending and social welfare spending make up 75 percent of all government spending," he writes. "Both serve the interests of private enterprise. Welfare mollifies the discontent created by unemployment; military spending provides an outlet for surplus productivity and is a great source of profit" (p. 141). Corporations breed poverty and inequality, stress materialistic values, alienate the workers, and endanger democracy itself. Indeed, McGovern concludes (quoting Charles Lindblom), the private corporation "does not fit into this democratic process" (p. 316). McGovern joins his voice to a swelling chorus to proclaim that monopoly capitalism "is simply un-Christian" (p. 321).

Two Views of Human Nature

Socialists, whether religious or not, tend to articulate a common cluster of themes. I must say that I am sympathetic to many of the ends they propose. As Michael Harrington has said, "socialism is not only the work of creating a new economy to end poverty; it is the work of creating new human goals, new forms of spiritual life,"[19] in which the values of solidarity and cooperation, human dignity and full personhood, justice for all and a society borne up on the wings of love are emphasized. These are noble values; they are all noble values. I would like to see them realized. Who indeed would not? The problem comes

---

[17] Unpublished letter, John Cort to the *National Review*, March 31, 1980.

[18] Arthur F. McGovern, S.J., *Marxism: An American Christian Perspective* (New York: Orbis Books, 1980).

[19] In *Religious Socialism*, vol. 3, no. 4, p. 5.

in the matter of means. The very real strengths of socialists are vision and criticism of existing states of affairs; socialists have a keen sensitivity to unmet human needs. But with respect to practical programs and a firm grip on empirical realities, they most often come a cropper. Many socialists admit as much. Arthur McGovern's final chapter is not untypical of what we read in the literature. "A decentralized, democratic socialism in principle," he says, "is quite consistent with democracy, Christianity, and even traditional Roman Catholic social thought. But whether it is only an ideal, and how a transition to such an economic system could occur, remain serious problems (p. 320).

One might begin by questioning the socialist equation of Christianity with democracy and entertain the notion that socialism is, on the contrary, perhaps inconsistent with both. I am especially puzzled by the easy manner in which religious socialists postulate an identity between their goals and the essence of the Judeo-Christian tradition. For that tradition rests most fundamentally upon the dialectic of sin and redemption. It proclaims that we are fallen creatures, capable of redemption to be sure, but only because fallen. The prophets especially did not ignore this reality. The human heart is deceitful above all things, and exceedingly corrupt (Jeremiah 17:9). I want to argue first of all that socialism founders on an idealized conception of human nature and secondly, that socialists are wrong about democracy and because wrong about democracy, wrong also about the nature of corporations.

The assumptions of both Biblical and classical morality seem to me in agreement in their assessment of human nature as a reed shaking in the wind. We are fallible and imperfect creatures, driven by passion and self-interest, misled by our illusions, divided in our loyalties, forever tortured and tempted by the world, the flesh, and the devil. As Niebuhr shrewdly observes, because Marxism fails "to understand the perennial and persistent character of human egoism in any possible society [it is led] to make completely erroneous estimates of human behavior . . ."[20] In both Biblical and classical morality, the affirmation of freedom and love, of our capacity for redemption and transcendence, is always closely governed by a somber assessment of the springs of human action. This pessimistic avowal of human limitation paradoxically goes hand in hand with a generally optimistic belief in human potential. Moral realism did not in the main lead to despair or fatalism, for fallen creatures are yet capable of glorious deeds. Morality was seen to be the artful business of balancing the conflict of opposites in the human personality.

---

[20] Quoted by John Cort, "Can Socialism be Distinguished from Marxism?" *Cross Currents* (Winter 1979–80), p. 427. (The quotation is from the third chapter of Niebuhr's *Children of Light and Children of Darkness*.)

In a highly useful essay Arthur Lovejoy has reminded us that the great framers of democratic theory in the seventeenth and eighteenth centuries operated on these assumptions of Biblical and classical morality.[21] He convincingly refutes the thesis advanced by Carl Becker in *The Heavenly City of the Eighteenth-Century Philosophers* that men are "natively good, easily enlightened, disposed to follow reason and common sense, generous and humane and tolerant, easily led by persuasion." Not at all, says Lovejoy. This may have been true of some philosophers, but it is "a radical historical error" to think that such optimism characterized the thinking of most philosophers of that time. It certainly did not characterize Anglo-Scottish thinkers. Much more typical of the age, says Lovejoy, was the method of counterpoise, a method by which desired results were achieved by balancing harmful things one against another. This view was influenced by Newton's celestial mechanics, according to which the planets were held in their orbits by a balance of centripetal and centrifugal forces, either of which operating independently would cause the planets to disintegrate in space. Political theorists adopted a similar model and sought to accomplish social goals by artfully balancing "competing egoisms." The two premises underlying the political method of counterpoise, Lovejoy states, are "that men never act from disinterested and rational motives, but that it is possible, nonetheless, to fashion a good whole, a happy and harmonious state, by skillfully mixing and counterbalancing these refractory and separately antagonistic parts" (p. 42).

This was the task confronting the founders of the American Republic. They attempted to apply the principles of the prevailing moral theory to a workable political constitution. Madison, in particular, articulated the premises of the method of counterpoise in *Federalist*, No. 10. He saw, as Plato did, that the great danger to popular governments was the spirit of faction. People pursue different interests, and these inevitably conflict. Madison envisaged two ways of dealing with the spirit of faction: either eliminate its causes or control its effects. To opt for the first of these alternatives would be to abolish freedom and deny citizens the right to their self-interest. This alternative is unacceptable because it is contrary to human nature. Therefore the solution must be sought by controlling the effects of self-interest through an effective division of powers. In this way individuals who favor their self-interest can be enlisted in the service of the general good, and wills that are fallible and divisive can be brought to a degree of harmony. Madison was no great believer in the powers of human rationality. Nor were the majority of

---

[21] Arthur O. Lovejoy, *Reflections on Human Nature* (Baltimore: Johns Hopkins University Press, 1961).

his compeers, who had little faith in the political acumen of people acting as individuals. But they did believe staunchly in a republican form of government. With Alexander Pope they thought that "jarring interests" will "create / Th' according music of the well-mixed state." Their position in politics was analogous to that of Adam Smith in economics: given the proper mechanisms (whether of the market or of a constitutional distribution of power), the pursuit of self-interest would approximate the general interest.

Democracy and capitalism are the twin products of similar historical circumstances and a similar philosophy of human nature. Given this coincidence, the only way in which socialists can assert their incompatibility is by advancing a different understanding of human nature. This they in fact do, but only by seriously distorting the clear message of Biblical and classical morality as well as by ignoring the actual historical conditions in which modern democracies emerged. The presumption of conflict rather than harmony guided the formation of democracies. They are governments for fallible creatures, setting as they do strict limits to human possibility. As a consequence, socialists place a tremendous onus upon their shoulders. The democratic capitalist wonders why so many eggs have to be broken for such a dubious omelette.

The Primacy of Technology

Let me now shift the angle of my critique and point out another difficulty in the socialist understanding of democracy. The missing middle term in virtually all its arguments is technology. This leads socialists to misread the relationship between democracy and capitalism in yet another way. Historically, technology antedated and made possible both democracy and capitalism, and it remains the most conspicuous feature of our modern culture. Modern technology as it began in the medieval monasteries and as it was philosophically elaborated by such pioneers of modern thought as Descartes and Bacon was essentially a redemptive act, an *imitatio dei*; that is to say, it was viewed as a means of repairing the ravages of original sin. Two things were lost in the fall, according to Bacon: innocence and power. The first is recovered by faith, the second by technology. Modern technology is, then, in some fundamental aspects, a religious phenomenon. When socialists attack capitalism they are often in reality attacking technology. The question is not, Is capitalism compatible with democracy? but rather, Is socialism compatible with technology? If technology is the necessary condition and primary shaper of both democracy and capitalism, it follows that the development of the former will affect the workings of the latter. One could say, simplifying somewhat, that as technology goes so goes democracy and capitalism (although I by no means wish to deny the dialectical relationship between these three cultural forces). Socialists often talk a kind of town-meeting idiom, demanding as they do a direct, participatory democracy. But this reveals their ignorance about the commanding presence of technology in modern society.

I want to draw on Don Price's *The Scientific Estate* to illustrate my point.[22] Price maintains that the development of scientific technology in the nineteenth and twentieth centuries has altered the Founding Fathers' understanding of democracy in three principal ways:

- It has brought the private and public sectors closer together.
- It has introduced a new order of complexity into public affairs.
- It has changed the original scheme of checks and balances in government.

Price's first point calls attention to the fact that all economies today are mixed economies. There is no pure socialism or pure capitalism anywhere in the world. This is the inevitable result of large-scale, highly sophisticated technologies. Today, Price writes,

> our national policy assumes that a great deal of our new enterprise is likely to follow from technological developments financed by the government and directed in response to government policy; and many of our most dynamic industries are largely or entirely dependent on doing business with the government through a subordinate relationship that has little resemblance to the traditional market. (p. 15)

Modern technology demands new forms of collaboration and new concentrations of human energy. As a result, much socialist talk about control of the modes of production is rendered obsolete. The corporation is industry's natural response to the development of technology (it is too big to handle any other way), and the government is itself in precisely this sense a corporation that has entered as a full partner in the planning of the economy. Conversely, it is increasingly true that corporations are taking on roles that might otherwise fall to government.

Price uses the expression "a diffusion of sovereignty" to refer to the way power in a technological society is exercised. Political authority is no longer exercised solely by the government; rather, it is diffused through what he calls the "four estates," of politics (elected officials), administration (managers in both the private and public corporations),

---

[22] Don K. Price, *The Scientific Estate* (Cambridge, Mass.: Harvard University Press, 1965). I am indebted to Langdon Winner's discussion of Price's theory in his *Autonomous Technology* (Cambridge, Mass.: MIT Press, 1971).

the professions (including medicine, education, engineering, and the media), and finally, the scientific estate, which is made up of those in government and industry who are doing pure research. As Price notes: "The process of responsible policy making . . . is a process of interaction among the scientists, professional leaders, administrators and politicians; ultimate authority is with the politicians but the initiative is quite likely to rest with others, including scientists in our government" (p. 68). That, I suspect, is why there is so much voter apathy. We do not expect too much from politicians any more, because they have less to give, and in any event, the royal road to power is through estate allegiance. It is perhaps true that such traditional rituals of politics as primaries and even the two-party system have had their day. Some of my political scientist colleagues argue that without the two-party system the Constitution is unworkable. That may also be true. I firmly believe that sooner or later the Constitution will have to be rewritten to accommodate the central role of technology.

The new system of checks and balances operates not merely within the government but in society as a whole. Because of this our former notions of power and property, of the nature of democracy and capitalism, have been proportionately altered. In Price's words: "We are now obliged to think about the political functions of various types of people not on the basis of the property they own but of what they know, and of the professional skills they command" (p. 69). This, as I recall, is what Galbraith means by the technostructure. More political and industrial power has been transferred to the respective estates; it is knowledge-based and knowledge-intensive. We have, it might be said, a new democracy of knowledge.

I am surprised that socialists do not see in this arrangement of power support for their cause. There is no doubt that wealth is more widely distributed in the corporate structure; and it is equally certain that more people have a voice in the modern corporation than in any previous form of industrial power. Earlier I quoted McGovern to the effect that the principal decisions in the top 200 corporations and twenty banks are made by fewer than a thousand persons. But he misconstrues the corporate nature of the decision-making process, rather like saying that the president's cabinet makes the decisions in a liberal arts college. In reality that process in modern organizations, whether governmental, business, or educational institutions, is complex, pluralistic, and effected at many different levels because it involves large numbers of people representing many different interests within the corporation.

I have often argued with socialist friends that the corporation might be considered one of the principal forms of community in our time because it allows very different kinds of people to work in harmony for common goals, to form friendships, make choices, and deploy their talents; it generates an esprit de corps and common loyalties and it distributes power—in brief, it affords an opportunity to practice a significant range of democratic virtues. Price's estates correspond fairly well to corporations, which, as I said before, represent the way government and business have adjusted to technology. Socialists have yet to make that adjustment. They are graveled every time they come up against the technological imperatives.

Let me cite a recent example. I recently reviewed a little volume by Bernard Gendron entitled *Technology and the Human Condition*.[23] In the course of his discussion Gendron ties himself into a triple bind. On the one hand, he requires a clearly articulated theory of socialism and its relationship to technology to successfully criticize other positions. But, as he admits, no such theory exists anywhere, except in "vague and unfinished form." A third complication is that no socialist societies exist—no real ones, that is. So we are back on the familiar horns. With one voice Gendron maintains that "real socialism seems to provide the only hope now for a technologically sane future" (p. 224). With another voice he holds that socialists are "saddled with the burden of showing that real socialism, though it has not yet appeared, is historically viable and will emerge with the demise of advanced capitalism" (p. 252). Then back to voice one: "Socialism has not yet been refuted, and it remains the most promising of the global views on technology and society" (p. 252). What is the basis of this promise? Intuition, faith, hunch, and hope, for these "are not unreliable springs of human action." (Moreover, all the evidence is not yet in. Gendron maintains a patient vigil over the historical process, awaiting an eventual epiphany.)

I have attempted to show that socialism is fallacious on two fundamental points: its understanding of human nature and its understanding of democracy (which implies a misunderstanding of technology as well). Let me point out here that if we are to have a developed theology of democratic capitalism, we will need concomitantly a theology of technology. It astounds me that about the only example is provided by Jacques Ellul. One could now proceed to a point-by-point critique of other socialist beliefs. I have tried to go to the heart of the matter and will not at this time press my critique further. Let me turn instead to the third task I have set myself and indicate some ways in which we might speak of modern corporations in philosophico-theological (or theologico-philosophical) terms.

---

[23] Bernard Gendron, *Technology and the Human Condition* (New York: St. Martin's Press, 1977).

Capitalism and Existentialism

Our modern money economy is rooted, insofar as I can determine, in medieval theories of grace. Both have a common purpose of healing and making whole a corrupt human nature. When we read, for example, Thomas Aquinas's treatise on grace we find that his principal concern is with the transformation of the human personality, with redirecting it toward higher goals. He speaks of grace in terms of integrity, strength, fitness, and so forth. Grace is what moves us to fulfill our natures; it changes the quality of our being; it leads to freedom. Aquinas, of course, discusses grace in a supernatural context, but his thoughts are translatable into secular language. In fact, this was the tendency in the late Middle Ages. Indulgences were, so to speak, an effort to technologize the intangible signs of election. Through indulgences, one's spiritual, and therefore human, worth was given quantifiable embodiment. I do not know anyone who has worked this out, but if I were doing a theology of wealth (and wealth-generating agencies like corporations) I would begin there. It is ironic that Martin Luther clashed with the church over the issue of indulgences, because the money economy was in the ascendancy at that time, and religion itself was becoming increasingly secularized. John Calvin was astute enough to notice the salvific symbolism of wealth. But theologians today are not mining that vein, and we nowhere have anything like a developed theology of money.

More proximately, I have found a close correspondence between the morality of capitalism and some basic insights of existentialism. This might seem odd, the more so because it is commonly thought that many existentialists were led by their philosophy to socialism, preeminent among them Jean-Paul Sartre. But in fact not many existentialists have been socialists. Sartre and Tillich are the best known of those who were. But Tillich abandoned socialism in later years and Sartre abandoned existentialism. Existentialism, as I have argued elsewhere, is the most traditional of all modern philosophies. Like capitalism, it is rooted in the major tenets of Biblical and classical morality. There is a historical congruence here that has been almost universally overlooked.

For the sake of brevity let me propose in a somewhat schematic fashion five correspondences between existentialism and the morality of capitalism.

First, they have in common *a pessimistic anthropology*. Both agree on the fallen condition of human nature. Capitalism assumes that self-interest is the mainspring of human action, that we are prideful and tangled creatures. Existentialism speaks of this under such familiar rubrics as estrangement, absurdity, homelessness, nothingness, meaninglessness. We live, as Gabriel Marcel said, in a "broken world" that is

167

populated by the specters of fallenness. The existentialists have all drawn detailed pictures of inauthentic existence. The raw materials of humanity are not very promising, but for both capitalists and existentialists, pessimism is a cause for optimism, for striving and overcoming.

Second, *the philosophy of freedom*. The strongest case for capitalism is the argument from freedom. As Edward R. Norman summarizes it: "The morality of capitalism has first to do with the morality of choice; with the individual's freedom to select, either as producer or consumer, from among alternative sources of economic enterprise. It is the freedom left to the individual to have control over his own labor."[24] Existentialism is by any other name the philosophy of freedom, of freedom radical and indivisible. "We are condemned to freedom," as Sartre put it in a dramatic turn of phrase. I believe the core and lasting value of his philosophy is his relentless exploration of the difficult paths of freedom and the dilemmas of choice. For Sartre, we do not merely have freedom; we *are* free. Freedom is not a quality added onto or a property of our natures. It is the very stuff of our being, that which constitutes humanity in its essence. Though we are hemmed in on all sides by determining forces—heredity, environment, the massive presence of others, the subconscious, or whatever—we are still free: capable of choosing within any conceivable situation.

Mathieu, in Sartre's *The Age of Reason*, suddenly becomes aware that it was by his own agency that everything had to happen. Sartre writes that "even if he let himself be carried off, in helplessness and despair, even if he let himself be carried off like an old sack of coal, he would have chosen his own damnation; he was free, free in every way, free to behave like a fool or a machine, free to accept, free to refuse, free to equivocate, free to marry, to give up the game, to drag his dead weight about with him for years to come. He could do what he liked, no one had the right to advise him, there could be for him no Good or Evil unless he brought them into being." Albert Camus dramatized the absoluteness of existential freedom in the image of Sisyphus, who imagined himself happy in order to turn the tables on the gods (although it should be pointed out that Camus opted for a more measured freedom than Sartre's).

Third, *the formation of moral character*. In the same article, Norman points out the connection between enterprise and personal moral character. "The competitive deployment of personal resources and talents is a tremendous stimulus to moral self-consciousness; it encourages,

---

[24] E.R. Norman, "Denigration of Capitalism," in *The Denigration of Capitalism*, Michael Novak, ed. (Washington, D.C.: American Enterprise Institute, 1979), p. 8.

rather than discourages, the individual in the cultivation of a practical scheme of responsibility for his actions, and imposes, as a condition of maintaining living standards, a sense of moral duty" (p. 9). The existentialist, who faces an absurd world in freedom, is similarly stimulated. The refractory character of the world becomes a challenge to ingenuity, a test of character, a demand upon our powers of choice. Kierkegaard has many fine things to say about the relationship between choice and moral character. Choice, he says, "is the power by which we acquire ourselves. . . . To think that for an instant one can keep one's personality a blank, or that strictly speaking one can break off and bring to a halt the course of one's personal life is a delusion."[25] In him as in all the existentialists there is a kind of Puritan fear about wasting our self-powers, about missing opportunities for self-improvement. We find Nietzsche espousing such old-fashioned virtues as courage, creativity, independence, compassion, heroism, honesty, love of man, energy of spirit, even obedience. What, then, is he against? A morality of prohibitions, brutality and laziness, unfreedom. Sartre, for his part, declares that freedom makes us responsible not only for ourselves but for all others as well. From one point of view, existentialism is the morality of rugged individualism, stressing as it does the tough virtues of risk-taking, personal responsibility, and courage in the face of adversity. But a host of other virtues are favored as well: the intersubjectivity of Gabriel Marcel, the I-Thou of Martin Buber, the sense of community and solidarity that emerges so beautifully in the writings of Albert Camus. It is not true to say that existentialism is merely individualism. In like manner, it is not true to say that corporate morality is merely a morality of individualsm. There is a place in it for communal values.

Fourth, *the will to power.* This is a very important idea we find primarily in Nietzsche. The essence of the world is the will to power, he affirms. Nietzsche saw the existential problem as the release of energy and the design of human experience. How can the Dionysian forces that churn and boil within us be given fitting shapes? Through the will to power, Nietzsche answers. He does not mean (as some have thought) that the will to power is some kind of brute military or political domination. It is not primarily a physical notion at all, but rather a spiritual ideal. What Nietzsche says about the will to power is analogous to what Aquinas says about grace: it is a metaphor of vitality, it is the fundamental drive of all living things to become more.

Specifically, by the will to power Nietzsche means two things: self-overcoming and striving for excellence. We must first do battle with

---

[25] See Robert Bretall, *A Kierkegaard Anthology* (New York: Modern Library, 1946), pp. 102–103.

our own weaker parts and then direct our energies to enhancing ideals. In the end, the will to power becomes one with our powers of choice. We stand before reality as before a blank, evanescent text that we must interpret. To interpret reality is to assert one's subjectivity as free, as creative. Reality thus becomes a function of our various wills to power, our respective abilities to organize our choices into coherent action. Our knowledge and values are tantamount to the creative annexation we make of the script of reality that unfolds before us.

If it is true, as I suggested, that we moderns interpret reality and release our human energies in a fundamentally technological way, and if it is also true that the corporations are the monasteries of a scientific age by means of which our energies are directed, then it might be useful to attend to how well they channel these energies and how fittingly they shape human experience. It might be useful as well to explore the alternatives from this angle. How well, for example, could the socialist ideal orient human energies? I was struck in reading a recent article on Alexander Hamilton[26] by how he anticipated Nietzsche's will to power. He justified the monetary system he was trying to advance by a moral appeal. A market economy, he said, would offer new opportunities to the busy nature of man to rouse and exert itself, and thus add new energy to the general effort.

The fifth and final correspondence (which is implied in the will to power) is *the theme of creativity*. Nietzsche speaks of the need to fictionalize our experience, to write imaginatively on the script of being as it unrolls before us. There is nothing humanly meaningful on the script until we put it there. No theme is more constant in existentialist literature: the imperfections of existence can be overcome by creative action. The existentialists overcame their own temptations to despair and nihilism by creating the works they have left us. My favorite illustration of this theme is the character of Roquetin in Sartre's *Nausea*. The novel is a long description of the absurdity of existence, and just when we think that Roquetin is about to commit suicide (or at any rate should commit suicide), he sees a way out. The trick is "to catch time by the tail." We do this by turning our lives into a story that has the permanence of a melody. Roquetin decides to write a novel with the hope that then "he could remember his life without repugnance and succeed in accepting himself."

Capitalism can be defended on imaginative grounds, in terms of inventiveness, ingenuity, and innovation. Whenever I go to the supermarket with my children I delight in their delight in the display of soaps and cereals and other foodstuffs, a seemingly endless rainbow of colors

---

[26] F. McDonald, "Understanding Alexander Hamilton," *National Review*, vol. 32 (July 11, 1980), pp. 827–830.

and shapes. This is a trivial example, of course. But more serious ones could be adduced. I do not think enough work has been done on the aesthetics of technology and capitalism, that is to say, on its fictive dimension, the sheer play of surface forms. The majority of people in our culture create through some form of corporate activity: in education, in government, in industry. Corporate funding, as we are all well aware, supports much (most?) of the creative work in the arts, in science, and in education. (Note the recent rescue of *Harper's* magazine.) The existentialist critique of the socialist ideal on this score makes some sense. Karl Jaspers states the critique succinctly. "A life that is entirely thought out in advance is not challenging or even interesting. Boredom, ennui, the immense tedium that attends the exclusion of all competition and the elimination of all hazards would render life futile and banal . . . eventual dehumanization would result.[27]

In conclusion, I have a suggestion for corporations and corporate leaders. They should make periodic retreats for a kind of examination of conscience, to take stock of their situation. In particular they should do three things: they should study their own spiritual, moral, and philosophical foundations so that they can be at least as well armed ideologically as their opponents; secondly, they should enter into dialogue with other estates. They do, of course, to some extent—with government officials, union leaders, lawyers, and others. But I believe they have not yet undertaken a sufficiently extensive dialogue with the intellectual estate. (A philosopher in residence for each corporation might not be a bad idea.) Finally, corporations should increasingly develop their social consciousness. I know there are those who say that the sole business of corporations is to make profits. But that is too simplistic, and in any event it is not the case and has not been the case for a long time. Corporations have for some time been responsive to criticism from environmentalists and others. Santayana's words that I have taken as an epigraph may be invoked for this concluding thought: Corporations have done well in furnishing the material base of our culture. There is more to do in exploring the ideal fulfillment of that base.

---

[27] Quoted in Charles F. Wallraff, *Karl Jaspers* (Princeton, N.J.: Princeton University Press, 1970), p. 71.

Discussion

QUESTION: I wonder if your anthropology is too pessimistic; that is, would not the role for theology be to talk about the sinner's redemption, but to stress the redemption more than the sin? Let me give a concrete example.

Mr. Jones has mentioned that there is no discipline on the Hill. We have too many interest groups, each pushing in its own little area. Isn't it time we thought of the common good?

Theology can speak to that issue because if we stress the fact that nobody has absolute good, that we each have to seek our partial goods, then we will develop our own interest-group pluralism, growing out of the kind of pessimistic anthropology, perhaps, that Niebuhr stresses.

I like Niebuhr. But I always wish that he did not stress sin, and relative and partial insights, to such an extent. Would it not be a role for the theologian, in training and educating our people in universities and churches, to say, granted, we have a partial insight, but let's try to move toward a picture of the common good because, although we are shot through with sin, we are also redeemed, and we can respond to God's grace and try to move out of our own selfish interests and look at the larger picture?

MR. MURCHLAND: I agree. In any dialectic, as in the dialectic of sin and redemption, there is always a spectrum; at certain times the positive is emphasized and at other times the negative.

When modern technology sprang on the scene as a redemptive agency in the seventeenth century, it ushered in a great age of optimism. Now, because of the problems that technology has run into, we are perhaps moving into a more pessimistic phase in some places.

I agree, in general, that we should emphasize the common good, the redemptive aspects, and the positive. I was interested in what was said earlier about the chaos on the Hill, as opposed to the kind of consensus politics that operates within the corporation.

The reason why, it seems to me, we have such adversarial politics is because we have a two-party system. I think, more and more, that poli-

172

tics is going to have to take a page from corporate life and build more politics of consensus rather than fight in the primaries, which no longer makes much sense.

I think that the times and circumstances dictate which pole is emphasized. There came a time when technology became hubristic, when science became hubristic and lost sight of its redemptive roots; then it has to be criticized. There is now a large body of negative criticism about technology, but we have not yet got our theology of technology, which might point out those positive aspects, something that we all might be working on.

QUESTION: If you go along with the picture of the critique and the critique of the critique, how central to your conception of it is the existentialist philosophical scheme? For those of us who find that scheme difficult, do you feel the critique is valid, or can it be attached to other philosophical explanations as well as yours?

MR. MURCHLAND: Existentialism is simply an example of how you might bring two realms of discourse together. I thought it was interesting, and one way the matter could be approached; but one could also use process philosophy or any kind of philosophy at all. Existentialism is difficult; it has so many bad features; it is difficult to read; all the existentialists are eccentric, and so on. But I think the points I singled out are valid points; there are nuggets in existentialism. It is very difficult to teach because the nuggets are valuable and the students ought to know about them, but there is no single work of existentialist philosophy that one can give an undergraduate student to read.

QUESTION: Corporate capitalism—managerial capitalism—to me signifies quite a different form of capitalism from that which prevailed in the nineteenth century and the first third of this century. This is an age of professionalism—property ownership really does not count for much any more. What matters are the professional, educated skills, the hierarchy based on these skills, and how these skills are developed.

I look on the corporation as a compromise or a working out of a synthesis of that part of the socialist critique that has some validity to it. Maybe unfettered capitalism is not all good. Look at the anxieties of existentialism that you point to—maybe man just can not stand that much freedom.

The corporation, essentially, has restricted man's freedom greatly. There is a great deal of paternalism in the corporation, and a great deal of community that comes with that paternalism; can you comment on that?

MR. MURCHLAND: I think you are absolutely right, that mankind can bear only so much freedom, and I think it has always been the role of social institutions, such as the corporations, to channel freedom and govern freedom and tame the energies of freedom, if you will; that is a problem I have with the socialist reliance on the prophetic tradition.

The prophetic tradition, it seems to me, has been a very small part of the whole picture. That has been said here before, and elsewhere. It is a necessary dimension, because the prophets always remind us of the freedom we do not have and have had in certain historical circumstances. But to base a political program on prophetism would be disastrous, and when we talk about freedom, I think we have to cherish it as a root value, a necessary value but an absolutely limited value, and I think we must always guard against the excesses of freedom.

Camus wrote a beautiful book, *The Rebel*, on the excesses of freedom. These excesses lead inevitably to slaughter and to murder as a political weapon. That is the decisive work on that point.

QUESTION: I am fascinated with your comments in regard to socialists and socialism in technology. Once again, we seem to see coming from socialism a critique of technology, rather than a proposed answer or solution. . . . There is a kind of oppressiveness in both East and West, the centralization of power, the centralization of technology, that would serve oppressive ends rather than liberating ends.

MR. MURCHLAND: Marxists of that stripe generally look upon technology as an instrument of freedom. But then, when you look closely at what they are saying, you find it is an instrument of centralization and planning. Lenin said that we must steal—and I think that was his word —the technology of the West in order to advance the cause of revolution. I think that we see something like that going on in Russia today.

There are two kinds of Marxist response to technology. One is the orthodox determinism that the modes of production, which include the whole technological apparatus of society, determine everything else in society. It is, in other words, a radical, rigid determinism. Then there is the other, more moderate school, which holds that technology is a means to fulfill the aims of Communism, which, of course, includes a strongly centralized state and a centralized economy.

Some American Marxists, for example, talk about a liberation technology, saying that technology is a means of advancing the revolution because technology will, in the final analysis, put everybody in charge of his or her own material destiny—that everybody can have an electric generator in the back yard.

But what such socialists inevitably miss—and the religious socialists, I think, miss it almost completely—are the imperatives of technology, the nature of modern technology, the bigness of modern technology, the sheer creativity of modern technology, and the knowledge base of technology. How will we plan democratically, control democratically, and share democratically Texas Instruments or Boeing Aircraft? Boeing airplanes cannot be built in someone's back yard. The socialist position for a democratic equality seems, to me, to entail an equality of knowledge which is, in the nature of things, impossible.

QUESTION: If it is true that the role of ownership is significantly less in the modern corporation, would it not be possible to think of another model of the corporation, in which shareholders were less significant and the public and workers, including management, were more significant; in which the shareholders, in effect, became lenders to an operation that existed not principally for their benefit but, for the benefit of the people who do the producing, including management? The loyalty and control of the board would be given not to shareholders but to the people who work in the corporation.

MR. MURCHLAND: Yes, indeed, but isn't that the case in many kinds of corporation? Take *Time* or *Newsweek*, for example; who has the effective power in those organizations? The writers, and those who make the editorial decisions. Somewhere at the top, policy is set, but if the departmental editors and the writers are not out doing their jobs, there will be no magazine. And isn't it true that effective power in automobile corporations rests with the engineers who design the cars, who get the materials out of the ground, who create the paint, and so on?

I think power is a pluralistic concept. There is power and there is power and there is power. And the power of a chairman, as Reginald Jones so beautifully said, like the power of a university president, is real; but I do not think that the president of my university has more power than I do, except in some quantitative sense. I think I have more power than he does, because I am doing something that is more central to the purpose of the university. I am sure that many writers and engineers and draftsmen and so on feel that way about the corporation. It is a good point. And of course, other kinds of corporations could be imagined.

QUESTION: Can't there be socialist corporations that are better than capitalist corporations?

MR. MURCHLAND: I guess you are asking what it is that distinguishes a capitalist corporation from the kind of corporation you find in, say, Yugoslavia.

175

Look at productivity, for example, at how effective each kind of corporation is at generating wealth, raising the standard of living, and so on; how happy and fulfilled are the workers within that particular type of corporation? Or take one of those existentialist criteria, as I would be inclined to do, and ask what kind of expression of the will to power this organization is. Is it ticking along? Is everybody operating at levels of maximum creativity? Could there be a socialist corporation, which would be largely worker controlled, that would be very much like a capitalist corporation?

It is an interesting question. Everything is so mixed these days. Everyone is part socialist, part capitalist; everyone is part Protestant, part Catholic, part atheist. We live in a kind of age of convergence, and it would be easy for me to say that there is little difference between a Yugoslav corporation and General Electric. But I know there are differences, and the question is an empirical one; we would have to take a look at the facts. It is an interesting question, but I am going to pass on it.

QUESTION: It seems to me that none of the things we have been talking about—capitalism, democracy, socialism, technology—are in themselves capable of having theologies. They all operate at a level that is beneath the concerns to which theology, religion, and spiritual and moral insight ought to direct our attentions. In that sense, the need is always for any of these things to be judged.

People of spiritual and religious insight have always understood that. Jesus talked about who would find it hard to get into the Kingdom of Heaven. I think if he'd known socialist managers and economic planners, and if there had been elephants where he lived, he would have had another analogy for how hard it was to get into the Kingdom of Heaven. And Bacon's notion that there was salvation in technology and science is probably one of the most grotesque and misguided ideals anybody ever had. That was how Milton and Pope and Swift saw it, which is the same kind of critique, I suppose, that Gandhi or Solzhenitsyn or others would make in our day. It seems to me that the whole point is always to find in what seem to me to be the rather shallow and ignoble conceptions that go along with capitalism, and even democracy, the main point, that in a democracy things are decided by the majority.

That may lead to all sorts of grotesque decisions, as we know well. We need to have a standpoint of certain judgment.

MR. MURCHLAND: I disagree with that position. I am willing to grant a role to prophetism, but it seems to me that one of the important things that philosophy and theology, in this case, have to do is to draw up a phenomenology of the redemptive agencies in the world.

One of the courses I teach is the history of medieval philosophy. What impresses me about the medieval theologians and philosophers is that they were fully a part of their society. They served in important administrative roles, in important educational functions, and they were in the vanguard of scientific and technological developments of their day.

Roger Bacon has written a scientific treatise in code, which has not yet been cracked, and it is a source of fascination in certain scientific circles. In the history of science and technology, it was the theologians and the philosophers who were front and center in that whole development, and they melded their scientific ideas very well with their theological and philosophical insights. I think the separatist position that you advance, while it has its place, mostly with respect to a prophetic role, leaves us with the very problem that we now have: no theology of capitalism, no theology of this, no philosophy of that, and so we become deaf and mute citizens of the world in which we live.

QUESTION: Could we go back to Madison and to what you had to say about the modern-day diffusion of sovereignty? I wonder if we can't say that Madison still lives, that what you referred to as the diffusion of sovereignty may be a twentieth-century version of factionalism all over again; that the factionalism that Madison was concerned with in the *Federalist Papers* was really the factionalism that came out of the new enterprise, out of the growth of commerce and of agriculture in the United States. The factions really just take on a different appearance, and rather than there being a diffusion of sovereignty, there really may be a modern-day diffusion of factionalism, and those factions really are administration, the professions, the scientific establishment, and politics itself.

If that is the case, I agree with you that we expect little from politicians, but not so much because they have little to offer as because the modern-day politician suffers from myopia, that he does not see what new tasks need to be undertaken.

MR. MURCHLAND: I think that is right. Of course, in the same papers, Madison had good things to say about factionalism. He was not against factions, if there is a constitutional framework in which they can operate —and I think one of the significant features of the present political situation is this new element of technology. Technology has caused the factionalism that Mr. Jones mentioned. Why? Because everybody is educated these days. Everybody is an expert.

But we do not have the constitutional controls that Madison

worked out for his time, and it is a fairly frequent refrain in the literature on this subject that the great, political challenge to political theory today is to do for our time what Madison did for his time. Now that means taking into account the central role of technology, which has created these estates in the first place.

QUESTION: On that point of technology again. In Article I of the Constitution, the word *progress* is mentioned—and this is the only place it appears in the whole document—in the phrase that allows Congress to guarantee the rights of individuals to hold their patent, to provide for progress, and I would probably disagree with you that we need to restructure the Constitution in order to allow for it. I think that the Founding Fathers understood very well just what progress is and where it could be had. Modern secular progress is, I think, much more metaphysically unreal than the progress the Founding Fathers had in mind.

MR. MURCHLAND: But technology is an active force in our society. It is an agency, an instrumentality. It is the most powerful means that we human beings have today for making choices. Modern technology is qualitatively different from what it was in previous ages. We cannot compare neutron bombs to clubs in caves, because that ignores the qualitative nature of technology.

Now, Ellul says that technology is an independent force, that it is demonic and is doing us in. Most of the literature on technology from philosophers and theologians and political scientists sees technology as an autonomous force in our midst. I am not saying that, and if I did say it, I wish now to correct myself.

Technology is the most powerful agency, the most powerful means that we have to express our choices in freedom today. This is another way of saying that the major choices we make involve technology.

But we live in a chosen world. We always live in a chosen world. That is my answer to the autonomy school—that technology is being used by free agents. Decisions are being made in industry, government, and elsewhere to do this, that, or the other thing with technology. So, it is not an autonomous force, but a very powerful means.

QUESTION: The idea that the technology out there is somehow an active force that demands that the U.S. Constitution be rewritten seems to me to be extremely naive.

MR. MURCHLAND: *Active force* is creating a problem here. Could you think of it as a very powerful means of realizing human intentions and of human projects?

QUESTION: No more so than a plowshare.

MR. MURCHLAND: Then you do not grant a qualitative distinction between modern technology and primitive technology?

QUESTION: I grant the qualitative distinction, but I do not grant that this modern technology has a greater power over my ability to choose.

MR. MURCHLAND: Well, we are in disagreement there. Would you agree that our technological choices today are more fraught with consequences than they were in the days of the bow and arrow? Would you agree that a decision to launch a nuclear war is more fraught with consequences than the Hundred Years' War with bows and arrows?

QUESTION: Yes.

MR. MURCHLAND: Then the quality of our choices has been changed, and the way in which we exercise our freedom in this technological situation is existentially different from the way Henry IV exercised his freedom.

QUESTION: Quantitatively, not qualitatively.

MR. MURCHLAND: I would argue with you on that. That is one of the real bones of contention here, and it is one of the major points that I was trying to make.

QUESTION: I liked what you said about the "fictive" dimension of experience but wouldn't "imaginative" be a better word?

MR. MURCHLAND: "Fictive" is Nietzsche's word, but I think it would work quite well here. Nietzsche talks about fictionalizing our experience, and that basically means putting something there that was not there before. You put up a plant or you invent money. Money is a form of technology. It is a fiction, something that we create and something that we assign purposes to; something that would not be there and would not have those purposes if we did not assign them. So I will not quibble with the words "fictive" or "imaginative."

Take television ads, for example. They are "fictive," and good fictions illuminate reality. We are not lost in a world of fictions; fictions have their own logic and their own tests of reality, and some fictions are better than others.

Camus said that we live by our images. He said that in a letter to a

German friend, and his objection to the German occupation of France was not so much the brutality and the physical oppression but that the Germans were taking away the images by which the French lived.

So "image," "imagination," "fiction"—they are all okay, as long as we understand their function here.

QUESTION: My question has to do with the theological dimensions of input into technology, with technology as having been born in a medieval monastery and with the corporation as a modern monastery. I wonder whether the theology we are talking about could be worked in a broader vein.

MR. MURCHLAND: Most histories of technology begin with the Middle Ages, and three technologies stem from that medieval perspective. There is the technology of machines, which is what we normally mean by technology; there is also the technology of money; and thirdly, there is the technology of law. Lawyers may not look upon law as a technology, but I think it is, in precisely the same sense that machines and money are technologies. But that is a kind of medieval perspective, and it is helpful insofar as we get at the immediate roots of some of our contemporary dilemmas; but it is by no means adequate to get at the remote and mythic and fundamental roots, which are important.

Incidentally, I think that more work might be done on the mythology of technology. A little bit has been done, and I think it is a first step to the theology of technology.

QUESTION: Does this involve a discussion of Bacon's idea about man exercising dominion over nature?

MR. MURCHLAND: Yes. I think we ought to go back to Bacon. Lynn White wrote a famous essay on modern technology in which he said it is all corrupt because it is a dominion; but he had not grasped Bacon. Bacon saw technology as a redemptive act. I definitely think we ought to reread him. People like Hamilton must, I think, have read a little bit of Bacon.

The Foundation
as a Nonbusiness Corporation

Merrimon Cuninggim

It is my intention to discuss private foundations, using the foundation as an example of a nonbusiness corporation, but still a corporation in remarkable measure. Perhaps we shall uncover some problems that pose questions of ethical, if not theological, significance.

The foundations were in trouble in 1969. Testimony before the House Ways and Means Committee had not gone well, and everyone was nervous about what Mr. Wilbur Mills might do to the foundations he did not like. He and his committee did not seem to like Ford and Rockefeller or a great many others, especially the big ones. The representatives of these foundations had not coordinated their testimony in regard to the pending Tax Reform Act, and as a result, they gave the impression of not knowing what they wanted to do.

It must be admitted, I think, that the Tax Reform Act in 1969 (TRA-69) did not harm the foundations as much as they had feared. But it was bad enough. That year has been called a watershed for foundations in American society. Discussions were held in Congress for ten and one-half months in respect to foundations and their programs. In February 1969, when those discussions first began in the House Ways and Means Committee, most foundations did not know they were in serious trouble. By late December 1969, many foundations were greatly alarmed.

The major concerns in the new federal legislation on foundations had to do with an audit fee, imposed for the first time, of 4 percent (although cut recently to 2 percent); a pay-out requirement of 6 percent; fewer tax incentives than for other charities; and a prohibition against "any attempt to influence legislation."

If the language of that prohibition had stopped at that point, I think no foundation person would have been alarmed by this particular provision. But the act went further, providing a prohibition against "any attempt to influence legislation, through an attempt to affect the opinion of the general public or any segment thereof." Would foundation activity be limited to things nobody would have an opinion about?

Finally, the foundations were disturbed by the general adversarial tone and the punitive attitude toward them that pervaded the new legislation.

Those were the major concerns. There were clearly some beneficial results recognized then and certainly recognized more recently. There was, for example, an effort to stop self-dealing: the act was an incomplete effort in this regard; it did not go as far as some of us in the foundations wanted, but it did begin a process. Also, there was an effort to encourage full disclosure: the new law provided that foundations must tell the public what they had been doing, to whom their grants had been made, and so on. This, too, was an inconclusive effort; there was no requirement for full disclosure to ensure that the public could easily find out what it wanted to know.

The act required something called "expenditure responsibility," a concept that was poorly defined. It spoke of an improved investment policy. The clear intention of the act was to require foundations to engage in self-examination beyond what they had ever done before and to cooperate with each other. As one result, the first trade association in the foundation field, the Council on Foundations, was greatly strengthened soon thereafter and has been a great help.

All those matters, the pros and cons of TRA-69, are not yet ancient history because many of the issues are still alive. The problems not solved by that act are still with us. In addition, we have a body of reaction to the act to deal with, as well as new problems that are arising to plague the world of organized philanthropy. I think it is important to address all these issues, because I see the foundation as a corporation facing serious problems, and before we can begin to ask about any kind of corporation what the ethical implications of its status and work are, we need to be franker about the problems than we are often tempted to be. So much of our talk about corporations of whatever kind is, it seems to me, defensive and protective in character, that I see no point in dwelling here on the achievements of foundations. This record can be read in many other places—though I am sorry to report that my book on that subject is now out of print!

Organized Philanthropy

Philanthropy in the United States is considered a big business, though in comparison with many other businesses, its dollar volume does indeed seem small: $39.6 billion in 1978, $43.3 billion in 1979. It is notable, however, that, despite the dollar increase, philanthropic spending as a percentage of the gross national product decreased slightly, from 1.88 percent in 1978 to 1.83 percent in 1979. Giving by individuals, together with bequests, adds up to approximately 90 percent of all philanthropy. The remaining 10 percent of that $43.3 billion figure comes from organized philanthropy, including the philanthropy of business corporations.

By the term *organized philanthropy* I mean to refer to foundations of various kinds or to charitable committees of a business corporation that has chosen to siphon its benevolence through a committee, rather than through a separate incorporated foundation body.

There is immense diversity in this field. As limited in scope as it is, the foundations differ from one another across a much broader spectrum than would be true for, say, colleges and universities or even for churches.

I once tried to define a foundation in the following fashion. Foundations are nongovernmental agencies, privately established and managed, but in which the public has a stake and which are answerable to government, possessing financial resources, usually in the form of endowment, and existing to serve the general welfare or some chosen segment of it, usually in the form of grants.

All of that wording is necessary in order to pin down exactly what we are talking about. Take the term *nongovernmental*, for example. Most of the shorthand definitions would say that foundations are private agencies. But *private* here is a slippery term. It is a misnomer. The money that foundations have to spend is public money, not private money. It has been set aside by some private donor, to be sure, but for the service of the general welfare or some chosen section of it. This has been recognized by the law, to the extent that the donor was given some kind of tax benefit for having set money aside for public purposes. So the money that foundations possess is public money. Many a foundation has not made that as clear to itself as it should. Nongovernmental, therefore, is a more accurate term than private.

A foundation's activities as well as its money are public. It is now required to report to the public what it does. The word private can properly be applied to a foundation only insofar as the decisions it makes with respect to where the money will be spent are privately arrived at. We must be careful, however, to realize that the decisions are not private in the sense of being secret; rather, they are in private hands.

The definition indicates that the resources of a foundation usually, but do not always, consist in endowment. Some foundations receive income from a family or a company; some have other resources than endowment. The phrase *usually in the form of grants* came last in my long definition because there are foundations that do things with their money other than make grants to a designated recipient.

There are three main types of foundations—independent, community, and company-sponsored, into which last category are usually thrown those charitable committees of corporations to which I referred earlier.

There are some 230 foundations in the community field. Their annual grant-making now runs in excess of $90 million. Their assets are about $1.4 billion. They receive gifts from many sources and thus have a preferred status in the eyes of the law—preferred vis-à-vis all other types of foundation. They qualify as *public charities*—that is the technical term in the Tax Reform Act—and this status entitles their donors to a special tax break. The best thing anyone can do with his or her millions right now is not to set up a private family foundation, but to give the money to the local community foundation.

Corporate foundations and charitable committees are the benevolent arm of business corporations. The philanthropic activity of businesses has grown rapidly in recent years, from $2 billion in 1978 to $2.3 billion in 1979. The charitable gifts of business corporations represent a little over 5 percent of the total of all philanthropy.

Business giving exceeded giving by independent foundations for the first time in 1979. Purely in terms of the amount of money being made available for charitable uses this past year, company funds of various kinds exceeded all private foundation funds.

But there is still much room for growth in business giving. Businesses are allowed to deduct gifts from their taxable income up to 5 percent of pretax profits. The $2.3 billion that was given by businesses last year represents less than 1 percent of pretax profits, so there is still a considerable way to go if businesses want to choose it.

Independent foundations, the group we usually have in mind when we think of foundations, now probably number around 21,000. There were about 26,000 in 1971, according to the Foundation Center's estimate at that time. The number has decreased because, as one result of the Tax Reform Act, people did not form new independent foundations and did close up many old ones. Almost half—47 percent—of the existing independent foundations have assets of less than $100,000; 85 percent of these have assets under $1 million.

The annual giving of foundations, including the community foundations but excluding the corporate ones, runs to something over $2 billion, compared with the $2.3 billion from the corporate area, and the amount may be going down.

Everyone is aware of the big boys in this field; but they are relatively few. There are perhaps as many as thirty-five having $100 million or more in assets.

The foundations are a peculiar product of American society. We do not find them in quite the same fashion anywhere else in the world.

There are some parallels in Western Europe and increasingly in Japan, but in the main, the foundation is an American creation, a child of American capitalism, of the profit-making impulse in American life.

You could say it is a child of semifree enterprise. If there were no government regulations and no government provisions giving tax benefits to those who set aside money for benevolent purposes, then it is highly unlikely that foundations would exist. It is not free enterprise, therefore, but semifree enterprise that has produced our foundations. Furthermore, foundations are clearly the result of, among other things, peculiarly American religious understandings, in particular of the so-called Protestant ethic, to which I will refer in a moment.

Organized philanthropy, then, is a massive endeavor in the United States, soon approaching a $5 billion total annually, or around 10 percent of all philanthropic activity. It is, of course, minuscule in comparison with spending by government or business corporations. Yet, because it is, so to say, free money, the lifeblood of the nonprofit sector, and the major support of many important agencies, concerns, and services, it has an influence in society and a significance for society that far outweighs its relatively limited financial strength. It is because organized philanthropy is so important to the health of our society that we must pay close attention to its condition. We are back at the beginning—the foundations have serious problems.

Not long ago, *Change* magazine sponsored a symposium on "The Future of Foundations," which pointed out that there is a "growing doubt" about foundations in American life, an "erosion of public confidence" in them, and "an equal erosion of competence inside." "A new intellectual rationale for foundations" is needed, said the symposium. Washington can be expected to take another look at them, perhaps fairly soon. The recent Dallas convention of the Council of Foundations gave voice to a host of concerns that dedicated foundation people face. "The birth rate of foundations has dropped sharply" since TRA-69. It all adds up to the feeling that "foundations need all the friends and partners they can get."[1]

I want to single out four groups or clusters of problems that have to do with the foundation as an economic entity, as an important and specialized kind of corporation.

Problems of Grant-Making. The first cluster of problems centers on programs and other activities of foundations, and on proposers and recipients. It is through its program that the foundation is, of course,

---

[1] Landrum Bolling, Council of Foundations, *Annual Report*, 1979.

most visible. It is grants that most people think of in respect to foundations.

First of all, foundations have problems in their relations with petitioners, and some foundations solve that problem by paying no attention to them and throwing letters wholesale into wastebaskets. The problem centers on the inability of most large foundations to respond to more than 5 percent of the petitions or proposals that they receive. This means that at least 95 percent of all the proposals that are received have to be turned down; the money is not there.

Relations with recipients are another troublesome area for foundations, and these relations are coming to be more and more difficult because recipients are more and more litigious, and the whole business of reacting and negotiating takes longer.

Pressures in respect to programs come in the form of criticism from organized groups, from other agencies, from government, and from other foundations. Every now and then one hears from a foundation the kind of plaintive complaint a business corporation might make in respect to the criticism it receives from the university or the church. My own feeling is that criticism from the university and the church is inevitable. Where else is there likely to be the sensitivity to the kinds of issues in our society that we think these great bodies of power and influence raise?

One feature of the program life of a foundation that has come in for a good bit of criticism lately, although earlier almost no attention was paid to it, is the process of grant-making, which is no longer as arbitrary as many foundations wish it still could be.

Related to this is the process of follow-up or evaluation of the grants. There was a time when foundations did no follow-ups at all, and although that is changing, if there is one area in which the foundations are clearly ill-prepared to defend themselves, it is in respect to the evaluation of their own work.

Compared with other nonprofit enterprises and organizations, foundations also suffer from the lack of a constituency. Consider, for a moment, that almost any other large agency in American life can call upon some kind of constituency. But a foundation has literally none— a fact that became manifest in Washington in 1969, when very little support for foundations was forthcoming from other quarters.

Problems of a slightly different kind, but having to do with program, point toward the future. Foundations face problems concerning new opportunities for service, concerning priorities among those opportunities, and concerning strategies for meeting the most promising opportunities. These problems are plaguing all philanthropic enterprises and are much more serious than in the old days, when everyone assumed that helping was easy.

Are there ethical implications to these problems having to do with program? I think there are a number. Let me simply note briefly that foundations think they exist to do good, to serve human beings and their institutions; they think they exist, in other words, to improve the lot of humankind, which means to change things. Their work would be meaningless if they did not make the assumption that doing good, improving, changing something or other in the area within their own range of vision, was called for.

In other words, foundations exist to make a difference, not to confirm the status quo. This, I submit, is a kind of moral implication of a foundation's program that has some exceedingly difficult and serious repercussions.

Problems of Structure and Management. A second crucial area for foundations today is that of structure and management. Many of these problems are relatively new because, for a long time, foundations themselves assumed that they were among the easiest organizations to run. They now recognize that this is not true, and they consciously face many problems in this area. Not long ago, for example, I was talking to the president of one of the best known American foundations, and he confessed to me that he is deeply puzzled these days about the composition and function of his governing board.

Although a recent volume by John Nason about trustees has helped greatly,[2] there has been very little study of what trustees of foundations ought to do and how they should be used. Nothing like the amount of study that has been devoted to the proper functioning of trustees of, say, colleges and universities, has been addressed to the trustees of foundations.

Take the particular matter of payment, for example: Ought trustees to be paid? Most foundations think not. But one prominent foundation in this country pays each trustee over $50,000 a year. It is not Ford; Ford pays $5,000. Nor is it Rockefeller, which pays $3,000. Carnegie pays only $250 per meeting. These matters, however, concern the whole field, lest any one or several foundations give all of them a black eye. The pattern, in matters of payment and certain other important areas is for foundation boards to follow the practices of the boards of other nonprofit, tax-exempt agencies rather than the boards of profit-making corporations.

---

[2] John Nason, *Trustees and the Future of Foundations* (New York: Council of Foundations, 1977).

In addition, there are questions as to the functions of advisory committees and consultants, and the quality and the functions of the professional staff. Foundation personnel come from a wide variety of backgrounds; there is no particular training for a foundation executive.

In the United States there are only about a thousand *philanthropoids*—a peculiar name given to a professional staff person of a foundation—as distinct, of course, from *philanthropist*, which is the word most often applied to the person making the benevolent gesture.

For boards of directors, there is the serious question about where the line between policy and management should be drawn. We learn, from other kinds of boards, profit and nonprofit in character, that a board is concerned with policy, the administration is concerned with management, and the two had better be kept clear. The line is not so clear in foundation work, and that constitutes a serious problem.

There is also the problem of interlocking memberships and relationships, and foundations have solved it in all kinds of strange ways. We had a rule of thumb at Danforth against accepting honorary degrees, though we allowed staff to accept honoraria for speeches. Only staff people who had been intimately connected with an institution, either as a faculty member or as a student, could accept honorary degrees. But one of our sister foundations had just the opposite rules: no honoraria, but as many honorary degrees as one could come by!

There are financial problems concerning structure and management: the shrinkage of assets, especially in the light of inflation; the liberty of making investments, or whether a foundation can invest wherever it wants to unless some restriction has been imposed by the donor; the artificiality of operating budgets. The operating budget of a symphony or a hospital or a college is, after all, not artificial, but is related to what comes in. But when a foundation, unlike its sister nonprofit institutions, prepares a budget, there is a little unreality about it, because the money is there; it is simply a question of how much is going to be used for administration.

Thus, salary scales have come to pose a serious problem in foundation affairs. Most foundations, incidentally, follow the practice of colleges and universities; presidents of most of the major foundations have salaries comparable to those of the presidents of major universities, not major business corporations. There are one or two exceptions, however, and they are proving an embarrassment to the field.

I could go on at length, but I want simply to note a few other factors that have ethical implications in this area of structure and management: the "dead hand," as it has been called, and its influence; the donor's wishes, oral or written; questions of self-dealing and self-serving versus selflessness on the part of the foundation; continuing feelings of the donor that the foundation money is still his or her personal treasure chest; and conflict of interest versus disinterestedness. All of these problems raise ethical concerns of complexity and increasing sensitivity, and no foundation can escape them.

Problems of External Relationships. A third area I want to touch on briefly is that of external relationships, especially with government. There are all kinds of problems here, from the residue of TRA-69 and how to deal with it, to the pressures exerted by government agencies today. A number of government agencies now in the business of making grants have chosen to do so by way of challenge grants, which put a none-too-subtle pressure on foundations to come across, to help, not to let a particular good cause fail. On the other hand, foundations these days must deal with the issues of when and how and how much of a common cause they can strike with government, with other foundations, with churches, with universities, or with other groups.

The central problem here, I believe, is one of independence from government. How can a foundation remain free when so many nonprofit and, of course, profit-making enterprises these days face the perils of collaboration?

I want to mention, with regard to these outside relationships, problems which apply only derivatively or secondarily to foundations but which are still very serious because of that second-hand effect. I refer to changes in tax policy generally, for although one might think that such matters affect individual donors only, the foundations are also affected. If the recipients of private donations can no longer expect the help they are used to—from the person who has been contributing $100 to his college or $10 per Sunday to his church or whatever—then the balance will have to be picked up by the foundations.

The greater dependence of all nonprofit institutions on tax dollars is a related problem, and one to which the newly formed organization, Independent Sector, is addressing itself in excellent measure.

The growth of the government vis-à-vis independent institutions in general is another problem with which foundations are concerned.

What about the ethical implications of these outside relationships? Foundations have discovered that they must give primary consideration to the good of the donee, or else they will be caught up in some kind of self-dealing or conflict of interest. The central operating question is not, therefore, how best to advance this or that foundation, but how best to advance the good of the donees. This will be the main operative criterion of a foundation that is sensitive to the ethical implication of its own nature. Asking that kind of question leads inevitably to some kind of cooperation, to striking some sort of common cause in programs or in activities. Yet foundations place great value on their freedom to make decisions as independent entities.

One feature of a foundation, then, that must not be proscribed in its outside relationships is its own freedom. Foundations have come to believe in pluralism, openness, and accountability; and in all of those things, there are ethical implications for the foundation's work.

Ethical Problems and Fundamental Values. The fourth group of problems has to do with the purpose and the ethical position of foundations.

One of the central questions that foundations face these days concerns their purpose. Why is it so difficult for foundations to speak about what it is they mean to do? In what does a foundation's accountability consist? How is it to be exercised? How are foundations viewed in the public mind? Finally, what are the ethical implications of philanthropy? What is its ethical base?

I have already referred to ethical questions concerning behavior. What I am now suggesting is that when foundations examine their central purpose, this calls for them to find a conscious rootage in ethics, not just the practice of ethical behavior on the surface of their daily activities.

All kinds of ethical implications inhere in the foundations' existence and essential nature. There are basic premises and values that foundations must affirm. I am not at all sure that we can speak of a theology of foundations, but we can consider foundations from an ethical, and perhaps even a theological, perspective.

The old trilogy of the Protestant ethic was supposed to have been "Earn all you can, save all you can, give all you can." Somehow, practitioners of the ethic always did a better job of emphasizing "earn all you can," a good job on "save all you can," and the least good job on the third and in a sense, the redeeming, admonition of the ethic, "give. . . ."

One gave not because of guilt, although philanthropy has indeed used this rationalization on occasion. One gave not because of condescension, although philanthropy certainly has practiced that from time to time. Nor did one give because of an effort to practice restitution or to buy some virtue, although philanthropy has undoubtedly been so motivated now and then. One gave because, in the nature of the situation itself, the moral integrity on which the organization was built demanded it.

I have several concerns about the values that foundations affirm, and I want to mention a few that seem to me to need special attention these days.

Foundations are by definition concerned with the national interest, or with those parts of it that they have chosen especially to address.

They are concerned with the national interest in the sense that the United States is a free society, and they want to do what they can to keep it free. The government cannot and should not do everything. Complementarity of public and private action is called for. Foundations thus find a great measure of their justification these days in taking the action necessary to maintain and strengthen the United States as a free society.

This is more or less what most foundations will say when asked what their purpose is. But, sadly, this is about as far as the justification usually goes.

I think that to say as much as I have just said—that the foundation is concerned with the nation as a free society and with finding its appropriate place in maintaining and strengthening that freedom— means that the foundation itself has come to accept and espouse the central values of our society. Therefore, a foundation is, by essence, not amoral. It cannot sustain the pretense that it is morally or ethically neutral.

Foundations do not define the good, but they must want to do it. It may be the church or it may be some other agency or aspect of society that defines the good. But the foundation makes certain moral presuppositions by virtue of the very work in which it is engaged. Whenever an individual foundation is untrue to these, it is clearly eligible for condemnation, by virtue of its being an unsatisfactory member of its kind of organization.

Let me mention two or three of the values that are implicit in the character of a foundation. I have already indicated one of them, integrity in its dealings. A second is universality of outlook. This does not change the particularity of a foundation's strategy. When a foundation makes a grant to a school for helping Chicano students, it is because it believes that education is a good thing for all youngsters, not just for a particular group. The universal in the particular must be its raison d'être.

A third premise so often unspoken and yet clearly necessary in the work of a foundation is concern for humanity. Foundations, ultimately, are not concerned about the American Council on Learned Societies, or Harvard University, or the Cleveland Symphony, to mention only highly reputable organizations. They are concerned about people, or at least they must be if they understand their own nature and their own implicit value system.

Finally, the value that is perhaps least often mentioned, even though it may be the most important, is the foundation's recognition of its own frailty, or, if you will, in theological language, its sin. That is to say, a foundation must understand—though I will have to admit that

I do not know a single one of them that does fully understand—that giving is potentially an immoral act. There is such a terrible danger in the assumption of virtue by the giver. The desire to help, which is implicit in the foundation's nature, can so easily move the short distance to become the desire to be the helper, which itself can so easily move that next distance to the desire to be recognized as the helper, which, in turn, can so easily move to become the desire to make decisions for the helpee, to dictate, to paternalize, to manipulate. A foundation, if it is able to understand its own ethical premise, needs to be aware of those dangers. I know of none that is.

I hope that, among other things, I have indicated something of the fragility of the philanthropic enterprise in general and of foundations in particular. And yet I think the foundation world is still a strong and terribly important aspect of our society. It has within it the strength of caring.

There is a place in the New Testament in which we are told that Jesus once said it is more blessed to give than to receive. Actually, scholars dispute the quotation's authenticity, I believe. In any event, and however we feel about blessedness, I do believe giving is much harder than receiving, especially when one takes seriously the ethical implications of the philanthropic enterprise. Conscientious foundation work is hard work!

Discussion

QUESTION: You spoke about the concern of foundations for American values. One of the main things that Americans value is pluralism. Are foundations pluralistic?

MR. CUNINGGIM: The large foundations, which have a great measure of choice, are, with very few exceptions, committed to the proposition that pluralism is part of our national heritage. Granting that they have made program-area decisions, they manage to practice it pretty well.

That is, there are things that even Ford, the largest foundation, does not do. But within the areas in which Ford does act, it tries to spread its own perspective broadly. This is much truer than it was twenty-five years ago, I believe.

QUESTION: Do foundations act or just react? Must foundations merely respond to, say, government, or can they initiate things on their own?

MR. CUNINGGIM: The chance for foundations to play the kind of enabling role that your question refers to was reduced by the Tax Reform Act, for prior to that time, foundations could have said, "We can take this ameliorative position because we do not want anything." Unfortunately, the Tax Reform Act changed some of that, as far as the foundations were concerned, because they now do want some things from government, and they themselves are sometimes in a pleading posture. They need the help of other outside agencies to represent the concern that they have and to indicate their importance.

But apart from the dilution of their own status that was caused by these somewhat restrictive measures, the foundations still have a chance to play the kind of role you are talking about.

I mentioned earlier the American Council of Learned Societies (ACLS). At one time that Council got most of its nonmembership money from foundations, but in recent years, the largest proportion of support for the Council has come from the National Endowment for the Humanities (NEH). I think it is very healthy that the NEH regards the ACLS's dependence on the Endowment as less than desirable. NEH feels that it is important to find ways to work with foundations so as to bring a broader base of support to the various kinds of nonprofit and tax exempt agencies that are within its own purview.

QUESTION: You mentioned that foundations have to come up with money. The analogy in my mind is of my putting money in the collection plate at my church and the government not taking it because they allow me a tax deduction for it. By the same token, I think the foundation money should be considered private money, and not public money.

MR. CUNINGGIM: I disagree with you in respect to the use to which the money is put. It is supposed to speak to the issues and needs of a society. It is not money for the special help of those who happen to be placed in charge of the foundation. A foundation does not have money for the benefit of its own governors, donor, corporation, or anything else. Its resources are dedicated to public welfare or to that particular portion of public welfare that it has been given the remarkable privilege of concentrating upon. It is in this sense that I call it public money. Since the decision is indeed made by a private agency, however, it is possible still to think of it, in that sense, as private money.

QUESTION: In the Tax Reform Act of 1969, there are some attempts to improve the ethical standards by which foundation money is spent. I wonder what your sense of the motivation for these attempts was.

MR. CUNINGGIM: It was mixed, as would of course be expected, and a great deal went into it. There was the feeling that foundations had not used their own resources sufficiently for the good of the general welfare. A few people felt that some foundations had, in fact, used the money for political purposes. Then again there was some resentment of a very personal kind, not necessarily political in our usual sense of politics, but at the personal behavior of certain foundation executives.

The foundations were lucky to come out as well as they did, because at one time that bill had in it a provision that would have prevented any foundation from making a grant to any individual. That was a punitive measure, even though the grants at which they were directed were arbitrary and whimsical. Congress was displeased, and it got to the point of putting that provision in the bill. It was finally taken out.

At one time there was also a provision in the bill that every foundation must, by law, go out of business within a forty-year period. Various numbers of years were tried—twenty, twenty-five, thirty, thirty-five—and at one point an affirmative vote was obtained for a forty-year limit. That provision was not so much inspired by a desire to be punitive as it was the outgrowth of a determination to make a foundation spend its money, for there had been some few but spectacular abuses by foundations that thought they had been called into existence in order to put their income back in their own coffers and pay the members of the family on the board a nice little fee for doing so, and literally doing nothing else. The forty-year limit was an effort to penalize such behavior, but, much more importantly, it meant to say something about the need for active programs that would address some of the issues and needs of society.

On balance, I have been from the very beginning a supporter of most of the provisions of the Tax Reform Act of 1969, as they applied to foundations, even though the organizations I have worked for have indeed had many problems trying to meet some of the absurdities that crept into the act.

QUESTION: Where do foundations get their purposes? How do they take their bearings? Do they have their own value systems, or do they subscribe to the general American way of life?

MR. CUNINGGIM: I think that the American system of pluralism helps us here. Some foundations will be suspicious that the general temper cannot go far enough in defining what their purpose should be, and they want to go further, perhaps even opposing some popular value of the moment. Some will not so much take their bearings from Gallup polls or litmus tests as from church groups or other arbiters of national conscience and taste. Some definitely now take their bearings, in respect to what doing good consists in, from universities and colleges and the various interests that they are working on.

I believe it is inappropriate for foundations to set themselves up as definers of the values of our society. I worry when they begin to play that kind of role. There is already in foundation behavior too much temptation to be God, or to play God, or to get oneself confused with God, and so on. Much better that they seek their bearings elsewhere. I do not mean to suggest, however, that foundations need to take their bearings from one source or another. Rather, it seems to me that part of the pluralism that characterizes us and blesses us spills over into the foundation or the philanthropic field by allowing a number of sources for bearings to be available for foundation use.

QUESTION: You said that only a small percentage of proposals are funded. Once those funds are in, however, the foundations are the conduits of the great abundance. They dispense the surplus resources that are generated by the economic system.

Is there a schizophrenia here? Is there a sense that we live in a world of scarce resources and we are the policeman of them? And, on the other hand, that we live in a world of abundance, and we are the conduits of that abundance, through foundations? Is this a world of abundance or is this a world of scarcity? What is the world view of foundations?

Mr. Cuninggim: I assume that there is a residue of the so-called Protestant ethic still at work. "Earn all you can, save all you can, give all you can" is the shorthand. That is not the Protestant ethic. It certainly is not the full Christian ethic. But it is a useful, shorthand means of delineating a foundation's business. A foundation does not try to earn all it can in a profit-making sense. It does need to pay attention to its investment policy to make sure that it is being a good steward of its own resources. Foundations, however, with very few exceptions, do not bother a great deal about earning and saving. Their job is giving.

Now, is it an appropriate activity to give, from supposed abundance, whatever one can? Some will be able to give more abundantly than others. Is that an appropriate activity for any of us, whether we are incorporated as a foundation or simply individual members of society? I believe it is.

I do not see that the question of the propriety of my giving from my relative abundance arises merely because what I give can go only a short distance toward any particular scarcity that anyone would have in mind.

Question: Would you say something about philanthropy in the nineteenth century? The income tax was instituted in 1913. Yet there was enormous philanthropy, which was quite distinctively American, throughout the nineteenth century, independent of taxation.

Mr. Cuninggim: Nineteenth-century philanthropy was not organized into what we know now as endowed foundations. Those were very, very few. There was a Peabody Fund and a Slater Fund, and few others. Some of the work for the education of recently freed slaves was financed by early foundations. But it was a different style of trying to confess to the philanthropic impulse.

Question: I was trying to draw attention to the spirit in the country which antedates the income tax laws, a spirit that was already quite distinctive and already favored philanthropy. I refer to a form of organized giving, organized to the extent that very wealthy men, who acquired or accumulated money themselves, did not actually make the decisions about where it all was going; their staff members did.

MR. CUNINGGIM: There were, of course, individual gifts to help this institution, to establish that one, and so on, but there were no endowments of any large size set aside in the nineteenth century.

Carnegie and Rockefeller are products of the early twentieth century, and nothing of the sort that we have come to think of as the endowed foundation, with the possible exception of three or four tiny funds, spills back over into that other century as a style of giving. They gave in other ways.

QUESTION: I do not know the history, but I had thought that in many cases buildings were put up, for example, and funds for their maintenance and some of their activities supplied. Was that type of thing a fairly familiar practice?

MR. CUNINGGIM: Yes. What we would now call grants, gifts by individuals for a particular cause or task, were made. The establishment of colleges all across the country was certainly greatly aided in this way. Take Vanderbilt, my own alma mater. The Commodore saw fit to give—I think it was all of $1 million—to establish a university in Nashville, Tennessee, in 1876. Mr. Rockefeller helped to get the University of Chicago started by a personal gift.

But there was no such thing as a foundation then. The giving did indeed take place. Incidentally, it was not in anything like the measure that it now seems to be, even in terms of percentages, so far as I am aware. I do not have the figures to prove that, but my impression is that the disposition of Americans to give in small amounts, in large amounts through foundations and other corporations established for it, and through collection plates in church, has increased considerably in this century.

We have never attained in America anything like that $43 billion figure that I mentioned to you as the size of philanthropy at the present time. And that, incidentally, is philanthropy in terms of money. When we take into account gifts in other forms, which have been growing immensely in scope, the picture, I think, runs far beyond anything the eighteenth or nineteenth centuries can show.

You have asked a question that extends beyond my own personal expertise, but I do think that the nineteenth century represented a new surge of the disposition to give, which stretched far beyond what the eighteenth century had offered. The twentieth century has itself gone so far beyond, again, that I do not think we can learn much from the nineteenth-century record, certainly not in terms of organizations specifically incorporated by law to undertake the task of continuous and sensitive grant-making. That is new.

QUESTION: I was thinking of how we invoke the idea of fraternity in America and how the remarkable giving orientation, despite the tax laws, still springs out of a possible idea of fraternity. Will you comment on this?

MR. CUNINGGIM: At one time I had thought to try to indicate some of the values that seem to me to be implicit in the nature of a foundation's task. One of those that I did not say anything about, because of time limitations, is the relatedness of the human family. I did say that one of the central values, as I saw it, that a foundation could not escape, else it belie its own character, is a concern for humanity, and certainly that includes the recognition that all humanity is in some way kin.

Again, I would have to say that I do not think each individual foundation could possibly confess to this value in any meaningful way. I do believe that organized philanthropy in our society must totally confess to this value or demonstrate its presence in the shaping of their work, else in some fashion or other foundations are indeed missing their proper business.

QUESTION: Two major foundations have joined to save *Harper's* magazine, which had a deficit of approximately $4 million and was scheduled to go out of business. Was that an unusual move on the part of major foundations? What is your reaction to it?

MR. CUNINGGIM: Personally, I would not have wanted to be a part of that particular grant decision. I faced that kind of decision more than once when I was in foundation work at Danforth, and in one or two other instances that had to do with shoring up or salvaging a college.

In general terms, I think that when an institution such as a magazine or a college has come so close to proving its inability to find and continue an independent life of its own, it does not help in the long run, although it may indeed be a sentimental gesture for the short run, to give that college or magazine a peculiar boost.

I am against such a strategy. I am glad that not everybody in the foundation field agrees with me. In my time, I was a party to the saving of several institutions. I resigned from Danforth, however, because I was not willing to be a party to the sudden expenditure of $80 million to save an institution. This is a strategy that I have questions about, but one whose usefulness turns, in very special measure, on the particular circumstances of the situation: whether the college indeed has a chance, whether there is something about the *Harper's* picture that has not been said to the general public, and so on.

I think the foundations that are considering such action would be well advised to take careful stock. The answer might well differ from foundation to foundation. It might never be mine at all.

QUESTION: Since the foundation is the child of capitalism, it is obviously a part of a system. And we have heard Reginald Jones tell us that he feels the system is being threatened. My question, then, is why aren't corporate leaders giving more of their energies to supporting the foundations, since it seems to me that if the network and the benefits of the foundations can be extended, then the spirit of capitalism has a far better basis of surviving.

It seems, however, that corporate leaders do not give much to foundations. You seemed to indicate that this was an area for further growth. Why don't they have a missionary zeal to work through the foundations rather than work on their own? Is that a fair question?

MR. CUNINGGIM: Yes. First, the zeal is growing at a remarkable rate. Only a short time ago the total giving of corporations through foundations and through benevolent committees was much smaller than it is now. It has been growing faster than any other form of giving in American life. So the direction is right.

Second, corporate leaders have not developed an all-encompassing willingness to engage in corporation giving because many corporations do not believe it makes good sense for them as business entities. They can take as much as 5 percent. Only 1 percent is now being given.

That difference represents not only those who are not giving as much as they could but also many corporations, large as well as small, that do not give anything at all. The reason they do not give is that they think their stockholders would disapprove. Many of the stockholders of corporations that do give, do not approve and say so at stockholder's meetings.

The management does not want to get into that hassle, or they themselves do not believe. They fail to see a quid pro quo, and they think that if a corporation gives, there must be immediate and clear quid pro quo. So they hesitate. But it is remarkable, in light of these resistances that have characterized the picture for so long, that the trend is as it is.

QUESTION: Do the foundations give any thought to how much of their giving is simply in response to requests and how much involves creative thinking on their own part—initiative from the foundation's side to help create something better, new, or different?

MR. CUNINGGIM: More and more, the larger foundations are seeking to develop their own programs rather than merely respond to proposals and appeals. That is both good and bad. I feel that we should welcome increasing imagination, initiative, and leadership on the part of the foundations. I want to make sure, however, that this is not whimsy, that it is not arbitrariness, that it is not some special brand of self-dealing.

I think I could illustrate both kinds of initiative as now being exercised by large foundations: one foundation, whose staff is able and active in defining the work of that foundation and in finding the places where that work can best be done; and another which is doing more of this than they have ever done, but which is being hurt, because they are not good enough to know what ought to be done.

It is dangerous to say that every foundation ought to plan more of its own program instead of listening carefully to the world outside, even as I think it would be dangerous to say that every foundation ought to spend more time listening and never plan its own program.

QUESTION: I agree with you that there is a uniqueness in foundations. I wonder if we might find an analogy in the Muslim practice of *Zakat*, which is the command to give 2½ percent annually, gains and assets, unlike the 10 percent only of gains which we understand as the tithe. I even wonder if there might not be a moral imperative to effect a redistribution of accumulated assets; that is, if not enough was siphoned off when the wealth was first created, and it has accumulated somewhere and still needs to be further redistributed, perhaps a moral imperative governs that situation.

MR. CUNINGGIM: I am not happy with the specifics of a direction, Christian or Muslim or any other, of that sort as a guideline that can inform those who might without it be more reluctant than they should.

I suppose it has its use, but in the long run, it is the impulse that I would want to see fostered. The impulse is going to turn on many things beyond a mere prescription, and no prescription is going to be good enough to get me to give all of my tithe and do what I should, although perhaps it might help someone else. Someone else might be able to respond, whereas I would be reluctant, and some other kind of appeal would have to be made to me.

QUESTION: When you responded to the question about *Harper's*, you alluded to several cases in which you had been personally involved. Could you talk about any one of those experiences, illustrating the kinds of questions that arise and the kinds of issues that get discussed in the course of making such a decision?

MR. CUNINGGIM: In the early 1970s, Webster College came close to closing. This was our own hometown. The Danforth Foundation is located in St. Louis. We were given the opportunity to try to meet some of Webster's needs. We undertook an extensive factual survey, determining what Webster's assets were, what was real, what Webster itself knew about what it had and where its problems were, and so on. We discovered, incidentally, that Webster did not have adequate information, even though it was contemplating going out of existence for financial reasons before the end of that particular academic year. It did not know its own condition. But we did something which, to me, was much more important than simply getting the facts of the situation. We tried to come to as responsible a judgment as we could; we made our best effort at assessing the temper of the institution. How good were the faculty who were willing to stay and see this thing through? Was there now able leadership in place? Not just the president and so on, but a board? Would this leadership stay? We were not going to give a big piece of money unless the board were convinced that they, too, would do whatever they could to help.

We extended our survey of both the factual picture and the atmospheric picture, so to say, to the surrounding community, which included other, competing colleges and other sources of support, to see whether or not the factors that added up to continuance outweighed the factors that suggested discontinuance. It was on the basis of that kind of effort that our trustees made the decision to bail Webster out.

I have chosen an example that was a great success because the information on which we relied proved to be sound information. Similar efforts did not always produce such happy results.

Other foundations do similar things. Carnegie, Sloan, Ford, Rockefeller, Lilly, Kellogg—a considerable group of the large foundations have learned to operate pretty much this way.

QUESTION: How does a foundation arrive at the conclusion that Webster is worth saving in the first place? Were there discussions about that kind of question? Not only could it be saved, but should it be saved at all?

MR. CUNINGGIM: Yes. There is nothing mysterious about it. A foundation arrives at that decision by guess and by golly. By prayer and by sweat. By argumentation and discord, as often as by consensus and ease of conclusion. A foundation makes important decisions in its life in much the same way that any responsible person does for any organization of which he is a member, whose work and whose nature he cherishes.

A Theology of the Corporation

Michael Novak

Our task is to set forth some steps toward a theology of the corporation. We need such a theology so that the ministers who serve businessmen and workers might be able to preach more illuminating and practical sermons and so that critics might have at their disposal a theologically sound standard of behavior for corporations.

For many years one of my favorite texts in Scripture has been Isaiah 53:2–3: "He hath no form nor comeliness; and when we shall see him, there is no beauty that we should desire him. He is despised and rejected of men; a man of sorrows, and acquainted with grief; he was despised, and we esteemed him not." I would like to apply these words to the modern business corporation, a much despised incarnation of God's presence in this world.

When we speak of the body of Christ, we ordinarily mean the church, both invisible and visible, both sinless and marred by sin. God calls His followers to bring His presence to their work, to their daily milieu, to history. This is the doctrine of Christian vocation. A liturgy does not end without a word of mission: "Go out into the world of daily work to carry the peace and love of Jesus Christ." I do not mean by this way of speech to suggest that the Christian form is the only form of speech for this fundamental attitude. A sense of vocation infuses Jews, Muslims, and others of religious faith. Many who are not religious also regard their work as useful and ennobling. They feel called to the task of making life better for their fellow human beings. But I am a Catholic Christian, and it is better to speak in the idiom with most meaning for me than to pretend to an idiom that, by virtue of being no more than a common denominator, would appear superficial to all of us.

To work in a modern business corporation, no one need pass a test of faith or even reveal his or her religious convictions to others. But it would be a mistake to permit the business corporation's commendable acceptance of religious pluralism to mask the religious vocation that many see in it.

The Multinational Corporation

In speaking of the corporation, I will concentrate on those large business corporations that are found among the 300 or so multinational corporations, two-thirds of which are American.[1]

The reason one must first consider these *big* corporations is that all but very strict socialists seem to be in favor of markets, ownership, cooperatives, and *small* business. Religious socialists like John C. Cort favor the private ownership of small businesses, ownership through cooperatives, and some free-market mechanisms.[2]

What are multinational corporations? They are not those which merely sell their goods in other lands, buy goods from other lands, or trade with other lands. Multinationals are corporations that build manufacturing or other facilities in other lands in order to *operate* there. The building of a base of operations in other lands is an important condition for qualification as a multinational corporation in the strict sense. One should not think only of factories; banks and insurance firms —important for local investment—may also establish such operations.

The training of an indigenous labor and managerial force is not a strictly necessary condition for a corporation to be considered multinational, but it is a common characteristic, particularly of American companies. Thus multinationals make four chief contributions to the host country. Of these the first two, (1) capital facilities and (2) technological transfers inherent in the training of personnel, remain forever in the host country, whatever the ultimate fate of the original company. In addition, products manufactured within the nation no longer have to be imported; thus (3) the host nation's problems with balance of payments are eased. Finally, (4) wages paid to employees remain in the country, and local citizens begin to invest in the corporation, so that most of its future capital can be generated locally.[3] These are important

---

[1] Sperry Lea and Simon Webley, *Multinational Corporations in Developed Countries: A Review of Recent Research and Policy Thinking* (Washington, D.C.: British-North American Committee, 1973), p. 1.

[2] See John C. Cort, "Can Socialism Be Distinguished from Marxism?" *Cross Currents*, vol. 29 (Winter 1979–1980): 423–434.

[3] Ronald E. Muller estimates that 80 percent of the capital raised by multinational corporations in Latin America is local: "We find initially that, for the period from 1957 to 1965, of the total U.S. investment in Latin America only 17 per cent of the actual financial capital investments ever came from the United States. When we look at the manufacturing sector for the same period, we find that 78 per cent of all U.S. corporate investments were financed not from U.S. savings but from Latin American savings." "The Multinational Corporation: Asset or Impediment to World Justice?" in *Poverty, Environment and Power*, ed. Paul Hallock (New York: Interational Documentation on the Contemporary Church—North America, 1973), p. 42.

factors in any accounting of the relative wealth transferred to and from the host country and the country of the corporation's origin. Critics sometimes concentrate only on the flow of return on investment. They neglect to add up the capital investment, training, balance-of-payments relief, salaries, and stimulation of local investment.

Almost all of the 200 American multinationals are to be found among *Fortune* 500 industrial companies, though a few are among the largest banks and insurance firms. What less-developed countries want most today is manufactured goods, at prices made possible by local production, and the financial services of banks and insurance companies.

Generally speaking, only a company of the size represented by the *Fortune* 500 has the capital and skills to accept the risks of operating in an unfamiliar culture. As it is, 40 percent of all foreign sales of U.S. multinationals are in Western Europe, and another 25 percent are in Japan, Canada, Taiwan, Hong Kong, South Korea, Australia, and other industrial nations. Most concerns about the multinationals, however, focus on their role in the developing nations. Only about 12 percent of the business of U.S. multinationals is to be found in Latin America, and only a tiny fraction in Africa. Vast expanses of the whole world never see an American multinational.[4]

The vast majority of U.S. corporations are *not* multinationals. Many which could be do not wish to be, believing the headaches more costly than the rewards. Some which are refuse to build operations in unstable conditions, such as those which characterize most of the developing nations. That is why such a small proportion of overseas activities by U.S. multinationals is to be found in Latin America and Africa.

Other contextual matters should be noted. In most nations of the world—notably the socialist nations—private corporations are not permitted to come into existence. Only a relatively few nations of the world produce privately held corporations. Furthermore, some nations which do so (like the United States) were formerly colonies, and some others (Hong Kong) still are. Since economic development depends to a large extent upon home-based privately held corporations, differences in moral-cultural climate are significant. Some cultures seem to develop far higher proportions of skilled inventors, builders, and managers of industry than others. In some cultures, the work force is more productive than in others.

Over time, education and training may provide new moral models and fairly swift cultural development. Simultaneously, of course, such

---

[4] U.S. Bureau of the Census, *Statistical Abstract of the United States, 1979* (Washington, D.C.: U.S. Department of Commerce, 1979), table 944.

developments may provoke intense conflicts with guardians of the earlier cultural order. It cannot be stressed too often that corporations are not merely economic agencies. They are also moral-cultural agencies. They may come into existence, survive, and prosper only under certain moral-cultural conditions.

It goes without saying that private corporations depend upon a nonsocialist, nonstatist political order. Insofar as socialist governments in Yugoslavia and elsewhere now experiment with autonomous economic enterprises, take their signals from a free market, and reward their managers and workers according to profit and loss, they are moving toward a democratic capitalist political order. As their middle class grows, so will the demand for further political rights, due process, democratic methods, a free press, freedom of worship, and the rest. Economic liberties require political liberties, and vice versa. Historically, private business enterprise has not only grown up with liberal democracy, it has also been the main engine in destroying class distinctions between aristocrats and serfs, by making possible personal and social mobility on a massive scale.

The private business corporation is particularly active among Americans. As Oscar Handlin has pointed out, the United States, with a population of just over 4 million in 1800, already had more corporations than all of Europe combined. Some of these corporations began to grow into large-scale organizations—roughly following the railroads— at the end of the nineteenth century.

Nearly all American corporations, and particularly those from the *Fortune* 500, originated around a novel invention. They grew in sales, size, and capital either through products never before known to the human race or through novel processes for producing them. Entire industries, like those for airplanes, automobiles, oil, gas, electricity, television, cinema, computers, copiers, office machinery, electronics, and plastics, are based on corporations initially formed by the American inventors of their products.

Theological Beginnings

In thinking about the corporation in history and its theological significance, I begin with a general theological principle. George Bernanos once put it this way: "Grace is everywhere."[5] Wherever we look in the world, there are signs of God's presence: in the mountains, in a grain of sand, in a human person, in the poor and the hungry. "The earth is charged with the grandeur of God." So is human history.

---

[5] George Bernanos, *Diary of a Country Priest,* trans. Pamela Morris (New York: Macmillan Co., 1962), p. 233.

If we look for signs of grace in the corporation, we may discern seven of them—a suitably sacramental number.

1. Creativity. The Creator locked great riches in nature, riches to be discovered only gradually through human effort. John Locke observed that the yield of the most favored field in Britain could be increased a hundredfold if human ingenuity and human agricultural science were applied to its productivity.[6] Nature *alone* is not as fecund as nature *under intelligent cultivation.* The world, then, is immeasurably rich as it comes from the Creator, but only potentially so. This potential was hidden for thousands of years until human discovery began to release portions of it for human benefit. Yet even today we have not yet begun to imagine all the possibilities of wealth in the world the Creator designed. The limits of our present intelligence restrict the human race to the relative poverty in which it still lives.

During 1979 Atlantic Richfield ran an advertisement based on a theme first enunciated, as far as I can tell, by Father Hesburgh of Notre Dame; namely, that 40 percent of the world's energy is used by the 6 percent of the world's population residing in the United States.[7] This way of putting the facts is an example of the cultivation of guilt that Professor Bauer has described. A moment's thought shows that it is a preposterous formulation.

What the entire human race meant by energy until the discovery of the United States and the inventions promoted by its political economy were the natural forces of sun, wind, moving water, animals, and human muscle. Thomas Aquinas traveled on foot or by burro from Rome to Paris and back seven times in his life. The first pope to be able to make that voyage by train did so six centuries later, in the mid-nineteenth century. Until then, people traveled exactly as they had done since the time of Christ and before—by horse and carriage, by donkey, or by foot. History for a very long time seemed relatively static. The social order did not promote inventions and new technologies, at least to the degree lately reached. The *method* of scientific discovery had not been invented.

In 1809 an American outside Philadelphia figured out how to ignite anthracite coal. The ability to use anthracite, which burned hotter and more steadily than bituminous coal, made practical the seagoing steamship and the locomotive.

In 1859 the first oil well was dug outside Titusville, Pennsylvania.

---

[6] John Locke, *Second Treatise of Civil Government* (New York: Macmillan Co., 1947), p. 20.

[7] Theodore Hesburgh, *The Humane Imperative: A Challenge for the Year 2000* (New Haven: Yale University Press, 1974), p. 101.

Oil was known in Biblical times but used only for products like perfume and ink. Arabia would have been as rich then as now, if anybody had known what to do with the black stuff.

The invention of the piston engine and the discovery of how to drill for oil were also achieved in the United States. The first electric light bulb was illuminated in 1879 in Edison, New Jersey.

After World War II the U.S. government dragooned the utilities into experimenting with nuclear energy. They knew nothing about it. They did not need it; they did not want it. Oil and coal were cheap. The government, however, promoted the peaceful uses of the atom.

Thus 100 percent of what the modern world means by energy was invented by 6 percent of the world's population. More than 60 percent of that energy had been distributed to the rest of the world. Though the United States can, of course, do better than that, we need not feel guilty for inventing forms of energy as useful to the human race as the fire brought to earth by Prometheus.

The agency through which inventions and discoveries are made productive for the human race is the corporation. Its creativity makes available to mass markets the riches long hidden in creation. Its creativity mirrors God's. That is the standard by which its deeds and misdeeds are properly judged.

2. Liberty. The corporation mirrors God's presence also in its liberty, by which I mean independence from the state. That independence was the greatest achievement of the much-despised but creative 6 percent of the world's population. Advancing the works of their forebears, they invented the concept and framed the laws that for the first time in history set boundaries on the state, ruling certain activities off-limits to its interference. Rights of person and home, free speech in public, a free press, and other liberties came to be protected both by constitutional law and by powerful interests actively empowered to defend themselves under that law. Legal autonomy was such that even the king could not forcibly enter the home of a peasant; a peasant's home was as protected as a duke's castle—rights which the colonists in America demanded for themselves. Private business corporations were permitted to become agents of experimentation, of trial and error, and for good reason: to unleash economic activism. The state retained rights and obligations of regulation, and undertook the indirect promotion of industry and commerce. The state alone was prohibited from becoming the sole economic agent. A sphere of economic liberty was created.

The purpose of this liberty was to unlock greater riches than the world had ever known. Liberty was to be an experiment, for which Adam Smith and others argued, that might (or might not) prove to be in accordance with nature and with the laws of human society. Pleading for room to experiment, their practical, empirical arguments flew in the face of entrenched ideological opposition. The case for liberty prevailed.

The foundational concept of democratic capitalism, then, is not, as Marx thought, private property. It is limited government. Private property, of course, is one limitation on government.[8] What is interesting about private property is not that *I* own something, that *I* possess; its heart is not "possessive individualism," in C. B. Macpherson's phrase.[9] Quite the opposite. The key is that the *state* is limited by being forbidden to control all rights and all goods. It cannot infringe on the privacy of one's home or on one's right to the fruit of one's labors and risks. Herbert Stein has a useful definition of capitalism: "The idea of a capitalist system has nothing to do with capital and has everything to do with freedom. I think of capitalism as a system in which ability to obtain and use income independently of other persons or organizations, including government, is widely distributed among the individuals of the population."[10]

This is the distinctively American way of thinking about private property. In this framework, property is important less for its material reality than for the legal rights its ownership and use represent and for the limits it imposes on the power of the state. Such liberty was indispensable if private business corporations were to come into existence. Such corporations give liberty economic substance over and against the state.

3. Birth and Mortality. In coming into being with a technological breakthrough, and then perishing when some new technology causes it to be replaced, a typical corporation mirrors the cycle of birth and mortality. New corporations arise every day; dead ones litter history. Examining the *Fortune* 500 at ten-year intervals shows that even large corporations are subject to the cycle: new ones keep appearing and many that were once prominent disappear. Of the original *Fortune* 500, first listed in 1954, only 285 remained in 1974. Of the missing 215, 159 had merged, 50 had become too small to be listed or had gone out of busi-

---

[8] See Paul Johnson, "Is There a Moral Basis for Capitalism?" *Democracy and Mediating Structures: A Theological Inquiry*, ed. Michael Novak (Washington, D.C.: American Enterprise Institute, 1980), pp. 49–58.

[9] C. B. Macpherson, *The Political Theory of Possessive Individualism: Hobbes to Locke* (New York: Oxford University Press, 1962), p. 263.

[10] Herbert Stein, *Capitalism—If you Can Keep It* (Washington, D.C.: American Enterprise Institute, 1980), p. 6.

ness, and 6 were reclassified or had unavailable data.[11] Recently, Chrysler has been number 10. Will it by 1990 be gone from the list? Will Ford be gone from the list? It is entirely possible. As products of human liberty, corporations rise and fall, live and die. One does not have in them a lasting home—or even an immortal enemy.

4. Social Motive. Corporations, as the very word suggests, are not individualistic in their conception, in their operations, or in their purposes. Adam Smith entitled his book *An Inquiry into the Nature and Causes of the Wealth of Nations*. Its social scope went beyond individuals and beyond Great Britain to include all nations. The fundamental intention of the system from the beginning has been the wealth of all humanity.

The invention of democratic capitalism, the invention of the corporation, and the liberation of the corporations from total control by state bureaucracies (although some control always, and properly, remains) was *intended* to be multinational. Smith foresaw an interdependent world, for the first time able to overcome immemorial famine, poverty, and misery. He imagined people of every race, every culture, and every religion adopting the new knowledge about the causes of wealth. One does not need to be Christian or Jewish, or to share the Judeo-Christian worldview, to understand the religious and economic potency of the free economy. Smith did not exactly foresee Toyota and Sony. But he certainly would have been delighted to add a chapter to his immense study showing how the Japanese demonstrated the truth of his hypothesis.[12]

5. Social Character. The corporation is inherently and in its essence corporate. The very word suggests communal, nonindividual, many acting together. Those who describe capitalism by stressing the individual entrepreneur miss the central point. Buying and selling by individual entrepreneurs occurred in Biblical times. What is interesting and novel —at least what struck Max Weber as interesting and novel—is the communal focus of the new ethos: the rise of communal risk taking, the pooling of resources, the sense of communal religious vocation in economic activism. To be sure, certain developments in law and in techniques of accounting had to occur before corporations could be insti-

---

[11] Linda Grant Martin, "The 500: A Report on Two Decades," *Fortune*, May 1975, p. 238.

[12] Per capita savings deposits in Japan at the end of 1977 were $9,531, compared with $4,354 in the United States. See *Facts and Figures of Japan* (Tokyo: Tokyo Foreign Press Center, 1980).

tutionalized in their modern form. In this sense, too, they are social creations.

Corporations depend on the emergence of an infrastructure in intellectual life that makes possible new forms of communal collaboration. They depend on ideas that are powerful and clear enough to organize thousands of persons around common tasks. Moreover, these ideas must be strong enough to endure for years, so that individuals who commit themselves to them can expect to spend thirty to forty years working out their vocation. For many millions of religious persons the daily milieu in which they work out their salvation is the communal, corporate world of the workplace. For many, the workplace is a kind of second family. Even those who hate their work often like their co-workers. This is often true in factories; it is also true in offices. Comradeship is natural to humans. Labor unions properly build on it.

6. Insight. The primary capital of any corporation is insight, invention, finding a better way. Insight is of many kinds and plays many roles: it is central to invention; it lies at the heart of organization; it is the vital force in strategies for innovation, production, and marketing. Corporate management works hard at communal insight. Constantly, teams of persons meet to brainstorm and work out common strategies. Insight is the chief resource of any corporation, and there cannot be too much of it. Its scarcity is called stupidity.

Karl Marx erred in thinking that capital has to do primarily with machinery, money, and other tangible instruments of production. He overlooked the extent to which the primary form of capital is an idea.[13] The right to patent industrial ideas is an extremely important constitutional liberty. It is indispensable to the life of corporations, as indispensable as the copyright is to writers. Money without ideas is not yet capital. Machinery is only as good as the idea it embodies. The very word "capital," from the Latin *caput*, "head," points to the human spirit as the primary form of wealth. The miser sitting on his gold is not a capitalist. The investor with an idea is a capitalist. Insight makes the difference.

A momentary digression. Money was more material before capi-

---

[13] Stephen B. Roman and Eugen Loebl write: "Economy is essentially the transformation of natural forces and natural goods into forces and goods that serve humanity. It is an order created by thinking people, and one that has developed as a result of people's intellectual and spiritual growth. Further, it should be clear that when we regard economy as the creation of thinking human beings, economic wealth becomes nothing more than the transformation of natural wealth. There is no material wealth except that of nature and that created by humans from nature." *The Responsible Society* (New York: Regina Ryan Books/Two Continents, 1977), pp. 22–23.

talism, when it was gold and silver coin, than it came to be afterward. Under capitalism, perhaps a majority of transactions are intellectualized "book" transactions. Moreover, paper money is necessary, as are stocks, bonds, constitutions, and legal contracts. Materialism is more and more left behind as money depends for its value less on material substance than on public confidence, the health of the social order, the stability of institutions. Let these be threatened and investments flee because deteriorating social health reduces the value of the amounts registered on paper. Materially, money is often "not worth the paper it is printed on." Its real value depends on sociality, trust, a sense of health and permanence. In this respect, a theological treatise on the symbolic nature of money is badly needed. Such a treatise would have to deal not only with the fact that most money exists only in the intellectual realm but also with the impersonality of money, which transcends discrimination based on race, religion, sex, or nationality, and with money's remarkable indeterminacy, according to which its moral value springs from how persons, in their liberty, use it. Money opens a vast range of freedom of choice. Accordingly, it is more closely related to insight and liberty than to matter. It no longer functions as it did in Biblical times.

7. The Risk of Liberty and Election. A corporation faces liberty and election; it is part of its romance to do so. Tremendous mistakes in strategy can cripple even the largest companies. Easy Washing Machines of Syracuse once made an excellent washing machine, but Maytag's discovery of a new technology took away part of Easy's market. Easy had all its assets sunk in a plant that it could not redo quickly enough to incorporate the new technology, and the company collapsed. Thus a sudden technological breakthrough, even a relatively minor one, can cripple a company or an industry. A simple strategic mistake by a team of corporate executives about where to apply the company's energies over a year or two can end up dimming the company's outlook for many years. A failure to modernize can bring about bankruptcy. The corporation operates in a world of no scientific certainty, in which corporate leaders must constantly make judgments about reality when not all evidence about reality is in. Such leaders argue among themselves about strategic alternatives, each perhaps saying to himself, "We will see who is right about this," or "The next year or two will tell." But a judgment must be made and the investment committed *before* the telling is completed. Thus decision makers often experience the risks inherent in their decisions. At the very least they always face the risk of doing considerably less well than they think they are going to do.

In these seven ways, corporations offer metaphors for grace, a kind of insight into God's ways in history. Yet corporations are of this world. They sin. They are *semper reformanda*—always in need of reform.

Problems of Bigness and Other Accusations

Big corporations are despised and rejected even when the market system, small businesses, and private ownership are not. Some religious socialists do not absolutely reject certain elements in the democratic capitalist idea. But they commonly bridle at the *big* corporations. Their accusations against such corporations—many of them as true as charges made against the universities or against any large institution—are many.

One accusation is that the corporations are autocratic, that internally they are not democratic. In trying to decide how true this charge is, one could undertake a survey of the management techniques of the *Fortune* 500 corporations. How are they actually managed? How does their management differ in practice from the internal management of universities, churches, government agencies, or other institutions? Let us suppose that some autocrats still function in various spheres of authority today, including business. What sanctions are available to autocrats within a corporation? Leadership in all spheres today seems to depend upon large areas of consensus; leaders seem to "manage" more than they "command." I have roughly the same impression of the chief executive officers I have met as of the American Catholic bishops I have met; namely, that out of the office they would find it hard, as Schumpeter says, to say boo to a duck. Few, as I see them, are autocrats. Would that the world still saw the likes of Cardinals Spellman, Connell, Cushing, and Gibbons; or of industrial autocrats like Carnegie, Mellon, and others. Such types seem to have perished from the earth. In their place are men who, if you saw them in sport shirts at a Ramada Inn, would make you think you had dropped in unawares on a convention of real-estate agents from Iowa. Very pleasant, nice men, they are nowhere near as assertive as journalists. They do not often have the occupational arrogance of academics. But empirical tests are in order to see how many autocrats are in corporations, as distinct from any other sphere of life.

A second frequent accusation against big corporations is the alienation their employees experience in the workplace. To what extent is such alienation caused by the conditions of modern work under any existing system or under any imaginable system? Do laborers in auto factories in Bratislava or Poznan work under conditions any different from those faced by laborers in the United States? One ought to compare hours of work, conditions of the workplace, salaries, working procedures, and levels of pollution. There is no evidence that any real or imagined socialism can take the modernity out of modern work. Nor is boring work unique to the modern factory; it surely dominated the ancient work of European peasants and continues to dominate the fourteen-hour day of the modern potato farmer. Farming is not, in my experience, inherently less alienating than working seven hours, with time off for lunch, on an assembly line.

Alienation is not a problem peculiar to capitalism or to corporations. Is work less alienating within a government bureaucracy? Instead of condemning political activists or politicians to jail for various crimes, suppose one simply condemned them to filing the correspondence of congressmen from states like Ohio and Arkansas for periods of up to three months.

A third accusation against corporations is that they represent too great a concentration of power. What is the alternative? There is indeed a circle within which small is beautiful, a relatively small and beautiful circle. But "small is beautiful" does not apply across the whole large world. When Jane Fonda and Tom Hayden made their pilgrimage to seventy-two cities carrying the word on economic democracy, they did not fly in airplanes made in mom and pop stores. Their travel arrangements were made not by small organizations working off a telephone in a back room, but by agencies with computers and Telex connections to operating stations in all airlines and in all airports, giving them the instantaneous information required to synchronize such a trip in a very short time.

Socialist economist Robert Lekachman has argued that the big corporations should be reduced in size to more manageable proportions.[14] Maybe so. To my mind the question is a practical, experimental one. Consider the largest of all corporations, General Motors. It is already broken up into more than 200 units in more than 177 congressional districts in the United States. Its largest single facility, in Michigan, employs no more than 14,000 people. Many universities—

---

[14] "A second characteristic I would seek from socialism is a reduction in the scale of the corporation in our country. Now, this is not 'small is beautiful.' I do not think you are going to build large aircraft with E. F. Schumacher's intermediate technology—nor, for that matter, large computers in local workshops. Nevertheless, by every account, the scale of the large corporation is much less related to technological economies of scale than to various advertising, marketing, financial, and legal benefits—including the opportunity to control markets.

"Now, free enterprise economists, of course, would be alarmed by the idea of limiting the size of corporations. I would argue that competition only works where it exists; and the scale of the large organization frequently limits the amount of effective competition that can occur. Diminishing the average size of the productive units would increase their number, and thereby the potential for competition." Robert Lekachman, "The Promise of Democratic Socialism," in *Democracy and Mediating Structures*, ed. Novak, p. 40.

the University of Michigan and Michigan State, to name two—comprise human communities two or three times that size. Corporations already follow the principle of subsidiarity far more thoroughly than Lekachman seems to take into account. One might argue that they should be still smaller. Yet one must note that the smaller U.S. auto companies—American Motors, Chrysler, and Ford—are apparently in danger of perishing because of inadequate capital to meet the enormous expenses of retooling for new auto technologies. The foreign auto companies competing with General Motors (even in the United States) are also very large. If small is beautiful, its beauty seems precarious indeed; big may be necessary.

In practice, I cannot imagine how human capacities and human choices of the sort needed by mass markets could still be made available except through large organizations. Small organizations may suit a small country, but it seems to me absurd to imagine that a continental nation with a population of 220 million can be well served in all respects only through small organizations in small industries. If somebody can invent a system of smallness, fine; I am not, in principle, against it. I just cannot imagine that it can work in practice.

Corporations are further accused of being inherently evil because they work for a profit. Without profit no new capital is made available for research, development, and new investment. Further, there is a difference between *maximization* of profit and *optimization* of profit. To aim at maximizing profit—that is, to obtain the greatest profit possible out of every opportunity—is to be greedy in the present at the expense of the future. The profit maximizer demands too much for products that can be produced more cheaply by somebody else and in the process narrows his market and destroys his reputation. Inevitably, he damages himself and, in time, destroys himself. Adam Smith made this point a long time ago, and history is replete with examples of it. By contrast, to optimize profit is to take many other factors besides profit into account, including long-term new investment, consumer loyalty, and the sense of a fair service for a fair price.

The profit motive must necessarily operate in a socialist economy, too. Every economy that intends to progress must have as its motive the ability to get more out of the economic process than it puts in. Unless there is a return on investment, the economy simply spins its wheels in stagnation, neither accumulating nor growing. Capital accumulation is what profits are called in socialist enterprises. If the Soviets invest money in dams or in building locomotives, they must get back at least what they invest or they lose money. If they do lose money—and they often do—then they must draw on other resources. And if they do that throughout the system, economic stagnation and decline are inevitable.

The same law binds both socialist and capitalist economies: Economic progress, growth, and forward motion cannot occur unless the return on investment is larger than the investment itself.

It is true that under socialism profits belong to the state and are allocated to individuals by the state for the state's own purposes. Such a procedure can be institutionalized, but the costs of enforcing it are great. It tremendously affects the possibilities of liberty, of choice. It deeply affects incentives and creativity.

Objections to corporations are many. Some are clearly justified. Some are spurious. A full-dress theology of the corporation would properly evaluate each one fairly, from many points of view. A convenient summary of some of them is to be found in *The Crisis of the Corporation* by Richard J. Barnet.[15] Barnet makes three major accusations: (1) that the multinational corporations have inordinate power; (2) that they weaken the powers of the nation-state; and (3) that their actual practice destroys several "myths" about corporations.

The power of the multinational corporations, Barnet believes, springs from their ability to internationalize planning, production, finance, and marketing. In planning, each part can specialize, so that the whole pursues "profit maximization." In production, resources from various lands are integrated. In finance, computerization allows multinational corporations to take advantage of fluctuations in capital markets. In marketing, goods and consumption are standardized.[16]

From another point of view, these accusations seem to list *advantages*. Any economic organization which can work as Barnet describes would seem to be well placed to produce the maximum number of goods at the lowest cost. This efficiency should have the effect of making the most practical use of scarce capital, while increasing that capital through profitable investment. (We have already noted an important difference between "profit maximization" and "profit optimization.") The purpose of an interdependent world economic order is to match off the strengths of one region with those of another: a region with capital reserves and high labor costs is needed by a region without capital reserves but cheap labor. The cost of ignoring each other would be high for both regions. Cooperation should produce benefits for both.

Barnet argues that the powers of nation-states are weakened because multinational corporations make intracorporate transfers of funds without the knowledge of national governmental bodies. In addition, he asserts, they shift production to low-wage areas with fewer "union

---

[15] Richard J. Barnet, *The Crisis of the Corporation* (Washington: Institute for Policy Studies, 1975).

[16] Ibid., pp. 7–8.

troubles", move productive facilities to regions where tax advantages are greatest, have no loyalty to any one country, and use dominance in one national market to achieve dominance in others bcause they can "out-advertise" smaller local companies.[17]

If all of these assertions are true, at least sometimes and in some places, not all their effects are evil. Consider, for example, the competition between Japanese, European, and U.S. automakers. The new reality is that market competition has been internationalized. Every such new development has advantages and costs. It appears that U.S. citizens benefit in quality and cost from this competition. Obviously, foreign autoworkers would seem to benefit. Unless U.S. automakers can do better, U.S. autoworkers will continue to suffer.

Would the world be a better place if each nation-state tried solely to protect its own industries? At various times, protectionism has triumphed. Nations do have the power to expel, close out, restrict, and nationalize foreign industries; often they do. This course, too, has costs as well as advantages. Barnet does not show that its costs are lower than those of the competition he opposes. No matter how Chrysler advertised during 1979, it did not seem to move the cars it tried to sell. Advertising is far less exact than he imagines.

Barnet argues, finally, that monopolization undercuts competitive free enterprise. He concedes that monopoly scarcely exists, but hastens to substitute for it oligopoly (four major firms, for example, controlling a majority of sales in several industries) whose "effects are much the same."[18] He argues that efficiency is undercut by intracorporate transactions (as when tax laws encourage the shipment of products over long distances, when similar products could be acquired locally);[19] that income distribution between the top 20 percent and the bottom 20 percent of income earners in the United States has "remained the same for forty-five years";[20] and that democracy is not enhanced by a free economy.[21]

Since Barnet himself is in favor of state monopolies in the socialist pattern, his objections to "oligopolies" do not have an authentic ring. Surely, four large companies in an industry are better than one state monopoly. Moreover, in the international field, the three major U.S. auto companies, for example, compete not only with each other but

---

[17] Ibid., pp. 8–11.
[18] Ibid., p. 14.
[19] Ibid., pp. 16–17.
[20] Ibid., p. 20.
[21] Ibid., pp. 21–22.

with Volvo, Fiat, Peugeot, Volkswagen, Toyota, and many others. In other industries, international competition is also a reality.[22]

It is true that prices in a complex, highly technological industry are not simpleminded, but to suggest that they are "no longer a useful indicator" of cost and value falls short of sophistication. Consumers today make economic choices not only between which car to buy but whether to buy a car at all, or to invest the money, or to build an addition on the house, and so forth. In seeking the consumer's dollars, producers compete not only with others in their own industries but with other industries altogether. Pricing, however sophisticated the process through which it is arrived, still affects the decisions of purchasers, as alternative marketing strategies amply demonstrate.

With respect to income distribution, most socialists today recognize that incomes are not and cannot be perfectly equal. They certainly are not in socialist countries. If persons at the top end of the income ladder receive eight times as much as those at the bottom, it follows that the total share of income of those at the top will be significantly higher than that of a similar cohort at the bottom. This relationship is strictly arithmetical. Imagine that Barnet himself earns $50,000 a year from his salary and royalties. This income would rank among the top 3 percent of all U.S. households, seven times as high as the official poverty level for a nonfarm family of four.[23] Arithmetically, his class must accumulate a disproportionate share of all U.S. income.

There is a further point. One must not compare only percentiles—snapshots of groups at one point in time. As a graduate student at Harvard Law School, Barnet's income was certainly lower than it is now; it may even have been below the poverty level. This did not, except technically, make Barnet "poor." At each decade thereafter one would even then have expected his future income to place him in a different percentile. While *percentiles* may remain relatively constant, *individuals* (at least in a free, mobile society) rise and fall between them. Moreover, a family's relative *wealth* depends in the long run—over, say, three generations—to a great extent on the sort of *investment* it makes with available funds. Investments in consumption at each moment preclude growth; investments in education, property, and the like make future material improvement probable. Thus, in many families, one generation

---

[22] Lester C. Thurow, "Let's Abolish the Antitrust Laws," *New York Times*, October 19, 1980.

[23] "The poverty threshold for a non-farm family of four was $7,412 in 1979." U.S. Bureau of the Census, *Money Income and Poverty Status of Families and Persons in the United States: 1979 (Advanced Report)* (Washington, 1980), p. 1.

works not solely for itself but for its future progeny. As it happens, families once wealthy sometimes experience economic decline, and families once poor sometimes become better off than in earlier generations. One must track not simply the statistical percentiles but the rise and fall over time of individuals and families within these percentiles. One would expect some individuals and families to be more intelligent, wiser, and luckier over time than others. Inequality of income is no more a scandal than are inequalities of looks, personality, talent, will, and luck. Inequality of income appears to be an inevitable fact in all large societies.

There is a peculiar historical link—which even Marxists recognize —between the emergence of liberal democracy in Great Britain, the United States, the Netherlands, and a few cognate lands and the emergence of a free economy. One might be satisfied to stress the *historical* character of the link. But it also seems to have a *necessary conceptual* character as well. If individuals lack fundamental economic liberties (to earn, spend, save, and invest as they see fit), they necessarily have few effective political liberties. If they are dependent upon the state for economic decisions, they must be wards of the state in other matters. Moreover, to believe that state bureaucrats are competent to make economic decisions beneficial for the common good is to make a great leap of faith, when one considers the actual economic well-being of workers in the U.S.S.R., Poland, Cuba, Yugoslavia. Even the democratic socialists of Sweden and West Germany insist upon vital economic liberties for individuals and corporations.

Socialist societies do not permit private corporations. They operate on the assumption that state officials know best what is for the common good. In reflecting on their actual practice, one may come to believe that democratic capitalism is more likely to meet the goals of socialism—plus other goals of its own—than socialism is. The social instrument invented by democratic capitalism to achieve social goals is the private corporation. Anyone can start one; those who succeed in making them work add to the common benefit. Yet corporations do not live (or die) in a vacuum. They must meet the demands of the moral-cultural system and of the political system. While corporations spring from some of our most cherished ideals about liberty, initiative, investment in the future, cooperation, and the like, they must also be judged in the light of our ideals. They are moral-cultural institutions, as well as economic institutions. Their primary task is economic. One cannot ask them to assume crushing and self-destructive burdens. Yet they are more than economic organisms alone and must be held to political and moral judgment.

Three Systems—Three Fields of Responsibility

The most original *social* invention of democratic capitalism, in sum, is the private corporation founded for economic purposes. The *motivation* for this invention was also *social*: to increase "the wealth of nations," to generate (for the first time in human history) sustained economic development. This effect was, in fact, achieved. However, the corporation—as a type of voluntary association—is not merely an economic institution. It is also a moral institution and a political institution. It depends upon and generates new political forms. In two short centuries, it has brought about an immense social revolution. It has moved the center of economic activity from the land to industry and commerce. No revolution is without social costs and sufferings, which must be entered on the ledger against benefits won. Universally, however, the idea of economic development has now captured the imagination of the human race. This new possibility of development has awakened the world from its economic slumbers.

Beyond its economic effects, the corporation changes the ethos and the cultural forms of society. To some extent, it has undercut ancient ways of human relating, with some good effects and some bad. After the emergence of corporations, religion has had to work upon new psychological realities. The religion of peasants has given way to the religion of new forms of life: first that of an urban proletariat, then that of a predominantly service and white-collar society. The productivity of the new economics has freed much human time for questions other than those of mere subsistence and survival. The workday has shrunk and "weekends" have been invented. After work, millions now take part in voluntary activities that fill, in effect, another forty-hour week (meetings, associations, sports, travel, politics, religion, and the like). Personal and social mobility has increased. Schooling has become not only common but mandatory. Teenagerhood has been invented. The "stages of human life" have drawn attention as room has been created for the emergence of the private self.

But the corporation is not only an economic institution and a moral-cultural institution. It also provides a new base for politics. Only a free political system permits the voluntary formation of private corporations. Thus, those who value private economic corporations have a strong interest in resisting both statism and socialism. It would be naive and wrong to believe that persons involved in corporations are (or should be) utterly neutral about political systems. An economic system within which private corporations play a role, in turn, alters the political horizon. It lifts the poor, creates a broad middle class, and undermines aristocracies of birth. Sources of power are created independent of the power of the state, in competition with the powers of the state, and sometimes in consort with the powers of the state. A corporation with plants and factories in, say, 120 congressional districts represents a great many employees and stockholders. On some matters, at least, these are likely to be well-organized to express their special political concerns. Political jurisdictions often compete to attract corporations, but their arrival also creates political problems.

Corporations err morally, then, in many ways. They may through their advertising appeal to hedonism and escape, in ways which undercut the restraint and self-discipline required by a responsible democracy and which discourage that deferral of present satisfaction on which savings and investment for the future depend. They may incorporate methods of governance that injure dignity, cooperation, inventiveness, and personal development. They may seek their own immediate interests at the expense of the common good. They may become improperly involved in the exercise of political power. They may injure the conscience of their managers or workers. They are as capable of sins as individuals are and, in the fashion of all institutions, of grave institutional sins as well. Thus, it is a perfectly proper task of all involved within corporations and in society at large to hold them to the highest moral standards, to accuse them when they fail, and to be vigilant about every form of abuse. Corporations are human institutions designed to stimulate economic activism and thus to provide the economic base for a democratic polity committed to high moral-cultural ideals. When they fall short of these purposes, their failure injures all.

Private corporations are *social* organisms. Neither the ideology of laissez faire nor the ideology of rugged individualism suits their actual practice or their inherent ideals. For corporations *socialize* risk, invention, investment, production, distribution, and services. They were conceived and designed to break the immemorial grip of mercantilist and clerical systems upon economic activity. On the other hand, they cannot come into existence, and certainly cannot function, except within political systems designed to establish and to promote the conditions of their flourishing. Among these are a sound currency, a system of laws, the regulation of competitive practices, the construction of infrastructures like roads, harbors, airports, certain welfare functions, and the like. The state, then, plays an indispensable role in democratic capitalism. The ideals of democratic capitalism are not those of laissez faire. The relations between a democratic state and a social market economy built around private corporations are profound, interdependent, and complex.

The ideals of democratic capitalism are not purely individualist, either, for the corporation draws upon and requires highly developed

221

social skills like mutual trust, teamwork, compromise, cooperation, creativity, originality and inventiveness, and agreeable management and
personnel relations. The rugged individualist of an earlier mythology
may be, if anything, an endangered species.

Great moral responsibility, then, is inherent in the existence of
corporations. They may fail economically. They may fail morally and
culturally. They may fail politically. Frequently enough, they err in one
or all of these areas. They are properly subjected to constant criticism and
reform. But types of criticism may be distinguished. Some critics accept
the ideals inherent in the system of private business corporations, and
simply demand that corporations be faithful to these ideals. Some
critics are opposed to the system *qua* system. Among these, some wish
to restrain, regulate, and guide the business system through the power
of the state and through moral and cultural forces like public opinion,
shame, ridicule, boycotts, and moral suasion ("do not invest in South
Africa," and the like). In the theory of "mixed systems," the ideal of
democratic capitalism shades off into the ideal of democratic socialism
—one leaning more to the private sector, the other leaning more to
the public sector. Still other critics wish to make the business system
directly *subject* to the state. These last may be, according to their own
ideals, corporate statists or socialists. They may be state socialists or
local participatory politics socialists. Criticism from any of these quarters may be useful to the development and progress of democratic
capitalism, even from those who would wish to destroy it.

There is plenty of room—and plenty of evidence—for citing
specific deficiencies of corporations: economic, political, and moral-
cultural. To be sure, there is a difference between accusations and demonstrated error. Like individuals, corporations are innocent until proven
guilty. A passionate hostility toward bigness (or even toward economic
liberty), like a passionate commitment to statism, may be socially useful by providing a searching critique from the viewpoint of hostile
critics. But unless it gets down to cases and sticks to a reasoned pre-
sentation of evidence, it must be recognized for what it is: an argument less against specifics than against the radical ideal of democratic
capitalism and the private corporation. It is useful to distinguish these
two types of criticism, and helpful when critics are self-conscious and
honest about which ideals actually move them. To criticize corporations in the light of their *own* ideals, the ideals of democratic capitalism,
is quite different from criticizing them in the name of statist or socialist
ideals incompatible with their existence. Clarity about ideals is as necessary as clarity about cases.

Theologians, in particular, are likely to inherit either a pre-
capitalist or a frankly socialist set of ideals about political economy.

They are especially likely to criticize corporations from a set of ideals foreign to those of democratic capitalism. To those who do accept democratic capitalist ideals, then, their criticisms are likely to have a scent of unreality and inappropriateness. Wisdom would suggest joining argument at the appropriate level of discourse: whether the argument concerns general economic concepts, whether it concerns the rival ideals of democratic capitalism and socialism, or whether it concerns concrete cases and specific matters of fact. Each of these levels has its place. Wisdom's principal task is *distinguer*.

Managing a free society aimed at preserving the integrity of the trinitarian system—the economic system, the political system, and the moral-cultural system—is no easy task. An important standard set by Edmund Burke is cited as the epigraph of a masterly work by Wilhelm T. Roepke, *A Humane Economy*:

> To make a government requires no great prudence. Settle the seat of power; teach obedience: and the work is done. To give freedom is still more easy. It is not necessary to guide; it only requires to let go the rein. But to form a free *government*; that is, to temper together these opposite elements of liberty and restraint in one consistent work, requires much thought, deep reflection, a sagacious, powerful and combining mind.[24]

To govern a free *economy* is yet more difficult than to form a free government. It is hard enough to govern a government. It is difficulty squared to govern a free economy—to establish the conditions for prosperity, to keep a sound currency, to promote competition, to establish general rules and standards binding upon all, to keep markets free, to provide education to all citizens in order to give them opportunity, to care for public needs, and to provide succor to the unfortunate. To have the virtue to do all these things wisely, persistently, judiciously, aptly is surely of some rather remarkable theological significance. It may even represent—given the inherent difficulties—a certain amazing grace. To fall short is to be liable to judgment.

Christians have not, historically, lived under only one economic system; nor are they bound in conscience to support only one. Any real or, indeed, any imaginable economic system is necessarily part of history, part of this world. None is the Kingdom of Heaven—not democratic socialism, not democratic capitalism. A theology of the corporation should not make the corporation seem to be an ultimate; it is

---

[24] See Wilhelm T. Roepke, *The Humane Economy: The Social Framework of a Free Society* (Chicago: Henry Regnery, 1960), facing p. 1; the quotation is from Edmund Burke, *Reflections on the Revolution in France* (1790).

only a means, an instrument, a worldly agency. Such a theology should attempt to show how corporations may be instruments of redemption, of humane purposes and values, of God's grace; it should also attempt to show their characteristic and occasional faults in every sphere. Like everything else in the world, corporations may be seen as both obstacles to salvation and bearers of God's grace. The waters of the sea are blessed, as are airplanes and ploughshares and even troops making ready for just combat. A city in Texas may be named Corpus Christi, and a city in California Sacramento. Christianity, like Judaism, attempts to sanctify the real world as it is, in all its ambiguity, so as to reject the evil in it and bring the good in it to its highest possible fruition.

Most Christians do not now work for major industrial corporations. Instead, they work for the state (even in state universities), for smaller corporations, restaurants, barbershops, and other businesses, and in other occupations. Still, a Christian social theology that lacks a theology of the large corporation will have no effective means of inspiring those Christians who do work within large corporations to meet the highest practicable Christian standards. It will also have no means of criticizing with realism and practicality those features of corporate life that deserve to be changed. Whether to treat big corporations as potential vessels of Christian vocation or to criticize them for their inevitable sins, Christian theology must advance much further than it has in understanding exactly and fairly every aspect of corporate life. The chief executive officer of General Electric needs such a theology. So do those critics of the corporation at the Interfaith Center for Corporate Responsibility. If we are to do better than clash like ignorant armies in the night, we must imitate Yahweh at Creation when he said, "Let their be light." We have not yet done all we should in casting such light.

Discussion

QUESTION: Isn't the poverty of the third world caused by the exploitation by the huge multinationals, which are larger than any single state?

MR. NOVAK: As Reinhold Niebuhr stated many times, the U.S. economy over the last two centuries has depended so little on foreign trade, particularly with Latin America, Asia, and Africa, that there is no rational way of linking U.S. prosperity to the poverty of those continents. Even today, three-quarters of U.S. overseas investment, sales, and profits are with other industrial countries in Western Europe, Canada, and Japan. Investment, sales, and profits from the third world constitute about 1 percent of U.S. economic activity.

Besides, which theory of the cause of poverty underlies your question? Actually, the poverty of the third world goes back thousands of years. There is no interesting "cause" of poverty. For most of history, poverty was not a problem. It was fact, and it created no moral urgency because there was nothing anyone could do about it, except give alms. The notion that poverty could be diminished was born with John Locke and Adam Smith. Economic development was an invention —if you want to put it in accusatory terms—of the white race and the Anglo-Saxon peoples and, indeed, of a few philosophers. Their ideas were not universally accepted—not then and not afterwards. Indeed, many Continental philosophers and theologians—Latins, Germans, Slavs —opposed "Manchester liberalism" all through the nineteenth century, disliking it intensely. The papal encyclicals treat it as a Protestant heresy. Yet the theory of economic development, the inquiry into the cause of the wealth of nations, did introduce a new ethical problem. If we can eliminate poverty, don't we have a moral obligation to do so? The road to that elimination is production. The fundamental ethical problem, the fundamental problem of justice, is how to produce more. The second ethical problem is how to distribute what is produced; what is the best mechanism of distribution?

In my view, there is room here, as anywhere else, for experiment. Socialist societies, like Cuba, have decided to give a high priority to raising the living standards of the lowest 20 percent of the population. As I understand the reports, they have done well at that. They have, however, deeply penalized the other 80 percent of the population to do that. The economic situation in Cuba is worse, in most respects, than it was earlier, but the situation of the poor is not. Many people admire that. In Latin America, as a whole, you could raise the situation of the lowest 20 percent of the population above the subsistence level and to an adequate nutritional level with an annual investment equivalent to 6 percent of the present self-generated GNP of Latin America.

This is not an insuperable task, and governments in Latin America might well choose to attempt it. The better off the people at the bottom, the larger the market for mass production. The dollars of the many amount to more purchasing power than the dollars of the wealthy few. I note that most nations of the world, even socialist nations like Nicaragua and Zimbabwe, want U.S. corporations to build plants in their countries, to bring salaries, technology, and domestically produced manufactured goods. Without question, though, foreign companies bring a foreign ethos. Khomeini could not tolerate that. So the activities of multinationals have a cultural dimension as well as an economic dimension. As to the political dimension, the capital of large corporations is largely tied up in investments already made. To say that General Motors is "powerful" because its assets are large is also to say that it is pretty much locked into its investments. States like Iran have no trouble throwing multinationals out when they wish to, or expropriating their local investments, or establishing laws to govern their local activities. It would probably help to have an international currency board to prevent speculation in foreign currencies as dramatic shifts in monetary values occur, which they do. Companies need protection here, as do states. No doubt about it, multinationals cause headaches—and have headaches. That is probably why so many of them do as little as possible outside the stable industrial countries.

QUESTION: One thing we have to look at in terms of alienation is that we are dealing with a knowledge explosion that parallels the productivity explosion. Specialization is one source of alienation. People become accustomed to the narrowness of their own disciplines and then find their own limits intolerable. Then, in the wider society, we conclude that nobody can do theology except someone who has two or three advanced degrees in theology, and that nobody can do anything in economics without the requisite credentials, and so forth. I feel very much that I was educated in one discipline and then took up another. That has been the story of my life. When *Future Shock* came out, I already had lived it. The situation we live in demands, first, humility enough to let go of expertise and, second, the compassion not to label people and impute unworthy motives, but to be open to the truth in a wide diversity of perspectives. Don't we need a recognition that people are whole, that they have other interests in life besides their area of specialization?

MR. NOVAK: Well said. It is beginning to happen. Expertise, as an ideal, has had a very short history. In the 1930s, university professors used to be regarded as absent-minded professors. They were not thought to be experts, or hardly so. It was after World War II, with its great explosion of technical knowledge, that the cultivation of the expert took hold. I can remember at Harvard, in graduate school, being told that it is wrong to be too worried about the "ought"; the crucial thing is to be right about the "is." We were taught the importance of the descriptive and warned against the normative. John Kennedy remarked in 1963, at Yale, that we now know how to solve most of the problems of world poverty; the only question is whether we have the will to do so. To my mind, that was the high point of the hubris of the experts. Ever since then, there has been growing skepticism about them. In a sense, the experts are always wrong when they address a whole problem because, in the nature of the case, they are expert in one facet of a problem, while nothing in life comes with one facet only. In political campaigns I have served with, we always had fun when we were obliged to consult with experts. There always came a point in the lunch when, after congenial conversation, we got down to business, and voices suddenly shifted gears into "expert."

QUESTION: Is there not a danger that you are developing a bit of a bunker mentality here about the state of siege of capitalism? Isn't a majority of the American people—even in the academy—in support of American democratic capitalism? What is the extent of the threat, in your estimation?

MR. NOVAK: I believe, and I know that many people in corporations believe, that the threat is very real, that we may not have free corporations to pass on to our children. There is a powerful vested interest in the growing state. Sixteen million people work for government, and another 4 million get their money indirectly from the government through contracts let out to corporations. There are, in addition, all the people on Social Security and unemployment, and all the teachers.

The number of people who—to use a vivid expression I heard this week—"suck at the public teat" is already quite large. One day it may be impossible to vote them out. They may come to think it in their immediate interest to see to it that the government controls corporations, because agencies of control open government jobs.

Every bureaucracy in the Congress has a tentacle into the corporation now, and a low-grade GS-14 can cripple an industrial establishment's local plants for years. There are 38,000 pages of government regulations to be applied. Everyone is always in some sort of violation of something, and vulnerable to political reprisal.

I have heard people say there is not a plant in this country that could not be closed, at any time, in any period of our history, for the violation of some law. It is being done. Regulation is necessary, but the costs of it are extremely high. Everyone pays for these costs. Read what it costs Firestone, what it costs the auto companies in any one of these recalls, what it costs the steel mills and chemical plants. All these things are matters of check and balance. The real interest and real power, in my view, has now swung to the political sector.

Pretty soon, people may say, "I don't want to invest. I'd rather invest in Japanese companies." And people will also say, "I don't want to work in industry, it's too much of a hassle," and the best people will go elsewhere.

In personal terms, I have to say that among my peers, my reputation was higher when I was a democratic socialist. When I began to reexamine democratic capitalism, I heard calls of "traitor" and "sell-out." The moral pressure is very strong to be a statist, at least among most of those whose opinions are most important to an intellectual.

By far the majority of American professors are on the side of democratic capitalism—81 percent. The 19 percent are concentrated almost entirely in the humanities and social sciences.[1] But I can not find many people in the field of religion who are not socialists, especially among those who write in social ethics.

QUESTION: The threat is very real then?

MR. NOVAK: I think the threat is real. I think the legitimation for the increase of state power is well in place. People regard state power as liberal, moral, and noble. This view came to prevail in Great Britain; why shouldn't it happen here? I do not see the things in place, at this moment, to prevent it's happening here.

---

[1] In a 1977 faculty survey of 4,400 persons at 161 colleges and universities 81 per cent agreed with the statement: "The private business system in the United States, for all its flaws, works better than any other system devised for advanced industrial society." The social sciences and humanities, on the other hand, each had 58 per cent of their members claiming "liberal" ideology. See Everett C. Ladd, Jr., and Seymour Martin Lipset, "Professors Found to Be Liberal but Not Radical," *The Chronicle of Higher Education* (January 16, 1978).

I do not, however, think of myself as in a bunker; I think of myself as on the attack. Our case is the better case, and it will prevail.

QUESTION: You said earlier that you were unhappy about asking the business community to do too much planning and thinking ahead; you preferred that to be a task for the church. I do not like that, for two reasons: first, from the point of view of ecclesiology. If we are talking about the "church," what we mean is the people of God, and the people of God have no part in the planning and the dreaming and the strategy preempted by the church bureaucracy. We plan all week and ask them to come in on Sunday and give us their money, to do the mission we plan. I say "we" here, as a clergyman.

Secondly, I feel the same problem from the point of view of industry and business. Shouldn't there be a balance of people who dream and create and think, as well as those who can administer and get things done?

MR. NOVAK: A good correction. Still I do not want corporate executives, insofar as they are corporate executives, and in the name of their corporations, to enunciate in too much detail the moral vision of justice and freedom which the corporation is serving. Not everybody who works for that corporation or who deals with it is Christian, or whatever it may be that the executives' own commitments express. Corporations must respect pluralism. As Christians, corporate workers ought to nourish their own moral visions. But they should not make the corporation ideological in too concentrated a way. As for the church, I would rather have the church's social teaching written by a committee with three-quarters lay men and women from various fields, including economics, than solely by theologians.

I hope that next year someone will sponsor a symposium called *Nonagesimo Anno*—1981, the ninetieth year after *Rerum Novarum*, the fiftieth year after *Quadragesimo Anno*. The purpose would be to criticize the social doctrines of the churches: the Oxford documents, the papal encyclicals, from the point of view of sophisticated laymen. There are many good things in these documents. Still, the more I learn, the more unhappy I am with their assumptions, lack of empirical analysis, and capitulation to conventional biases. Economic matters deserve more care.

In conclusion, I want to mention the book by Arthur McGovern, a Jesuit, called *Marxism: An American Christian Perspective*. The book "Democratic Capitalism: An American Christian Perspective" has not been written, yet now we have one on *Marxism* in American Christian perspective. It is remarkable.

Interestingly enough, McGovern is extremely tentative. He is not ready to embrace Marxism yet, although he prefers it to the originality of the political economy that has nourished him. Why are so many Christians now attracted to Marxism? He answers that question as follows: "First, many Christians are deeply troubled by conditions in the world, by the vast gap between wealthy, affluent peoples and desperately poor ones; by vast expenditures on military weapons and luxury goods while basic human needs go unmet; by the growing power of giant corporations, and by a culture that undermines Christian values and true human needs."[2]

In other words, a vision is needed. A program for moral action. On the level of evidence that McGovern supplies, the vision of democratic capitalism, which he has been living under, is superior to the Marxism he tentatively praises. Reading his book, I thought, There, but for the grace of God, go I. That's the route I was following until I began to question democratic socialism as rigorously as I had been taught to disdain capitalism. The poverty McGovern mentions cannot be cured by socialism. The wealth of many nations must be raised to historically unprecedented levels. It is odd that theologians now explore the theology of Marxism, without ever having established a theology of democratic capitalism. Yet we will never understand the nature and causes of wealth until we do. Nor will the churches free themselves from their preference for authoritarian moral systems. The task we have begun this week sets a heavy agenda before us.

---

[2] Arthur McGovern, S.J., *Marxism: An American Christian Perspective* (Maryknoll, N.Y.: Orbis Books, 1980), p. 135.

Bibliography

BARBER, RICHARD J. *The American Corporation: Its Power, Its Money, Its Politics.* New York: E. P. Dutton, 1970.

BERLE, ADOLF A., JR. *The Twentieth Century Capitalist Revolution.* New York: Harcourt, 1954.

BROZEN, YALE; MOTT, WILLIAM C.; TYRMAND, LEOPOLD; ST. JOHN, JEFFREY; SHENFIELD, BARBARA; and HOWARD, JOHN A., *Corporate Responsibility: The Viability of Capitalism in an Era of Militant Demands.* Edited by John A. Howard. Rockford, Ill.: Rockford College Institute, 1978.

DAVIS, JOHN P. *Corporations: A Study of the Origin and Development of Great Business Combinations and Their Relation to the Authority of the State.* 2 vols. New York: Putnam, 1961, reprint of 1905 edition.

DAVIS, JOSEPH S. *Essays in the Earlier History of American Corporations.* 2 vols. Cambridge, Mass.: Harvard University Press, 1917.

DRUCKER, PETER F. *Concept of the Corporation.* New York: John Day Co., 1946.

FINN, DAVID. *The Corporate Oligarch.* New York: Simon and Schuster, 1969.

FRANK, ISAIAH. *Foreign Enterprise in Developing Countries.* Baltimore: Johns Hopkins University Press, 1980.

GALBRAITH, JOHN KENNETH. *The New Industrial State.* Boston: Houghton Mifflin, 1967.

HESSEN, ROBERT. *In Defense of the Corporation.* Stanford: Hoover Institution Press, 1979.

HEWLITT, SYLVIA ANN. *The Cruel Dilemmas of Development: Twentieth-Century Brazil.* New York: Basic Books, 1980.

HUNT, BISHOP C. *The Development of the Business Corporation in England, 1800–1867.* Cambridge, Mass.: Harvard University Press, 1936.

HURST, JAMES WILLARD. *The Legitimacy of the Business Corporation in the Law of the United States, 1780–1970.* Charlottesville, Va.: University Press of Virginia, 1970.

KRISTOL, IRVING. *Two Cheers for Capitalism.* New York: Basic Books, 1978.

MANNE, HENRY G. and WALLICH, HENRY C. *The Modern Corporation and Social Responsibility.* Washington, D.C.: American Enterprise Institute, 1972.

MOORE, WILBERT E. *The Conduct of the Corporation.* New York: Random House, 1962.

MORAN, T. H. *Multinational Corporations and the Politics of Dependence: Copper in Chile.* Princeton, N.J.: Princeton University Press, 1974.

NOVAK, MICHAEL. *Toward A Theology of the Corporation.* Washington, D.C.: American Enterprise Institute, 1981.

POWERS, CHARLES W. *Social Responsibility and Investment.* Nashville: Abingdon, 1971.

POWERS, CHARLES W. and VOGEL, DAVID. *Ethics in the Education of Business Managers.* Hastings-on-Hudson, N.Y.: The Hastings Center, 1980.

SIGMUND, PAUL E. *Multinationals in Latin America: The Politics of Nationalization.* Madison, Wisc.: University of Wisconsin Press, 1980.

VERNON, RAYMOND. *Sovereignty at Bay: The Multinational Spread of U.S. Enterprises.* New York: Basic Books, 1971.

WALTON, CLARENCE. *The Ethics of Corporate Conduct.* Englewood Cliffs, N.J.: Prentice-Hall, 1977.

WILLIAMS, OLIVER F. and HOUCK, JOHN W. *Full Value: Cases in Christian Business Ethics.* New York: Harper & Row, 1978.

Contributors

P. T. BAUER is professor of economics at the London School of Economics and Political Science, University of London. He is a fellow of Gonville and Caius College, Cambridge and a fellow of the British Academy. He was born in Budapest and educated at Scholar Piae, Budapest, and Cambridge University. He has taught at the University of London and Cambridge University. He is the author of numerous books and articles, including *West African Trade, The Economics of Under-developed Countries* (with B. S. Yamey), *Dissent on Development*, and the forthcoming *Poverty, Poor Countries and Political Economy*. His articles have appeared in *Commentary, Fortune*, and the *Wall Street Journal*.

MERRIMON CUNINGGIM is president emeritus of Salem College in Winston-Salem, North Carolina. He was educated at Vanderbilt University, Duke University, Oxford University, and Yale University. He was a professor of religion at several universities before becoming dean of the Perkins School of Theology at Southern Methodist University. He has served as adviser to the president of the Ford Foundation and as executive director of the Danforth Foundation. He is the author of several books, including *The College Seeks Religion, The Protestant Stake in Higher Education*, and *Private Money and Public Service: The Role of the Foundations in American Society*.

OSCAR HANDLIN is Carl H. Pforzheimer University Professor at Harvard University. He was educated at Brooklyn College and Harvard University and has taught American history at Harvard since 1944. He is the author of numerous books, including *The Uprooted*, which won a Pulitzer Prize, *Chance or Destiny, The Americans*, and *The Wealth of the American People*. He is a frequent contributor to *Atlantic*, the *New York Times Magazine, Commentary*, and the *Saturday Review*.

REGINALD H. JONES has been chairman of the board and chief executive officer of General Electric Company since 1972. He was born in England and educated at the University of Pennsylvania. He joined GE in 1939 and has held several key management positions in various

233

divisions. He is co-chairman of the Business Roundtable and chairman of the Business Council. In a 1980 survey, he was the top choice of 306 chief executives of large corporations as the most respected U.S. business executive; he was mentioned by about one-third of all respondents and by more than half the heads of the largest corporations.

PAUL W. MCCRACKEN is Edmund Ezra Day University Professor of Business Administration at the University of Michigan. He was educated at Pennsylvania College and Harvard University. He taught at Berea College and served as an economist with the Department of Commerce and the Federal Reserve Bank of Minneapolis before coming to the University of Michigan in 1948. A noted financial economist and theorist of monetarism, he has also served as member and chairman of the President's Council of Economic Advisers. He is the author of numerous articles and monographs, including *Balance of Payments and Domestic Prosperity* and *Economic Progress and the Utility Industry.*

BERNARD MURCHLAND is professor of philosophy and chairman of the Department of Philosophy at Ohio Wesleyan University. He was born in Canada and educated at the University of Moncton, the University of Montreal, the University of Ottawa, and the State University of New York at Buffalo. He is the author of over 100 articles and a number of books, including *The Age of Alienation, The New Iconoclasm,* and the forthcoming *The Death of Liberal Arts.*

MICHAEL NOVAK is resident scholar in religion and public policy at the American Enterprise Institute and adjunct professor of religion at Syracuse University. He has also taught at Harvard, Stanford, and the State University of New York at Old Westbury. He has published widely in *Commentary, Commonweal, Harper's,* and the *New Republic,* among others. His books include *Belief and Unbelief, The Rise of the Unmeltable Ethnics, Choosing Our King, The Joy of Sports,* and *The Guns of Lattimer.* His *The American Vision: An Essay on the Future of Democratic Capitalism* is another American Enterprise Institute publication in this series.

TIMOTHY SMITH is director of the Interfaith Center for Corporate Responsibility in New York City, an affiliate of the National Council of Churches. The center is active in bringing the social concerns of its member churches to the attention of corporate leaders and the general public; special emphasis is given to legal actions and stockholder resolutions. He was educated at the University of Toronto and Union Theological Seminary. He has held previous positions with the United Church of Christ and the Australian Council of Churches. He has testified before committees of the United Nations and the U.S. Congress.

A NOTE ON THE BOOK

The typeface used for the text of this book is
Times Roman, designed by Stanley Morison.
The type was set by
Maryland Linotype Composition Company, of Baltimore.
Thomson-Shore, Inc., of Dexter, Michigan, printed
and bound the book, using Warren's Olde Style paper.
The cover and format were designed by Pat Taylor.
The manuscript was edited by Barbara Kraft, and
by Anne Gurian of the AEI Publications staff.

SELECTED AEI PUBLICATIONS

AEI ASSOCIATES PROGRAM